Storytelling in Presentations

by Sheryl Lindsell-Roberts MA

for dummies®
A Wiley Brand

Storytelling in Presentations For Dummies®

Published by: **John Wiley & Sons, Inc.**, 111 River Street, Hoboken, NJ 07030-5774, www.wiley.com

Published simultaneously in Canada

For general information on our other products and services, please contact our Customer Care Department within the U.S. at 877-762-2974, outside the U.S. at 317-572-3993, or fax 317-572-4002. For technical support, please visit https://hub.wiley.com/community/support/dummies.

Wiley publishes in a variety of print and electronic formats and by print-on-demand. Some material included with standard print versions of this book may not be included in e-books or in print-on-demand. If this book refers to media such as a CD or DVD that is not included in the version you purchased, you may download this material at http://booksupport.wiley.com. For more information about Wiley products, visit www.wiley.com.

Library of Congress Control Number: 2023942992

ISBN 978-1-394-20100-6 (pbk); ISBN 978-1-394-20101-3 (ebk); ISBN 978-1-394-20102-0 (ebk)

SKY10053254_081423

Contents at a Glance

Table of Contents

Introduction

Stories are how we learn best. We absorb numbers and facts and details, but we keep them all glued into our heads with stories.

— CHRIS BROGAN, AUTHOR, MARKETING CONSULTANT, JOURNALIST, SPEAKER

Join the sensibility of today's industry giants who are renouncing slidezilla-type, data-laden PowerPoint monsters (and their clones). Instead, they're energizing audiences with storyopia. Storyopia, like utopia, represents the ideal. It's the ideal story that takes audiences on a journey from what *is* to what *could be.* Storyopia will make your audience feel like heroes and will lead to amazing results for them and for you. Your audience will see your presentation as personal, and you'll become a valuable resource.

This book will help you develop your own tales of adventure that will take your audiences on journeys to greatness through your insights, leadership, and storytelling, coaxing their brains into thinking they're experiencing the incidents themselves. And they're right there with you — engaged. Whether your presentation is in person, virtual, or hybrid and whether it's streaming or zooming into the metaverse, it all starts with storyopia. Then a storyboard maps it all out with what to tell and what to show.

About This Book

This book is the culmination of my many years of exploring the art of storytelling. I cherry-picked from an enormous body of the greatest raconteurs of all time — from Aesop to Lincoln to Jobs and others. Their quotes and stories are filtered throughout this book. Thus, the pages are somewhat like a big-picture briefing of storytelling in presentations — from preparation to presentation to a standing ovation. Here's a quick overview of what you'll find and where:

Part 1: Martians, Stories, and Heroes

Your presentations are stories. They have a beginning, a middle, and an end — that's a story. This part introduces you to the art of storytelling. It shows how your audiences can be heroes just like the heroes you read about in the news, fiction, and real-life situations.

Part 2: Nuts 'n' Bolts

This critical part takes you through the process of understanding your audience, starting strong, ending with a bang, and bringing your presentation to life with storytelling and storyboarding. It will help you pinpoint what you want your audience to do, think, learn, or feel.

Part 3: Adding Flourishes

This part shows you how slides can enhance your presentation with visuals when they speak more loudly than words. It also discusses how to kick handbooks and workbooks up a notch, how to write and present a stellar bio, and how to prepare and use evaluation forms.

Part 4: It's Showtime

When you get to this part, you're ready to take your show on the road. Find out how to be poised when presenting bad news and fielding difficult questions. Understand how to talk with a diverse audience. Journey with ease from the in-person world to the virtual world.

Part 5: Specialized Presentations

This part embodies specialized presentations from structuring a session, acing executive briefings, delivering a paper at a conference, and presenting someone else's content to make it your own.

Part 6: The Part of Tens

This part is a *Dummies* classic. You'll find tips for combatting stage fright, becoming more relatable, being interactive, and learning reasons presentations fail (with solutions so yours won't).

Part 7: Appendixes

Here's a checklist that will guide you from your presentation to preparing for a standing O, as well as a glossary of terms.

As you read through this book, you'll notice that each chapter abounds with best practices, including the following:

- Storyopia Archives are real-life accounts that I or others have experienced — all ending with the lesson learned.
- Visuals in each chapter enhance the narrative as well as stand alone when they speak louder than words.
- Each chapter opens with a quote that ties into the theme of that chapter. In addition to stories, quotes are one of several suggestions for openings to make presentations engaging from the get-go.

» Strong headlines and subheads give key information at a glance. They grab attention and provide a quick overview of the section.

Foolish Assumptions

I try not to make assumptions because everyone knows what happens when you *ass-u-me*. So, rather than making any foolish assumptions, I looked through my crystal ball and discovered that you probably fit into one of these categories. You're . . .

» On the verge of closing a major contract and need a compelling presentation to seal the deal.

» New in the job market and are making your first nail-biting presentation.

» Presenting a revised budget to executive-level managers that will have a negative impact on the bottom line.

» Looking for a consensus for a new idea.

» Teaching hardware, software, or a new concept.

» Applying for a large grant and your presentation will be the deciding factor.

» Delivering a paper at a large conference, and this is your moment to shine.

» Giving a presentation that was prepared by someone, and you want to make it your own.

» Shaking like an unbalanced clothes dryer when you have to make a presentation.

Whatever your reason, you'll want to wow your audience to ensure they heed your call to action and leave your presentation doing, thinking, feeling, or learning a pre-determined *something*.

Icons Used in This Book

Scattered throughout this book you'll find icons in the margins to highlight valuable information that call for your attention. Here are the icons you'll see and a brief description of each:

START-UP BRIEF

Grab your sleuth's magnifying glass to scrutinize the Start-Up Brief and gather all the clues you can about your audience.

REMEMBER

The nagging little voice in your head that won't let you forget anything, even if you try to ignore it like a pesky flying insect.

SHERYL SAYS

If I had a chance to speak with you personally, these are the things I'd say.

TIP

Find nifty tips that may be timesavers, frustration savers, lifesavers, or just about any other savers.

WARNING

Avoid these pitfalls to save yourself headaches, heartburn, and humiliation.

Beyond the Book

Beyond this book is a Cheat Sheet I've prepared that will get you rewarded (not busted). Here's what you'll find when you go to `www.dummies.com` and type **Storytelling in Presentations For Dummies Cheat Sheet** in the search box.

- Guidelines to rock your next presentation
- Avoiding the seven deadly slide sins
- Starting on the right foot with the Start-Up Brief

This Cheat Sheet is available as a handy reference at all times. Keep a copy on your wall, computer, tablet, and smartphone. And share it with your team.

Where to Go from Here

I realize you won't read it like a suspenseful mystery novel from cover to cover — but I strongly urge you to read Part II, Chapters 3-7 sequentially. These chapters offer the nuts 'n' bolts for casting your audiences as heroes through storytelling . . . bringing life to your presentations. For the remainder of the book, jump around to whatever topic interests you or applies to the presentation challenge you face. You may find something in one chapter that resembles something you read in another. (It's not a memory lapse or sloppy editing.) It's just that I don't know where you'll drop in, and there are certain things you shouldn't miss.

From here, you're on your way to becoming a presentation pro and giving top-notch talks that make you and your audience heroes.

1

Martians, Stories, and Heroes

IN THIS PART . . .

Create audience heroes with stories that sizzle, jettison slidezillas, use the story arc, and fire up your audience's imagination.

Take audiences on storyopia journeys from what is to what can be, get pointers from the all-time storytelling greats, and realize that everyone has a story (yes, even you!).

IN THIS CHAPTER

» Sharpening your axe

» Avoiding PowerPoint autopilot

» Beginnings, middles, and endings

» Storyopia to create audience heroes

Chapter 1 Sizzle Your Presentations with Stories

If history were told in the form of stories, it would never be forgotten.

—RUDYARD KIPLING (ENGLISH WRITER, POET, AND STORYTELLER)

Good storytelling can make your presentations sizzle in ways that slides can't.

Whether you realize it or not, you're already a storyteller. When you meet a friend, have dinner with family, or spend time with a colleague, you share small amusements and calamities of your day or week. It's in our nature to tell stories and share our life's events. And you probably use hyperboles (exaggerations) to make your stories more engaging — peppering them with statements such as, "I nearly died of embarrassment" or "My feet were killing me." While this casual sharing is different from being in front of an audience, you do know how to tell stories. You have lots of them. After all, you started telling stories when you made babbling sounds as a baby.

Storytelling Isn't Just a Buzzword

Storytelling has existed for eons, and it's more than a business buzzword. It's the way get your point across memorably. Think of your presentation as a story. *It has a beginning. It has a middle. It has an end.* That's a story! Aristotle is credited with having introduced this basic storytelling structure with his three-act plays.

- The opening is the setup, laying out the plot.
- The middle, which is typically the longest, introduces complications, twists, and turns.
- The third act brings the production to a close.

SHERYL SAYS

Throughout your lifetime, you'll likely give many types of formal and informal presentations: sales, educational, training, lectures, problem-solving, or simply a talk to a group for pleasure. Even giving toasts at weddings or delivering eulogies at funerals are types of presentations. They can all benefit from storytelling.

Storytelling Is Your Axe; Sharpen It

Abraham Lincoln is perhaps one of the best-known orators and storytellers of all time. He said, "Give me six hours to chop down a tree, and I will spend the first few sharpening the axe." Relating that to presentations, when you spend the time to prepare compelling stories, your presentation will be relevant and memorable, and you'll be able to chop through the clutter.

When you spend time planning properly, you'll become a confident and influential presenter, and you'll get the results and recognition you deserve — perhaps even get standing Os.

REMEMBER

Whether presentations are live, virtual, or hybrid, they're one of most effective business communication tools of our time. Strong presentation skills are a hallmark of strong leaders and people who aspire to become leaders. When you want to be seen as a subject matter expert (SME) or knowledge source, a presentation can showcase your skills and potential. Each time you pitch an idea, discuss solutions with a client, or interact with colleagues, you're presenting your skills. This can lead to

- Higher visibility
- Improved confidence

- Better communication skills
- Career growth
- Extended networks

Setting the Stage

At the outset of my signature workshop, "Storytelling and Storyboarding: Building Blocks to Influential Presentations," I divide the group into teams of two or three people and present the following scenario. (Although this may seem a little hokey, there's a method to my madness, so please bear with me and give it a try.)

It's the year 2050 and a group of Martians is scheduled to visit your facility. You plan to be at the space pad to greet them, but an important meeting has called you away. You know the Martians will be hungry after their long and arduous journey, and you'll be out of the office when they arrive. So, you hire a driver to bring them to your location. You need to prepare a presentation teaching them to make something easy — a peanut butter and jelly sandwich. They do speak English.

Grab a pen or pencil and a sheet of paper and briefly show how you'd approach this.

Welcome back... Did you start with a slide presentation? If so, you're in the majority. Most participants spend 5-10 minutes outlining what would become a slide presentation. They begin by instructing the Martians to put down two slices of bread. Open the jar of peanut butter. Smear some on one of the bread slices, etc. On occasion, I'd overhear someone say, "I don't think slides will work. Perhaps a video would work better." While that's insightful, few have thought through the details they take for granted when giving instructions. Here are just a few of the things you may take for granted:

- Although the Martians speak English, would they necessarily know what peanut butter and jelly are? (We only understand the words we've been exposed to.)
- Would they understand how to remove the lids from the jars? (Hmm. . . hit them with a sledgehammer?) If you said twist the lid, would that be clockwise or counterclockwise?
- How should they spread the peanut butter? (With their fingers?) If you told them to smear the peanut butter with a knife, would they know how to use the knife safely without spewing blood?

Then . . . once you've identified the level of detail you need to share, the next step is to identify the best means of communicating it. A live, interactive presentation would work best. If that's not possible, a video could be a viable substitute.

REMEMBER

When you're faced with a presentation you need to prepare, sharpen your axe. Consider your audience and the best way to present. Think of relevant stories they'll relate to. Chapter 3 offers a full discussion of knowing your audience and how to focus on their needs.

STORYOPIA ARCHIVES: PAIRING PEANUT BUTTER AND JELLY

The history of how peanut butter met jelly is a little uncertain, but one thing is for sure – they're a match made in heaven and are meant to be together. In the early 1900s peanut butter was a delicacy, bought and eaten only by the wealthy. At the time, peanut butter was frequently paired with pimento cheese, celery, cucumbers, and crackers.

Today's beloved pairing of peanut butter and jelly (PB&J) were first mentioned in the *Boston Cooking School Magazine of Culinary Science and Domestic Economics* written by Julia Davis Chandler in 1901. But the impetus that took the PB&J sandwich over the top came after World War II and the Great Depression. Here's the backstory:

PB&J were on the U.S. military ration menus in World War II. Peanut butter is high-protein, rich in vitamins, minerals, and fiber. Peanut butter also contains healthy fat, but the sweetness comes from the jelly's sugar. These sandwiches were easy to pack for long marches and were yummy to eat due to the bread that holds this dynamic duo together. Thus, after the war, soldiers craved PB&J sandwiches, and they became an American standard.

This sandwich is so ubiquitous that in the U.S. the average schoolchild eats about 15,000 PB&J sandwiches before the end of high school. (The growing number of kids with peanut allergies, however, is now threatening the popularity of this lunchbox staple.)

Lesson learned: Getting back to Kipling's quote, your story (or stories) can become part of your presentation's history — making it unforgettable.

Avoid Defaulting to Slides

SHERYL SAYS

Throughout this book I use the term *slides* to represent any presentation software.

Old habits die hard. When people hear the word "presentation," most of them automatically plummet into the slide abyss. When you ask these same slide-abyss people to describe the last presentations they attended, they use words like *boring, humdrum, uninteresting, waste of time, too many slides, too much text, no interaction*, and other negative phrases.

Poll everywhere, real-time audience response software, estimates that . . .

- 30 million PowerPoint presentations are shown each day.
- 500 million people view PowerPoint presentations every day.
- The average presentation lasts 4 hours.
- The average slide has 40 words.

If you think slides don't get in the way of good conversation, try showing a few at your next dinner party and see how well it goes over.

Eliminating slidezillas

Slidezillas are the presentation equivalents of Godzilla. Just as Godzilla is the towering, reptilian monster that plagued Japan, slidezillas are the data-laden technology monsters that plague audiences.

It's the twenty-first century. Don't continue inflicting boring, linear, static, text-laden slides on your audiences. Every presentation should be a conversation — a sharing of information — with active participants (the audience) and a facilitator (you).

As mentioned in the introduction, industry giants such as Amazon, Google, Apple, Starbucks, Airbnb, Netflix, Zappos, Facebook, LinkedIn, GlaxoSmithKline, and others have banned slidezilla-type slides from their meetings. Their presenters must use a narrative (or conversational) format, which means talking WITH the audience, not AT them. Too many presenters use slides as teleprompters. They have their backs to the audience much of the time as they read from their slides. They may as well have sent the slides to the audience and stayed home.

Whether your presentation is for training, fact finding, problem solving, brainstorming, selling, building consensus, or takes the form of instructor-led, online, mobile, gamification, or microlearning — tell stories. Sharing stories allows you to establish a good flow of communication so your main message reaches the audience in a way that engages and drives the call to action.

WARNING

Here are a few reasons why slide presentations are *not* effective:

- Slides are a crutch for the presenter, not a learning tool for the audience.
- They steal the limelight from the stars and heroes of the presentation — the audience.
- Displaying words and graphics on a screen while speaking decreases engagement, comprehension, and retention.
- There's always the risk of a technical glitch.
- The audience may be reluctant to ask questions or provide their own valuable insights because they know the presentation must end in the allotted time.

Visual storytelling can be exceedingly powerful

Visual stories are *not* slidezillas. They're stories communicated through visual content in the form of photographs, illustrations, slides, clip art, memes, jpgs, gifs, videos, charts, tables, graphs, infographics, word clouds, live demos, or more. The main goal of visual storytelling is to convey complex thoughts and emotions to hook the audience and drive storylines, emotions, and the call to action (CTA).

Why is visual storytelling so powerful? As humans, we're visual creatures. Ninety percent of the information transmitted to ours brains is visual, so it's no surprise that visual storytelling catches our attention in a way words can't.

TIP

Add visual storytelling to your repertoire of stories. You can find out more about visual storytelling in Chapters 8 and 9.

STORYOPIA ARCHIVES: STORYTELLING FROM THE CRYPT

While writing this book, I had the remarkable experience of making a long-awaited visit to Egypt where stories of Ancient Egyptians come alive through wall art. Like descriptive novels from one of the world's oldest and greatest civilizations thousands of years ago, the visual art shares narratives about the people and the times.

Egyptian tombs were intended to be secret art galleries. Stories on the walls were to help the pharaohs and the people buried with them on their journeys to the afterlife. Scribes wrote the tales on the walls, and then craftsmen carved and painted them. The tombs were never meant to be opened or viewed. However, with today's technology, tombs are being unearthed in Luxor's Valley of the Queens and Valley of the Kings. Thus, these venerable stories live on today and will continue sharing this rich history thousands of years from now. This photo is from the tomb of Rameses in the Valley of the Kings. This is visual storytelling at its finest!

Sailingstone Travel / Adobe Stock

Lesson Learned: Tell your stories. They'll live on, and you never know what will resonate with someone and have lasting impact.

Firing Up Your Audience's Imagination with Storyopia

This book is all about the game-changing storyopia. *Storyopia*, like utopia, represents the ideal. It's the ideal story that takes the audience on a journey from what *is* to what *could be*. A journey to where they see themselves as heroes along that same path.

Try to recall presentations you've attended. What drove the presentation? Bullet points? Charts? Tables? The monotonous drone of a facilitator plodding through a dry rendition of data? My guess is all of them. (A pretty tedious experience.)

Since people began to communicate, storytelling has been the lifeblood to getting points or ideas across and making them memorable. Stories make ideas and words come alive. They explain examples or points of view in a way that resonates. People naturally connect emotionally with stories, associating their feelings with their learning.

REMEMBER

Stories aren't meant to be objective. They're meant to sway emotions, generate suspense, add surprise, create wonder, facilitate the call to action, and take your audience on a journey to success.

TIP

If you're intrigued by this concept of storyopia, head to Chapter 2 for more details.

Using the Story Arc

Figure 1-1 shows the typical story arc (also known as dramatic arc or narrative arc). It represents storyopia. When creating a story using the arc as a guide, your story will have a natural, connected flow.

1. **Cite the incident (the plot) telling what is.**
2. **Build rising tension toward the climax.**
3. **Work towards the resolution, which is what could be.**

REMEMBER

Always create tension in your story. It's critical but often overlooked. If the tension isn't obvious, this is a good opportunity to embellish with a story. After you've filled out the Start-Up Brief, which you find in Chapter 3, you'll have a good idea of your audience's pain and what matters to them. Focus on storyopia — the gap between what is and what can be. Take them on that journey so they see themselves as heroes on the same path.

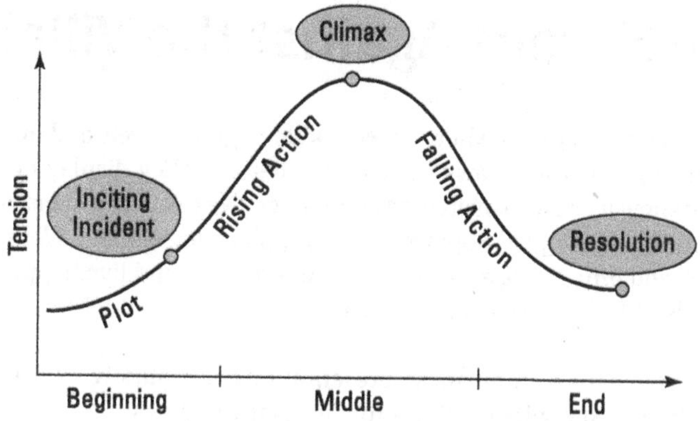

FIGURE 1-1: The story arc.

Your story will have characters: people, companies, or things, such as processes or equipment. There will be goals, struggles, challenges, and a positive or negative outcome. Either outcome serves as a valuable lesson. Let's see how beginnings, middles, and ends can become a story:

- **Beginning:** Introduce characters with the same challenge, problem, complication, or issue your audience is facing — the reason they're attending. You'll hook them because they'll feel like they're in the same situation. Edit the details to keep the story simple and relatable. You may start with, "One of my customers was dealing with your exact issue(s)."
- **Middle:** You've already sparked their curiosity. Now focus on the characters' problems and how your solution brought the change they needed. Don't merely go from Point A to Point B. The long cuts and shortcuts are what make the journey interesting, worthwhile, and relatable.
- **End:** This is where you tie it together, targeted to the CTA. Deliver the main takeaways and lessons your audience should remember based on the success of your characters. Let your audience see the happy ending where they imagine themselves as heroes achieving these same positive outcomes.

REMEMBER

Always give your characters names to make them more relatable, but change the names for the purpose of anonymity. People don't identify with words such as *attendee*, *coworker*, *colleague*, or *manager*. Also, provide a vivid description of your main character and the setting so your audience can envision the scenario and place themselves in the situation.

For example, if you're presenting to a group about sales strategies because sales have been slumping, you may share a story of [name] who worked for [company for x years] and how he was able to bring his sales and commissions up to a much higher level by [strategy].

Pitting the Heroes Against the Villains

From bedtime stories when we were kids to great novels and movies as we became older, a good story draws us. We love heroes. They display qualities we admire. They show us how to overcome challenges. We can recall superhero caped crusaders: Batman, Batgirl, Superman, Zorro, Shazam, Wonder Woman, Scarlet Witch, Thor, and others. We all want to be superheroes and live happily ever after in our worlds of family, friends, and business.

Are there heroes in business presentations? Absolutely — the audience! This is how heroes and villains play a role in happy endings:

» **Heroes:** Think of the character Yoda from the *Star Wars* series. Yoda was the legendary Jedi Master who trained Jedi Knights for 800 years. Yoda was cool. He was a hero in addition to being a mentor and instructor. He unlocked the path to immortality in characters such as Han Solo, Luke Skywalker, Obi-Wan Kenobi, and others who became heroes in their own rights. You can be the Yoda in your presentation, unlocking the path to slaying the villain and guiding your audience toward success.

  Heroes can even be antiheroes — people who display true human nature. People who make poor decisions that may harm those around them, intentionally or not. Some are even well intentioned, such as Robin Hood, the classical literary antihero. He stole from the rich (bad) and gave to the poor (good). Even Donald Duck has been labeled antihero for his short and often explosive temper.

» **Villains:** Without villains (often the most interesting characters) there would be no stories and no heroes. For example, if not for Cruella De Vil, *101 Dalmatians* would merely feature lots of spotted canines running around. Without Scar in *The Lion King* scheming to be next in line to seize the throne, there would be no story, and Simba wouldn't have become a hero.

  In business, the villain is the problem or challenge. That can be unscrupulous people, anti-technology diehards, a combative person, the competition, and so on. A villain may also be a non-person: a specific event, befuddled communication, meager lead generation, declining customer base, poor cash flow, inability to retain valuable employees, failure to balance quality and growth, software that isn't producing as expected, and so much more.

» **Happy endings:** You don't want the victory to be too easy or too predictable — it kills the interest and suspense. At the beginning of every story the villain must be strong, the victim's problems must seem insurmountable, and the hero's task must seem challenging. Your story needs an imagined future where the audience puts themselves in the place of slaying their villain and making themselves heroes.

Perhaps your audience will use the knowledge they learned from you to

- Add $$$ to their bottom line.
- Become more innovative.
- Discover the right tools or technology.
- Take a leadership position.
- Communicate with impact.
- Get the big contract signed.
- Procure a grant.

In Chapter 4 you find a process for mining your own stories from people, places, and things in your life — past and present.

STORYOPIA ARCHIVES: DITCHING SLIDES AND TELLING THE STORY

Carter came into one of the Storytelling and Storyboarding workshops I was facilitating at a major Boston hospital. He was very excited. He walked right up to me and said, "Hi, Sheryl, I'm Carter. The timing for this workshop couldn't be more perfect. I'm one of five finalist seeking a very large grant. We were each asked to prepare a PowerPoint presentation to strengthen our cases. And I present a week from now . . . I printed out the 25 slides I prepared and hope you'll have time to critique them. I really need this grant to continue the research I've been doing."

After a quick scan of 25 data-laden slides of charts, tables, and graphs, my response to him was *Yikes!* So I challenged him with the following idea:

"Imagine this: It's the day of your presentation. You walk into this large conference room with three stern-looking grantors sitting in black leather swivel chairs around a long, mahogany conference table. The room is modern, almost sterile looking. White walls. The only thing hanging is a white board that spans one entire wall. There are no windows, just bright lights. The five finalists are seated facing the projector and large screen in front of the room. (Pause) Let's assume that you're the fifth and final presenter. Do you think the grantors will still be listening attentively by the time you present? Or will they have been so bored by the data-laden presentations of your competitors, they're mentally packing for a trip to Hawaii? Then I asked him, "Have you ever seen the popular TV show Shark Tank where a group of investors hears pitches from people who are seeking funding from them? Think of your presentation as your shark tank."

(continued)

(continued)

He was quite taken aback by my comments because he was planning to blend in with the pack using slides, as he was directed. I encouraged him to see that the villains in this story were his competitors. I encouraged him to do three heroic things:

1. Ditch all his slides.
2. Prepare stories and deliver a narrative in conversational format.
3. Generate a dynamic handbook for each of the grantors.

At the outset Carter was reluctant. But after going through the workshop, he agreed to deliver a narrative telling stories of the successes of many recipients of his former grants. He left each grantor with a handbook of the stories and other information that made his research worthy of additional funding.

Rather than being the last to present, Carter was the first. The grantors were so impressed with the high bar Carter had set, that all the other presenters (who showed data-laden slides) paled in comparison. Carter was memorable. He was awarded the grant! He brought home the gold. Carter was the hospital's hero!

Lesson Learned: When you use a narrative approach to presenting, your audience pays attention. Don't burden them with slides, unless they're necessary to drive home a point. Tell your story, and they will listen.

On to Storyboarding. . .

In Chapter 7 you find out everything you need to know about storyboarding, which is basically a visual outline that incorporates your spoken and visual stories. When you use a storyboard to incorporate stories into your overall narrative, you'll engage your audiences. Storyboarding helps you in the following ways:

- See the continuity of your message.
- Identify any gaps.
- Discover if you told too much or too little.
- Turn your ideas into a narrative.
- Incorporate visuals when and where needed.
- Get your audience actively involved and keep them involved.
- Use your time efficiently.

IN THIS CHAPTER

» Sparking minds with stories

» Picking up pointers from the all-time greats

» Becoming a great storyteller

» Speaking in the first person, present tense

» Spanning industries with storytelling

Chapter 2

Storyopia: Sharing Stories from What Is to What Can Be

Stories create community, enable us to see through the eyes of other people, and open us to the claims of others.

—PETER FORBES, AUTHOR AND PHOTOGRAPHER

This chapter takes you on a journey to understanding how storyopia plays a part not only in presentations but also in our everyday experiences. For example, note the oversaturation of journey-based ads that inundate our TVs, smartphones, computers, and tablets. They're brief, impactful stories — combining words and visuals — aimed at pre-determined audiences taking us on journeys from what is (before) to what can be (after).

Companies pay ad agencies huge sums of money to target audiences with the appropriate messaging in order to create awareness, consideration, and decision. Here are just a few examples:

- » Financial organizations take us on journeys from saving our nickels and dimes to retiring as intrepid travelers hobnobbing around the world. These images of carefree, vibrant seniors stick in our minds.
- » Acclaimed celebrities (who are never seen without being professionally made up and looking years younger than they actually are) are selling beauty aids. The call to action is, "Buy the product and you too can look this awesome."
- » Pharmaceutical ads claiming to clear blotchy skin (among other conditions) open with a person disgusted with an ugly skin condition. After using the product, that person is part of a loving couple sitting on a sandy beach enjoying the sunset. The optic is alluring. Viewers tune out the litany of side effects that are jabbered quickly because they're focusing on what they see — the loving couple with beautiful skin sitting on the sandy beach watching the sunset.
- » The wonder remedy that will give you energy so intoxicating, you'll imagine that it's you sucking the marrow out of life by participating in unusual or even daredevilish activities.

These journey-based ads work remarkably well. Otherwise, the world's largest companies wouldn't dedicate so much of their marketing and advertising budgets to bombarding us with them.

Taking Your Audience on a Journey

The most effective storytellers frame the journey to convince their audiences to identify with the outcome. The stories — whether verbal, visual, or a combination — should grab attention, be memorable, relatable, persuasive, and evoke emotion and imagination.

START-UP BRIEF

Storytelling begins with filling out the Start-Up Brief, covered in detail in Chapter 3. It will help you to know your audience so you can incorporate clear signposts by gauging what's important to them. Who they are? What problems are they trying to solve? What compelling call to action will they relate to? Here are a few examples:

- » You're a financial planner trying to convince a group of millennials to let you manage their investments. Their concerns are saving for their children's education, having enough money to retire early, leaving money to the next generation. Take them on a journey of how successful your strategies have been with other clients to reach those goals.

- You're delivering sales training to a group of neophytes recently hired by a company. You'll want to tell rags-to-riches stories of how other salespeople have made tons of money in the competitive world of sales.
- You're presenting complex semiconductor equipment to a senior-level audience — potential customer. This company can add large sums of money to your company's bottom line if they select you. Stories can range from a journey of exactly how a customer implemented your solution and became successful. Or you can go in the opposite direction and share a story of a company that didn't implement your solution and things went awry.

REMEMBER

Not all stories are positive or have happy endings. However, there are still lessons to be learned. Don't shy away from them. A perfect example is George Orwell's *Animal Farm* written in 1945. It's a story about animals, but adult readers would recognize it to reflect the Russian Revolution of 1917, drawing attention to the unfair structure that exists in societies. The book is about corruption and oppression, and how one person in total power will eventually become corrupt.

Understanding why people respond to stories

There's a scientific reason why people respond so strongly to stories. People are biologically and neurologically wired to connect with stories through a feel-good hormone called *oxytocin*. Oxytocin lifts our feelings of trust, compassion, and empathy.

When you supercharge your presentation with stories that are well told, shown, and relevant to the goal of your presentation, you trick your audience's brain into thinking they're experiencing the incident themselves. And they're right there with you — involved.

Remembering that stories can be visual

When people think of storytelling, they often think of words only. However, visuals can be used in conjunction with the narrative, or they can stand alone. Visuals can range from simple diagrams, charts, or tables to infographics, photographs, memes, jpgs or gifs, videos, word clouds, props, and more. No matter the medium, the goal is always the same — to make complex stories easier to understand and, as a result, deliver a more impactful message.

REMEMBER

Note how even a simple photograph (see Figure 2-1) can bring a story to life, making it imaginative and relevant for readers. If you merely said, "A grandfather is reading a story to his granddaughter," that wouldn't evoke the same heart-warming imagery you see in the photo. It just wouldn't. To find out more about visual storytelling, head to Chapter 9.

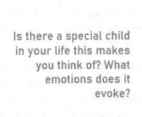

Is there a special child in your life this makes you think of? What emotions does it evoke?

FIGURE 2-1: Granddaughter relishing a story with her PopPop.

Photo courtesy of author

WARNING

Slidezillas, or data-laden slides, guarantee that your presentation will sink under the weight of overload. Examples would be an endless deck of spreadsheets or slides with so many bullets they'd be hard to read without a magnifying glass. Easy-to-read slides (whether text and/or graphics) that drive a point are *not* slidezillas.

Knowing that everyone has a story (Yes, even you!)

At the outset of the storytelling and storyboarding workshops I facilitate, I often hear people say, *I don't have any stories.* That isn't true. Stop and think about it. Stories are merely experiences — experiences you or others have had. Just by virtue of the fact that you're alive, you've had lots of experiences; therefore, you have lots of stories. Everyone has a story — in fact, everyone has loads of stories.

Check out Chapter 4 to discover how you can morph your experiences into stories so that you're engaging your audiences, not lecturing to them. As a preview, make connections between the people, places, and things in your life. Then tie them together into engaging stories. For example, perhaps you're giving a talk on mentoring. You may share a story of how you mentored a colleague at your former company, and that colleague went on to create an effective process that was very valuable to the company. That colleague even got the process patented. The lesson learned is the strong impact a mentor can have on a mentee.

TIP

Also think of storylines from popular movies or books that relate to your audience and your topic. They can be encounters and adventures that challenge the hero, occasionally giving a new perspective on life and on the world. Even stories of tragedies can have redeeming qualities, relaying how people rise above tragedy to do great things. You can use an endless amount of storylines that have lasted through the ages. This list offers you a few ideas:

- Rags to riches
- Voyages and returns
- Overcoming monsters or other evils
- Tragedies
- Comedies
- Thrillers and adventures
- Pursuits and rivalries
- Search and rescue

STORYOPIA ARCHIVES: SEEING IS BELIEVING

When my husband first heard I was writing a book on storytelling for presentations, he wasn't convinced of its efficacy. He's an engineer-scientist and is steeped in the world of data and analytics. (His slides reflect that.) We're a left-brain, right-brain couple, so I wasn't entirely surprised. Opposites attract and often clash (or at least disagree).

Then the January 13, 2023, issue of *SCIENCE* magazine arrived, and (Voila!) I was vindicated and so was the topic of storytelling for presentations. The magazine ran a three-page feature article titled "'Storylistening' in the Science Policy Ecosystem. Expert analysis of narrative can complement and strengthen scientific evidence." The authors Claire Craig and Sarah Dillon state, "Storytelling or narratives, when expertly incorporated, can help augment scientific knowledge." . . . Stories matter but,

(continued)

(continued)

particularly in the context of the use of research-based evidence, policymakers and experts rarely ask how, or why, or what to do as a result." My husband's comment after reading the article was, "Oh . . . I get it!"

The authors use an interesting word "storylistening." The inference is that there's rarely serious thought about how best to listen to stories." Murray, Nossel, author and founder of Narativ, says "Acknowledge your listeners. Thank them for listening. Let them know that their listening makes a difference to your story and that without it, your story would lose its potency."

Lesson learned: Across the board, storytelling is the way to teach and reach people. An interesting storyteller will have interested storylisteners.

Mapping Out Your Storyopia Journey with Storyboards

Storyboarding (in the form we know it today) was developed at Walt Disney Productions in the early 1930s. It's an essential step in the film, public relations, and marketing industries where it's critical to get the message across clearly and succinctly.

Storyboarding is the tool for effective storytelling. It involves creating a draft to plan how a presentation will evolve. And, as within every good book or movie, there are subplots with stories. In essence, storyboards are basically frames containing what you'll tell and what you'll show — whether your presentation live, virtual, hybrid, streaming, or zooming in the metaverse. (You can discover lots more about storyboarding in Chapter 7.)

REMEMBER

Successful presenters use storyboarding to outline their narratives and decide what, if any, visuals they need to show. If you think storyboarding is an unnecessary step that hardly anyone actually uses . . . think again:

- Business professionals storyboard to plan advertising campaigns, corporate videos, commercials, events, proposals, grant requests, and other presentations intended to influence and create a call to action.
- Storyboard artists often interpret screenplays from a script. Storyboards illustrate the visual and technical requirements of a production.

STORYOPIA ARCHIVES: LEARNING FROM YOUR AUDIENCE

For several years I presented my Storytelling and Storyboarding workshop without any slides. My goal was to demonstrate how slides aren't necessary to enhance the message. Each person received a workbook, and the sessions were very interactive. Over a few months, several people commented that they would have appreciated my showing at least a few slides to demonstrate best practices. Realizing that most people won't eliminate slides completely, I took those comments to heart and prepared several relevant slides — many of which you'll see throughout this book.

Lesson learned: There's much you, as a presenter, can learn from your audience. Listen to them and learn. I'm glad I did.

- Businesses use storyboards to outline the experience of new customers from purchase to after the sale. That is common practice in web and app design, and it's often called user experience design.
- Comic book artists storyboard for staging the scene and showing the positions of the characters in the story.
- Storyboarding proves valuable for team alignment. Planning a project with lots of people can be like juggling ten balls. It's a handy tool in the early stages for planning and envisioning the activities throughout every phase of a project.
- Storyboards are used for revamping websites and blogs to visualize what works best before implementing changes across multiple platforms.
- Novelists often write their stories by scenes rather than chapters, and storyboarding helps plot the sequence of events.
- This process is useful in software engineering. It helps users understand exactly how the software will work — much better than an abstract description would.

Speaking in the first person, present tense

Punctuate your story by telling it in the first person, present tense using *is* and *are*, rather than *was* and *were*. Use *I*, *me*, *my*, or *myself*. In the examples that follow, notice how the first person, present tense creates real-time immediacy — a sense of urgency. It gives the audience the feeling of plunging into the situation with you as it's happening, and they ask themselves, "What would I do?"

> **First person, present tense:** I walk onto the stage. Immediately there's a power failure. My instant reaction is, "What can I do?"
>
> **Third person, past tense:** Kate walked onto the stage. Immediately there was a power failure. Her instant reaction was what could she do.

Learning from the All-Time Storytelling Greats

What do Aesop, Abe Lincoln, Jerry Seinfeld, (Mr.) Fred Rogers, Winston Churchill, Volodymyr Zelenskyy, Steve Jobs, guests on TED talks, and many others have in common? From the title of this section you may have guessed: They're all master speakers and storytellers — some with words alone, some with lights, some with cameras, and some with actions.

They didn't wow audiences with tedious slide presentations chock full of numbers, graphs, and zippy animations or videos. They knew their audiences and brought the most important element to each speaking event — their relatable, human selves. They're also masters of storyopia, taking audiences with them on their journeys to what can be. We can learn many lessons by harnessing each of their examples.

Aesop

Aesop's fables are allegorical myths of animals or insects engaged in human- like situations. These fables — all teaching morals — have been interwoven into different cultures and have reached countless generations. Aesop's fables were among the first printed works and are currently written in more than 100 languages.

One of his most famous fables is "The Boy Who Cried Wolf." This story been passed down through generations by parents and teachers. It tells of a shepherd boy who keeps tricking people into believing a wolf is attacking his flock of sheep. When it really happens, nobody comes because he "cried wolf" too many times. The story ends tragically. It's a simple example of a story with a negative ending that teaches a valuable lesson about telling the truth.

Abe Lincoln

Lincoln's early years provided the perfect environment for storytelling. His family lived on the frontier during a time of great migration. Peddlers, adventurers, and pioneers making their way West would stop by his cabin and swap stories. Lincoln spent long hours translating what he heard into plain language. He longed for an audience and would present his version of the stories at any ad hoc gathering he could gather, usually kids in the neighborhood.

In *Team of Rivals,* historian and biographer Doris Kearns Goodwin writes that many scholars consider Lincoln to be one of America's greatest orators and storytellers of all time — a "Herculean act of self-creation." Lincoln became a great leader because he was a great communicator. And he was a great communicator because he was a strategic storyteller who took audiences on journeys with him. He deeply understood that the power storytelling has to influence the way people think and feel about an issue.

SHERYL SAYS

Imagine if Lincoln were here today and was asked to share the secret of how leadership is intertwined with great public speaking. He'd probably list the following:

- Share a good story and tell it convincingly.
- Help your audience see and feel the value and benefit of what you're saying.
- Speak from your heart with passion and purpose.
- Connect with your audience and take them on the journey with you.
- End with a relatable call to action.

Jerry Seinfeld

Comedians are natural-born storytellers. They share everyday stories about their lives with humor that engage audiences. *Seinfeld* is a sitcom about four friends weathering the trappings of life in New York City in the '90s. Many episodes start with Jerry and George sitting in the diner swapping stories about *nothing* — dates, sex, salsa, driving, money, baseball, and nothing of any relevance. Yet, it's one of the top shows in TV history, and reruns continue to air.

Why do you think that a program seemingly about nothing, has been so popular for decades? It's because *Seinfeld,* isn't about nothing. It's about something — storytelling. It validates the fact that stories, no matter how mundane they may seem on the surface, are relevant when told to the proper audiences. You may not have Jerry, Elaine, George, and Kramer, but you have friends, family, co-workers, and customers. All have had successes and failures, so your stories are just as relevant to your audiences.

(Mr.) Fred Rogers

Watching Tom Hanks portray Fred Rogers in "A Beautiful Day in the Neighborhood," made me think of why I enjoyed watching *Mr. Rogers Neighborhood* when I was a child and while raising my two sons. For 33 years Fred Rogers was part of the neighborhood, and he's still taking us on his journeys and teaching us.

Kids (as well as adults) always want to know *how* and *why*. Rogers always answered those questions with relatable stories. That's what made him so effective. He told relevant stories. His tone was warm and sincere. He kept a razor-sharp focus. His slow pacing made him easy to listen to.

Perhaps Fred Rogers' finest moment was in 1969 when he appeared before the U.S. Senate Subcommittee on Communications. His goal was to prevent $20 million in funding for PBS and the Corporation of Public Broadcasting being reduced to $10 million. Subcommittee Chair Sen. John Pastore was initially very antagonistic toward Rogers. Over the course of Rogers' six minutes of storytelling testimony, Pastore admitted to getting goosebumps as he was swept along on the journey.

The session ended with Pastore having a major attitude adjustment and saying to Rogers: "You just found your $20 million." And it was without a single visual! Just a powerful story. (If you want to view the exchange, go to `https://www.youtube.com/watch?v=fKy7ljRr0AA/`.)

Winston Churchill and Volodymyr Zelenskyy

I've paired these two historical figures because Zelenskyy has been compared to the late Churchill. During different points in history, each man delivered a powerful and passionate speech to the United States Congress to garner much-needed support for their nations under siege. Churchill's story took the audience on a journey about fighting on the seas, oceans, hills, streets, and beaches. Zelenskyy's journey was about fighting in the forests, in the fields, on the shores, in the streets. Both men used the storyline of David fighting the mighty Goliath, and each invoked the masterful art of storytelling.

Steve Jobs

Jobs didn't start out being a great storyteller. He made the choice to be one because he felt that good storytellers have power. He told audiences his plans in his presentation, not with slides but rather with a verbal roadmap. For example, when he introduced the iPhone, he heightened the anticipation by telling his audience he would be introducing three revolutionary products: a widescreen iPod, a phone, and an internet communications device. They turned out to be all in one devise. The audience went wild, whistling and cheering!

The secret sauce to Apple's success wasn't Job's inherent ability no one else had. He kept working on being a great storyteller. Jobs knew that he needed more than his own storytelling, he needed disciples who would tell their stories and drive people to Apple products. He taught others by his example. Stories helped to build the Apple empire, and the journey continues under new leadership.

Guests on TED Talks

If you ever watch TED talks (abbreviation for Technology, Entertainment, Design) you notice that talks are built around stories with personal anecdotes that bring ideas to life. They focus on one idea and stress the why. They

» Captivate with stories of triumph over extreme adversity.

» Create suspense to put audiences in the middle of the action.

» Bring characters to life with their fortunes and misfortunes.

» Taking audiences on the journey with them.

» End with a positive takeaway.

TED talks feature people of different nationalities and cultures, native and non-native speakers, and people with different levels of abilities. Many of them are afraid to speak in public, but they have something valuable to share and receive coaching to tell their stories.

REMEMBER

There are many lessons you can learn about presenting from watching TED talks: Tell stories. Focus on one idea. Start with your why. Speak less. Talk with your hands. Simplify your visuals. Have a strong call to action.

STORYOPIA ARCHIVES: HAVING STORIES IN YOUR HIP POCKET

Imagine you're a long-distance runner ready to start a major race. You've trained hard and can almost see yourself crossing the finish line, racing for the gold. You bought new running shoes. You even wore your lucky underwear. You're in the crouching position, and your adrenaline is pumping. Just as the starting pistol fires, one of your shoelaces becomes untied and you trip on it. Oh no! You forgot to double knot the laces.

I was the keynote speaker at a conference. Alexander was scheduled to give a 15-minute presentation before I was to be introduced. Alexander appeared to be a friendly man. Probably in his mid-50s. Average height. Average build. We chatted for a while, and he seemed ill at ease. He told me his daughter was to be married the following weekend. He was anxious that everything should go smoothly — both at the wedding and for this presentation. Trying to ease his tension, I kidded him that he was my warm-up act. Alexander smiled and walked on stage. He turned on his projector, and he had brought a thumb drive with the wrong slides. Red-faced, Alexander stood there for 15 minutes bumbling. I was embarrassed for him. The audience was embarrassed for him. He had no opening he could jump to and no stories to fall back on. He just had slides he couldn't use. He was totally unprepared to talk without them.

Just like the racer who didn't double tie his knots, Alexander didn't double check to make sure he had the correct slides, and he wasn't prepared if something went wrong and he couldn't use his slides. The vivid picture Alexander painted was not the one he intended to paint. (I surely hope the wedding went better than his presentation.)

Lesson learned: Always, always use a checklist to make sure you have everything you need. Practice without slides in case Murphy's Law strikes. And be ready with stories in case you have to pull a few out of your hip pocket.

2

Nuts 'n' Bolts

IN THIS PART . . .

Get to know your audience, focus on their key issues, know what questions you should be prepared to answer, and hit the bull's-eye every time.

Mine everyday experiences into engaging stories, create a narrative from data, craft your own repertoire, and coin a catchphrase.

Grab your audience's attention straightaway, introduce yourself and the program, open with engaging activities, and don't bury the lede.

Finish strong with a call to action your audience will heed, know what to cut if you're running short of time, give them something to remember, and extend your network.

Understand why storyboarding breathes life into presentations, get to know different types of storyboards, give presentations interesting titles, and create audience heroes.

IN THIS CHAPTER

» Assessing your last presentation

» Seeing your target

» Focusing on your audience, purpose, and key issue

» Understanding what questions your audience will want answered

Chapter 3

Knowing Your Audience to Make Them Heroes

To improve communication, work not on the utterer, but on the recipient.

—PETER DRUCKER, AMERICAN BUSINESS PHILOSOPHER AND AUTHOR

Every presenter must remember four important words: *It's not about me!* When your audience walks into the room, they're thinking, "What's in it for me?" Perhaps you think you already know your audience, but do you actually understand their (hidden) agendas or what keeps them up at night? In this chapter, you find out how to better understand your audience, their purpose and key issue, and the questions you need to address to create a presentation that will make each person feel like you're speaking directly to them.

SHERYL SAYS

If you don't get to know your audience at a deep level before your presentation, it will be like writing "To Whom It May Concern" as the salutation to a love letter. The presentation will feel impersonal, and it certainly won't deliver the intended message. The Start-Up Brief, which is the essence of this chapter, can help you connect with your audience and deliver your message — and have it received — as you intend. And your audience will leave feeling that the time with you was well spent because *what was in it for them* was valuable.

You Must See Your Target So You Know Where to Aim

Have you ever noticed how often you're targeted every time you turn on anything electronic? Commercials and ads target audiences incessantly with stories of overcoming obstacles, loving couples, happy families, smiling children, adventures, parties, successful businesses, and good times. What they're saying is: "This can be you."

Reaching targeted audiences is a proven strategy that works. Here are a few instances:

- During high-profile games, such as sports playoffs, there are abundant beer and car commercials.
- During evening news viewing, all kinds of drugs and health remedies are aired.
- During children's programs, kids are lured with junk cereal and snacks.

Do You Aim at the Needs of Your Audience?

Think of the last presentation you delivered. How do you think your audience would have answered the questions presented in Figure 3-1? Take a short break from reading this and check the appropriate answers in the columns labeled "Before." Be honest with yourself; you're the only one who'll see it. And it's okay to be unsure.

If you answered "Yes," those are areas in which you feel you're solid. If you answered "No" or "Not Sure," you have some work to do.

REMEMBER

The key is to start by understanding your audience, purpose, key issue, and questions you'll need to address. If you want to make your audience heroes, take them on a journey. Guide them to an improved future or solve a problem they've been grappling with — in much the same way commercials and ads do. This is called *storyopia.* It takes getting to know who they are so you can hold their attention, build anticipation, and lead them to a satisfying resolution.

Putting Yourself in Your Audience's Shoes

Question	BEFORE Yes	BEFORE No	BEFORE Not Sure	AFTER Yes	AFTER No	AFTER Not Sure
Was your key issue (or topic) crystal clear?						
Did your audience clearly understand what they were expected to do, think, feel, or learn?						
Did you consider the reaction your audience would have to your message?						
Was your message sequenced both strategically and logically?						
Was your message direct and personable?						
Did you limit your PowerPoints to 5-7 lines of text?						
Are you sure there were no errors—types or technical?						
Was your presentation interactive, allowing for audience participation?						
Did you let your personality show?						

Total *Yes* in Before column

Total *Yes* in After

FIGURE 3-1: Rate your presentation skills.

TIP

At the end of your next presentation go back and fill this in again posting your answers in the "After" column. You'll undoubtedly see a great improvement in the number of "Yes" responses and can run a victory lap! (You may even find that some of the areas where you thought you were solid, needed work.)

Using the Start-Up Brief to Target Your Audience

I compare understanding your audience to many of the courtroom scenes you've viewed in the movies and on TV. During the trial, attorneys pose leading questions they know will impact the jurors as they intend. They can do that because they've had the opportunity to get to know them beforehand through questioning. They can then relate stories aimed at strengthening their clients' cases to sway the jurors. The jurors become the heroes because they (presumably) reach a fair and equitable judgment. The selection of jurors can contribute to winning or losing the case even before it's even tried.

Let's relate this to presentations. Of course you won't select your audience, but the same principle of knowing them applies in order to have a winning presentation (for them and you). When you fill out the Start-Up Brief (see Figure 3-2), you learn all you can about your audience so you can target stories and the entire presentation toward the outcome you intend, and they'll leave as heroes.

START-UP BRIEF

AUDIENCE

1. What's the key issue — the one takeaway message I want my audience to remember?

2. Who's my primary audience?

3. What does my audience *need to know* about the topic?

4. What's in it for my audience?

5. Does my story need a special angle or point of view?

6. What will my audience's reaction be toward the topic? Positive? Neutral? Negative?

PURPOSE

7. My purpose is to________________ so my audience will ________________.

QUESTIONS

8. What *who, what, when, where, why,* and *how* questions will my audience want answered?

FIGURE 3-2: Use the Start-Up Brief to know your audience.

STORYOPIA ARCHIVES: STARTING WITH THE "WRITE" STUFF

For the past 15+ years I've conducted Storytelling and Storyboarding workshops for a wide variety of industries, including high tech, biotech, medical, manufacturing, and financial. Participants range from entry-level managers to those in the C-suites. They all bring to the session ideas for a presentation they need to prepare. Many of them are merely expecting to beef up slide presentations. The one overriding comment they have when I introduce the Start-Up Brief is, "I wouldn't have time to do it in the real world." However, after they fill it out during the early part of the workshop and develop their presentations during the session, they're amazed! Their presentations come together cohesively, rife with stories in a fraction of the time it used to take them. Many of them have gotten back to me later on with these comments:

- It now takes me 30 percent to 50 percent less time to get it right.
- I can't believe how many stories I've culled.
- I don't know how I ever did without the Brief.
- I'm telling everyone about it!

Lesson learned: Whether you're speaking or writing, when you clearly identify your audience, purpose, key issue, and questions your audience may need answers, your materials will be spot on. Use the Start-Up Brief before preparing every presentation.

Audience

When you see your target, you know where to aim and can hit the bullseye, as in Figure 3-3. The better you understand your audience, the better you'll be able to craft messages and stories they care about in terms of their interests, level of understanding, attitudes, and needs.

1. What's the key issue — the one takeaway message I want my audience to remember?

Your audience won't remember everything you say or show. What's the one message you want them to remember above all else? This is like an earworm. If you haven't heard that term, it's a tune you hear that plays over and over in your head that you can't seem to shake.

» What do you want your audience's earworm to be?

» What should they do? Think? Feel? Learn?

FIGURE 3-3: Know your target audience, so you know where to aim.

peterschreiber.media / Adobe Stock

REMEMBER

Condense the key message into one sentence. Until you can do that, you won't be focused. Imagine you have just one minute to get your key issue across clearly. What would that message be?

2. Who's my primary audience?

Why is it so easy to communicate with friends or close colleagues? Because you know them. You know their preconceived idea, level of expertise, probable reaction, and so forth. The same theory applies to your audience. Understand who they'll be and whether they're attending by choice.

There are so many types of audiences you may encounter. Here are just a few:

- Peers or subordinates
- Senior-level managers
- Middle-level managers
- Technical or non-technical
- Internal to your company or external
- Competitors
- Buyers
- Merchandisers
- Sales associates
- Customers (new and/or potential)
- Customer service

TIP

It would be helpful to determine the demographics of your audience prior to presenting. While there are limits as to what you can learn, on occasion it's apparent. For example, if you're addressing a technical group, you can assume that most are young, educated, and tech savvy. If the makeup of your audience isn't apparent, here are a few things you might try:

- Conduct surveys, questionnaires, or interviews with the event organizers. They may have knowledge of job titles, industries, and even a breakdown of age and gender.
- Survey the audience before the event. Ask what they hope to do, think, feel, or learn as a result of attending. Also inquire about their knowledge of the subject matter, organizations they belong to, volunteer activities, and so on.
- Tap into social media. If you have access to the event's social media accounts, check out who's following or engaging with them.
- Observe the audience and conduct informal conversations before the presentation starts.

WARNING

When presenting to all senior-level executives, different guidelines apply. Check out Chapter 20 to discover how to nail an executive briefing.

3. What does my audience *need to know* about the topic?

Please pay attention to the words *need to know*. Too often we give too much or too little information. For example, if you're discussing a specific aspect of genetic engineering but your audience isn't familiar with basic genetics, you'll have missed the mark. On the other hand, drastically underestimating the audience's knowledge may result in a presentation that sounds condescending. For a mixed audience, consider reviewing important key terms and concepts so everyone starts with baseline knowledge. Here are some things to think about:

- Does your audience have any preconceived ideas?
- Are there any barriers to their understanding (language, cultural, technical, or other)?
- Will there be any resistance?
- Will there be any adversaries?
- Will you have supporters?

4. What's in it for my audience?

Have you ever listened to WIIFM? The answer is "yes," you listen to it all the time — What's In It For Me? Whenever you listen to something, you unknowingly ask yourself, "Why should I care?" On the job, you might ask if this an opportunity to look good to superiors, make your job easier, solve a problem, or learn a new skill. If you didn't care, you wouldn't be listening.

REMEMBER

Dial in to WIIFM (Figure 3-4 shows a helpful visual reminder) to make sure you understand what's in it for your audience. Dig deeply. For example, if you're teaching them a new skill, will it impact their job performance? Help them look good to management? Ultimately get them a pay raise or promotion? You don't want anyone sitting in your audience waiting to find out what's in it for them. Let them know right up front.

FIGURE 3-4: Dial in to WIIFM to listen to your audience.

5. Does my presentation need a special angle or point of view?

Managers typically need the big picture to make big decisions. The lower down the chain of command, the more details may be needed. Technical people want all the details. Salespeople need benefits. Potential customers want to know why they should select you.

When presenting to hybrid audiences, key phrases may be:

- I'd like to take a few minutes to make sure we're we are all up to speed on the three key aspects of [topic].
- The crux of the matter is . . .

- The big picture is . . .
- Let me give you some examples . . .
- In practice this means . . .

6. What will my audience's reaction be toward the topic? Positive? Neutral? Negative?

You may not tell people what they *want* to hear, but you must tell them what they *need* to hear. What will their reaction be? Positive? Neutral? Negative? If you're not sure, ask yourself the following questions:

- Are you disputing existing data?
- Will you create more work for them?
- Are they attending by choice, or were they forced (strongly urged)?
- Are they interested in the topic?
- Will your information come as a surprise?
- What is their relationship with you and with each other?
- How will the presentation help them perform their jobs better?
- What are the most interesting parts of the topic?
- How much will the audience know about the topic?
- Which audience members may be more/less interested?

The following are suggestions for positioning positive, neutral, or negative topics:

- **Delivering a positive or neutral topic:** When your audience will be positive or neutral, use the BLUF (Bottom Line Up Front) approach. Your presentation isn't a joke where you need to put the punch line at the end. Tell them what they need to know right at the beginning. We've all sat through long, boring presentations waiting to hear the most important part we came to learn — the conclusion or findings.
- **Delivering a negative topic:** Strategically build up to your main message. Create a sandwich with good news, negative news, good news. Give reasons why. Offer options. Make lemonade. (Find out more about delivering negative news in Chapter 15.)

STORYOPIA ARCHIVES: CLEARING THE ELEPHANT FROM THE ROOM RIGHT UPFRONT

Jim was part of the Accounts Receivable department of a mid-sized company. The group was short-staffed and people were working lots of overtime. Morale was low, and people were calling in sick. This absenteeism created missed follow-ups on overdue invoices, errors on bills and invoices, and incorrect payment allocations. Jim requested a presentation to ask the management team to add two more people to the department. He knew there would be resistance because that would impact the bottom line. Of course, the people in attendance from his department were silently cheering him on.

He opened the presentation to address the "elephant in the room" to break down any resistance from the naysayers. "I know some of you may feel [he stated the reluctance]. I'm hoping to show you how my suggestion will be of benefit our organization."

After getting rid of the elephant, Jim presented a powerful case by sharing a few stories of where this was happening and what it was costing the company. He prepared a strategic graphic that showed how the cost of two more employees would be dramatically offset by the added revenue. Jim's argument was convincing, and the company hired two additional employees.

Lesson learned: When presenting to an audience of positive, neutral, and/or negative attendees, deal with the elephant in the room right up front and follow with story examples.

Purpose

Whether you think your purpose is to communicate, inform, sell, or whatever, chances are you're trying to "persuade" someone to do, think, feel, or learn something. Once you realize that most of what you present is to persuade — your message will be "strategic," not generic.

TIP

Keep peeling the onion (as the expression goes) because an underlying or unspoken purpose often boils down to money. For example, assume your presentation is to introduce a new corporate initiative. The unspoken message to those who embrace the initiative may be to perform better, look good to their superiors, increase the company's earnings, or perhaps be thought of more favorably when raises or promotions are due.

REMEMBER

The takeaway message you'll fill in on the second blank line (that follows) is the call to action. What do you want your audience to do, think, or feel, or learn? Your intention must be clear in your own mind so you can make it clear in theirs. What's their call to action? What's in it for them? Too many presenters don't get the action they wanted because they didn't make the expectation clear.

To state your strategic purpose and the call to action, fill in the blanks of the following statement:

7. My purpose is to ______________ so my audience will ____.

Questions

You may not think of every question your audience may have and need answered, but the following will help you consider as many as you can. They all relate to any or all of the following:

8. What who, what, when, where, why, and how questions will my audience want answered?

For practice, let's assume I'm inviting you to a meeting. There are questions you'll undoubtedly have when you receive the invitation.

Who else will be there?

What is the agenda?

When will the meeting be held?

Where will it be held?

Why am I being asked to attend?

How can I prepare and contribute?

REMEMBER

There are two sets of questions to think about when preparing a presentation:

- **Column 1:** Questions to ask yourself to prepare your presentation.
- **Column 2:** Questions you anticipate the audience will ask that you should include in your presentation or be prepared to answer.

Prepare two columns with who, what, when, where, why, and how. The following in Table 3-1 are possibilities to consider. Delete the questions that don't pertain to your presentation and add your questions that aren't listed.

TIP

Continue to Chapter 4 to find out how easy it is to create stories from your own experiences and the experiences of others.

TABLE 3-1 Questions to Ask When Preparing for a Presentation

	Your Questions	Audience's Questions
Who . . .	Will be supportive and make supportive comments? Will be adversarial and make combative comments? May feel threatened by my recommendations? Is my contact person for logistical and other issues? Should I bring in as a subject matter expert?	Is responsible? Will be impacted by the change?
What . . .	Are the major concerns of my audience? Can I tell or show to help them address those concerns? Stories can help them remember key points? Do they know about the topic? Is my relationship with them? Obstacles may I encounter? Discussion points should I encourage? Tough questions should I expect?	Are the alternatives? Are the advantages and/or disadvantages? Are the next steps? If we do nothing?
When . . .	Is the best time to deliver this presentation? Should I distribute the handouts?	Does this take effect? Do you need a decision?
Where . . .	Can the audience get more information? Can I get more information?	Will the funding come from? Can I get more information?
Why . . .	Is the audience attending? Was I chosen to make this presentation?	Are you recommending this?
How . . .	Much time should I spend on providing background? (Do they need any background?) Will I open/close the presentation? Does this relate to the strategic impact on the organization?	Will we measure success?

STORYOPIA ARCHIVES: GETTING TO KNOW YOUR AUDIENCE

I was contacted by a charitable organization to help six senior members of their staff design a presentation from the corporate office. Their presentation was to be presented to audiences with varied agendas: award recipients, community members, potential donors, current donors, business partners, volunteers, and the like. Each senior member came to the presentation with a different idea of what slides to use and the direction in which to take the presentation.

After filling out the Start-Up Brief, these six senior staff members came to the conclusion (which was my intention for them to realize) that each of their audiences had their own goals, their own agendas, different knowledge about the topic, different what's in it for them, different purposes, and different questions that needed answers.

The one common denominator for each audience, however, was *stories* — testimonials from recipients who received funding from the organization. Story testimonials are the cornerstone of nonprofits and are social proof of their value. With a twist of creativity, story testimonials connect emotionally and amplify efforts that create a meaningful connection for all audiences. This was an aha moment for them as each person was able to cull stories relevant to everyone in their respective audiences.

Lesson learned: It's critical to understand your audience at a deep level. Fill out the Start-Up Sheet and share stories to engage, evoke empathy, increase trust, and motivate action — and you'll hit your target each time.

IN THIS CHAPTER

- » Searching for compelling stories
- » Creating a narrative from data
- » Curating your own repertoire
- » Adding finesse to your stories
- » Coining a catchphrase

Chapter 4
Mining and Crafting Great Stories

You're never going to kill storytelling, because it's built into the human plan. We come with it.

—MARGARET ATWOOD, AUTHOR OF THE HANDMAID'S TALE

Open your eyes. Open your ears. Open your mind. Stories are all around you. The key is to aware and pay attention to your life and the lives of others. Be curious. Look about. Observe with all your senses. Try new things. Take up a new hobby. Explore different places. Talk with people. Ask lots of questions. Everyday life offers an endless plethora of experiences — all of which are potential stories.

This chapter helps you figure out how to mine experiences and craft great stories so you can make your point seamlessly and entice your audiences to heed the call to action.

STORYOPIA ARCHIVES: LEARNING FROM THE BARDS

Some of the best-known authors claim to have written fiction based on real-life experiences: birth, death, first kiss, graduation, marriage, divorce, career changes, overheard conversation, and more. Sometimes the tiniest detail recalled can be the nugget for a story such as how a kid was mistreated in school, the best day or your life, a politician who was convicted as a serial killer, a special event you attended, or a teacher who had a secret life as a drug dealer.

Others claim to cull stories from headlines in tabloids such as "An Owl Got Caught in My Hair," "Miracle Cure Kills Second Patient," or "Homicide Victims Rarely Talk to the Police." And some use their backgrounds as the vision. For instance, John Grisham relied on stories from his days as a lawyer. Patricia Cromwell created thrillers from her work as a medical examiner. Even Hans Christian Anderson wove aspects of his own childhood in his 150+ fairytales.

Lesson learned: Think of your life, novels you've read, or movies you've watched. They all have plots and subplots. Your plot is your topic and your subplots are the stories you weave in to make the presentation interesting and relevant.

Examining Ways to Mine Stories from Experiences

This section shares stories from my random experiences and the experiences of others in addition to how to incorporate them into presentations.

Some of the best stories come from just being around people. Schmoozing at networking events. Drumming up conversations at dinners, meetings, and conferences. Even chatting with strangers standing behind you in checkout lines. For example, I was on a long checkout line several years ago and started a conversation with a guy standing in back of me. He wound up being one of my best clients. Serendipity!

The more people you speak with — especially people with jobs and backgrounds different from yours — the more stories you'll find and the more interesting your life will be.

Becoming an active listener

Active listening is a communication skill that involves going beyond simply hearing the words someone else is saying, as you see in Figure 4-1. It will have a positive impact on your business and social relationships. Active listening can also harvest some interesting stories.

The following story was shared by someone during one of my workshops. I'm glad I was listening with my *ninja ears* because it's a winner. I made a note of this story to use at an appropriate time!

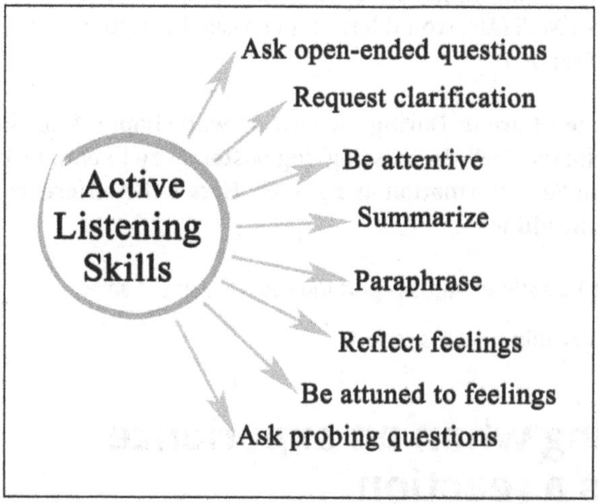

FIGURE 4-1: Attributes of active listening.

Dmitry / Adobe Stock

Story: Several years ago Nora attended my email workshop. She told the group of a very embarrassing situation. She'd sent an email to several hundred coworkers. In her rush to leave the office after working late, she didn't proofread carefully and wrote that she was pubic relations director, instead of public relations director. She learned of her mistake when she reported to work the following morning. Oops! I filed the story away for future use. It has provided a great introduction on the importance of proofreading *everything*.

How and when I use it: When I get toward the end of the writing workshop and discuss proofreading, I tell the story of Nora, the hapless PR director. I don't use the word pubic because I want the audience to use their imaginations. I merely say . . . *and she left the l out of public. Think about that for a moment.* People think momentarily, then chuckles start. Of course, I don't mention her name or company, but the story proves a valuable point about the importance of proofreading — *everything*.

Honing your skills of observation

We often go about our days on autopilot, not noticing what's around and in front of us. By consciously observing our surroundings, we can grow our awareness and flex our *noticing muscles,* thereby perceiving the world with higher resolution, detail, and clarity.

Story: I was stopped at a red light and noticed a sign posted on a poll. In large letters it said, MISSING DOG. Underneath was a small picture and some text, neither of which could be seen by passing in a car. The poster completely missed the mark. Had the owner put a larger photo of the dog and the type of breed in large print, passersby would have known what kind of dog too look for. For example, MISSING DALMATIAN, would have told passersby immediately the breed of dog to spot (pun intended).

How and when I use it: During my writing workshops I focus heavily on creating robust headlines. I tell the missing dog poster story to emphasize the importance of delivering key information at a glance. Here's the difference between a strong and a weak headline.

> **Strong headline:** Status report indicates 2% rise in sales
>
> **Weak headline:** Status report

Noticing when an experience sparks a reaction

When you have a reaction to something that happens or a reaction to something you hear or see, that could be fodder for a story. Whether it's funny, scary, heedless, upsetting, informational, negative, positive, or whatever, it may have story potential.

Story: I was sitting at my computer a little over a year ago writing another book. An email popped up on my screen from my friend Pam asking me to meet her for lunch. That message sparked such a strong reaction that my heart skipped several beats. Why? Pam had died six months earlier after a long bout with cancer. Her message must have been floating in cyberspace, and she probably wondered why I never responded.

How and when I use it: During my email workshop, I relate this story to convey how you should never assume someone received your message. Emails can get lost, wind up in the recipient's spam or junk folder, get blocked by the server, have an invalid address, or who knows what else. If you don't get an expected reply within a reasonable amount of time, either send another message or (better yet) phone the recipient.

Noting when you (or someone you know) beat the odds

These include experiences where you "just knew" that you (or someone else) couldn't do something. It was too difficult, too strenuous, too farfetched, too whatever. Discuss how you (or someone) wouldn't take "no" for an answer but kept on plugging away.

Story: Before I got my first book published eons ago, I sent manuscripts over a period of several years to dozens of publishers and got dozens of refusals. I had read that writers have a better chance of getting struck by lightning than getting a book published. However, I believed in myself and refused to give up. After several years of getting one rejection after another, I finally got a "yes." I've had 25+ books professionally published.

How and when I use it: I host a writing group for seven other people; we call ourselves the Scribe Tribe. They aren't professional writers, yet they're wonderful scribes. I've reminded them of my long journey to getting published as I encourage them to submit their work. Many of them started submitting their work (and after many rejections) have gotten articles published. One even published a book. I'm so delighted that my experience of beating the odds has inspired them.

Drawing upon what you've read

The stories we heard as kids taught us many lifelong lessons: Laugh at your mistakes; be a true friend; make yourself heard; there's no place like home; you can't always get what you want; everyone has a special gift; pick your battles wisely; be a good sharer; good things come to those who wait; and so much more.

As adults, our stories aren't that simple and they don't necessarily start with "Once upon a time." But the stories we opt to share will instill valuable teaching and learning lessons. In addition to your own stories, you'll find stories in newspapers, magazines, and on social media.

Presenters should feel comfortable telling other people's stories, as long as they give credit where credit is due. Here are two examples I include as a contrast:

Story example 1: When the Affordable Care Act (also known as ACA or Obamacare) was enacted in 2010, it was several thousand pages long. (The numbers vary depending on which site you look at, but it was veeeeery long.) The frightening truth is that our representatives routinely vote on huge, complex bills without having read anything more than an executive summary. This isn't a political statement. Most reps admit they never read more than the summary in the ACA, and the same is true for many other lengthy bills. Now, contrast that with the United States Constitution, often called the supreme laws of the land. It's only four pages long.

Story example 2: One of the shortest letters ever written was from Cornelius Vanderbilt, (business magnate who built his wealth in railroads and shipping). It read, *"Gentlemen, You have undertaken to cheat me. I won't sue you, for the law is too slow. I'll ruin you."* (19 harsh words)

How and when I used them: I make reference to these two examples when I'm presenting the workshop segment on keeping it short and simple (KISS) while stressing how to find a good balance and using tact. In all writing and speaking, include what's necessary and ditch what's not.

STORYOPIA ARCHIVES: SHARING FROM YOUR ARCHIVES

Dig into your archives and choose stories that fit the audience's values, goals, and interests as they relate to the topic of the presentation.

One of my clients, a mid-sized corporation, was looking for ways to cut costs. In the end, they decided to issue paychecks twice a month rather than every week. They knew that would cause hardships for many employees. They were offering employee budget assistance consulting for anyone needing it. Craig, the CEO, contacted me to critique the message they were planning to send. It read as follows:

> *To save money, starting on [date] we find it necessary to issue paychecks twice a month rather than every week. We hope this won't be a problem. If it is, we're offering free budgeting assistance through . . . .*

Yikes! I knew there was a better way to break this negative news. I asked what other cost-cutting options were on the table. Once Craig shared them with me, here's how we reshaped the message:

> *With operating costs rising, we have been looking for ways to cut costs without cutting jobs or benefits.* [Now we hit them with what could have been the worst-case scenario.] *Rather than cutting jobs, rather than asking you to pay more in health care premiums, rather than cutting your 401K match, rather than* [whatever else], *we have found a way to keep all your jobs and benefits intact.* [At this point, whatever they hear will be okay.] *Starting on* [date] *we find it necessary to issue paychecks twice a month rather than every week. We hope this won't be a problem. If it is, we're offering free budgeting assistance through . . . .*

Lesson learned: Delivering negative news can be tricky and you must use tact. Here are a few hints: (1) offer options, (2) give a reason, (3) change the order in which you deliver the information, or (4) make lemonade. In this case I helped my client make lemonade. Check out Chapter 3 for realizing when you're presenting negative news and Chapter 15 for a discussion on delivering it.

Avoiding Story Overload and Clutter

Storytelling is like salt. If you don't include any, the dish is bland. If you include too much, you ruin the dish. Just the right amount makes for a delish dish. So, how many stories should you tell? There's no magic formula, but there's one constant: Space stories out so audiences have time to absorb and reflect on each one. Here are some guidelines:

- If your presentation brings together many different layers, such as scientific data, evidence, or other hard content, interjecting stories makes the data more digestible — somewhat like sherbet served as a palate cleanser between courses. Each story should bring your point to life and transition from one topic to another.
- Consider a solid story for each major section of your presentation. However, don't include a story for the sake of telling one. It's better to tell no story than tell a weak or irrelevant one.
- If the presentation is less than a half hour or it's to share one specific idea, one story should suffice. Tell it near the beginning of your presentation to engage the audience.
- If the purpose of your presentation is to describe (for example) how people from different walks of life have benefited from a situation, you might think of sprinkling stories in two or three places.
- Referencing your opening story at the end is a really great way to tie the presentation together and lead into your call to action.

Regardless of how many stories you tell, cut the clutter. This relates to anything that doesn't increase understanding, such as inconsequential facts or figures. Remember that not all data are equally important. Ask yourself what you need to express the essence of your message and eliminate what's not relevant. As Blaise Pascal (French mathematician, physicist, inventor, and philosopher) famously said in the 1600s, "If I had more time, I would have written a shorter letter."

STORYOPIA ARCHIVES: REFERENCING OTHERS

Pablo Picasso is quoted as saying, "Good artists copy; great artists steal." If Picasso condones stealing from other artists, then it must be a good idea, right? My own interpretation of that comment is that Picasso doesn't actually mean "stealing"; he means "referencing." If you can't think of a personal story, there are experiences of others that may be relevant to your presentation. There are many that need permission, and many that don't.

Here's a great example that I'm "referencing": Airbnb has made its name by reaching out to customers to gather stories of people's satisfaction with the service. This story is shared online as a content marketing initiative. Good reviews lead to greater business. That's why people check Yelp, Better Business Bureau, Angi (formerly Angie's List), and other sites to learn of satisfaction or dissatisfaction with a group or company. These are stories you can use and reuse — no permission needed.

Lesson learned: When you incorporate stories from others, know what needs permission. Always check it out at the source and err on the side of seeking permission if you're unsure.

REMEMBER

Make sure to use the most current facts, figures, and statistics because data can change quickly.

Morphing Stories from Data

SHERYL SAYS

I want to start with a quick explanation about data visualization and graphics. Although they're often used interchangeably, *data visualization* is a graphic that's intended to be analyzed. Its purpose is to simplify complex information through graphs, charts, maps, infographics, and more. A graphic can be a photo, logo, illustration, clipart, and so on. It isn't necessarily for the purpose of being analyzed. Either one can have a story wrapped around it.

Simply put, data storytelling is intended to convey complex data by bringing it to life in a way the audience can relate to. This type of storytelling follows the same guidelines as any story with characters, settings, conflicts, and resolutions. It's meant to engage the emotional centers of the brain.

Knowing the tools

Data visualization tools such as Tableau, Microsoft BI, and Google Data Studio provide an accessible way to view trends and understand outliers, patterns, and more. Unlike standard slide presentation software, here's just some of what these tools can do:

- Generate different data points from the same data
- Create smart dashboards
- Allow interactive sharing so users can explore data in more detail
- Filter and sort
- Automate and customize tons of stuff
- Track key performance indicators (KPIs)
- Collaborate and real-time data sharing
- Visualize trends and patterns
- Compare performances over time
- Integrate with other tools

When done correctly, data storytelling and data visualization can combine to turn data into clear, concise, and actionable information. Finding and sharing the story within the data is powerful and memorable.

WARNING

Avoid using data storytelling or data visualization to be deceitful or misrepresent. That can have serious consequences such as a damaged reputation, job loss, or legal ramifications.

Crafting the data story

START-UP BRIEF

Use the Start-Up Brief in Chapter 3 to understand your audience. Consider what matters to them. Then find a story within the data, even if you need to craft one. Keep it simple while conveying insights.

Following is a hypothetical data story I crafted around the graph in Figure 4-2. This presentation would be to an audience of educators.

> *For 12 years, Tabatha taught AP (Advanced Placement) English in an upper-class rural school district in the Midwest. She credited herself with being a good teacher and helping her students attain high grades. One day she came across the graph you see in*

Figure 4-2. It made her think about a high school in a poor urban district not too far away. The dropout rate was high (and, of course, there were no AP courses). She realized that her students in the rural district were highly motivated and would do well with any attentive teacher, but the urban schools needed more dedicated teachers to motivate their students.

It was then Tabatha made the decision to switch schools and applied for the teaching position at the urban high school. It wasn't long before she was interviewing for the job of English teacher and was offered the position. Even though it was a lower salary and the school was in a rough part of town, she didn't hesitate to accept.

On her first day, Tabatha saw some of the harsh realities of the school's problems — the building was old and neglected, the classroom lacked supplies (including books), and many of the students weren't adequately trained to read. However, she didn't let this dissuade her passion for making a difference. Tabatha went out of her way to motivate and inspire students with a you-can-do-it *attitude. She introduced a variety of activities that got them involved. Over the course of five years, several of her students went on to college.*

Teachers have the power to make a difference in students' lives and contribute to shaping the future of the next generation.

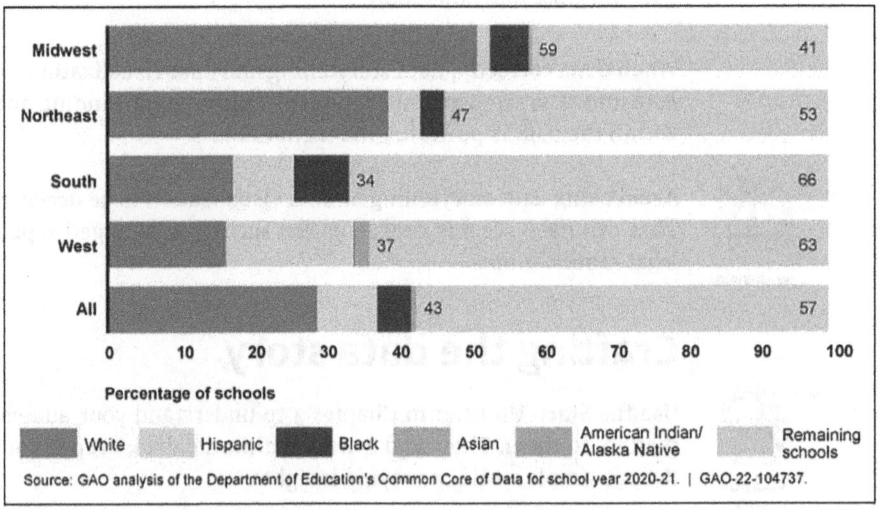

FIGURE 4-2: Inequalities in education based on ethnicity.

Using data to inspire action

When you couple data storytelling and visualization, you give data a voice and inspire action. For instance, you may use one of the data visualization apps to show sales trends for your company. The data story can include how the trends relate to future marketing and public relations campaigns, cash flow, staff retention, supply chain constraints, and so forth. This creates a framework your audience is familiar with, so they can better understand the relevance and importance of the data. That's data storytelling and data visualization in a nutshell.

Crafting Your Own Repertoire of Stories

During my Storytelling and Storyboarding workshops, people often come up to say they don't have any interesting stories to tell, or they can't tell a story because they're not funny. If you don't think you have any interesting stories or you think you're not funny, those are excuses. *I'm taking those excuses away from you — right now!* Just by the fact that you live each day, you have experiences, which are stories. We're all human beings with shared experiences that connect us. And nobody has to be funny to tell an engaging story. Sometimes a humorous anecdote or slide will do the trick.

The exercise that follows will help you think of the people, places, and things that have shaped your life. Consider those who have not only helped you think out of the box but made you forget there ever was a box. Also consider those who inspired you to do something different, who changed your outlook on something, or who encouraged you take a (non-dangerous) risk. These are all stories that may be worth sharing. Whether the results were positive or negative, they're valuable lessons others can benefit from.

TIP

Find your voice. Tell your stories. Practice. Pull back the curtain and shine. I've yet to find a person who didn't come up with at least one story relevant to their topic(s) when they used the following technique.

Starting with paper and pencil (or pen)

Yes, paper and pencil. For this type of exercise, you're more likely to be creative when using paper and pencil, rather than the computer. When you hand write something, you create spatial relations between each bit of information. This activates parts of your brain that makes you more open to critical thinking.

Now, take a short break from reading this and create a three-column table just like the one that follows. Include your own people, places, and things. Table 4-1 gives you an example of generic terms to draw from.

- Under **People,** write down past and present people in your life. Think of what each person represents, why they came to mind, and why they're important to you.

- In the **Places** column, note past and present places. Jot down the sounds, scents, and visuals these places trigger.
- Under **Things,** list stuff that reminds you of positive or negative experiences. (They both have value.) Think about what meaning they hold for you and why.

TABLE 4-1 **What's Your Story?**

People	Places	Things
Family	Neighborhoods you lived in	Books
Friends	The hallway in your school	Photos
Adversaries	A favorite vacation spot	Movies
Acquaintances	The desk at your first job	Gifts
Teachers	Your first job interview	Plants
Childhood friend	A teenage hangout	Sports
Coworkers	A place you walk or jog	Pets
Mentors or coaches	The worst place you've been	Religious item
Member of the clergy	House of worship	Big deal you closed
Others	Your happy place	Foods

Making the connections and creating a list

When you're done, you'll have planted seeds of stories. Start making connections between the people, places, and things you noted. See those seeds germinate and sprout. Some stories may be too personal to share; others may be very appropriate for certain topics. After you've curated a host of stories, categorize them and save them in folders on your phone, on your desktop, in a notepad, or wherever it's convenient. Each time something occurs to you, add it to your list. You'll be amazed at how many experiences you've had in your life that can enhance a presentation.

Before you know it, you may have more stories than Aesop had fables. When preparing for a presentation, look through your bank of stories and find one, two, or more that will be appropriate for your topic and your audience.

SHERYL SAYS

When I started collecting my list of stories, I put a reminder alarm on my phone for the evening, so I'd remember to notate things I'd heard, seen, or experienced that might one day become a story. After a while, it became a habit, and I no longer needed the alarm.

Introducing the Four Pillars of Storytelling

Every story has four pillars as you see in Figure 4-3. Before your fingers start clicking away on your keyboard, recognize how the four pillars of your story will fit into storyopia to take your audience on a journey from what is to what can be. This section provides an explanation of how to fit your setting, characters, conflict, and resolution into any story you reference.

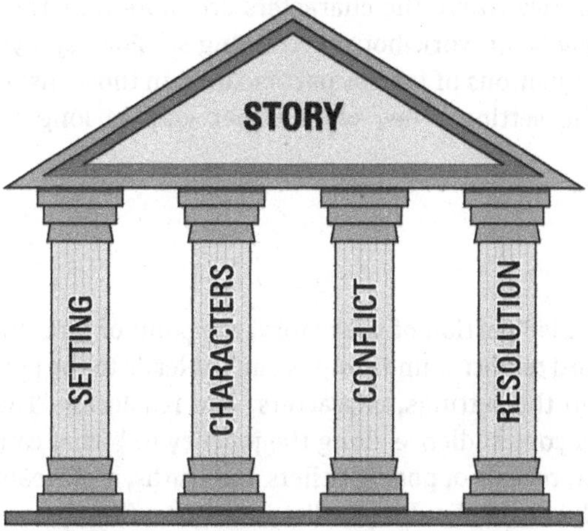

FIGURE 4-3: Four pillars to give your story structure

Setting

Anyone who's sat through a high school English class remembers, "It was a dark and stormy night" from Edward Bulwer-Lytton's novel *Paul Clifford.* Even in a business presentation you need to set the scene, which immerses the audience into where the story is happening.

The setting shows up early because it provides context and should be something your audience will relate to. This sets the tone for the plot. It can be a time of day, weather conditions, season, country, office, building or room, shopping mall, manufacturing plant, or any place from where the story unfolds.

Characters

Most stories are based around a person or group of people. They can be competitors, shareholders, coworkers, friends, heroes, antiheroes, villains, or others. Emphasize the parallels between your character and your audience. That means tying the challenges of your main character to the challenges of your audience. This will make your audience feel an emotional stake in the outcome. (You may say, *"Just like you, Jonathan had. . ."*)

REMEMBER

Be sure to give your characters names. Names breathe life into characters and create connections. Think of the Harry Potter series for example. The story wouldn't have been the same if J.K. Rowling merely called the hero, *boy wizard*.

TIP

This is where the Start-Up Brief will help you home in on their demographics, motives, goals, actions, questions they have, and what keeps them us at night.

There may be stories where the characters are more important than the setting. One example may be at workshops or training sessions and you're talking about the trials and tribulations of former participants. In those instances, put the characters before the setting. They work either way as long as they lead to the conflict.

Conflict

This is the "what is" portion of your story, the point of tension for your audience. Although the word *conflict* sounds unpleasant, it leads to the pot of gold — forming a bridge between the settings, characters, and resolution. The conflict fuels the story and moves your audience along the journey to "what can be." It creates the plot and drives it, reveals opposing beliefs and truths, and creates relatable context in an emotional way. Without a conflict in a story, film, or novel, the plot would be, well, boring and useless. Think of what your audience cares about and how the conflict will get and keep their attention.

Resolution

This is the ending, where you've taken your characters, setting, and conflict directly to your audience. Your resolution should one in which they can see themselves as heroes — "what can be" for them. Good resolutions should be memorable, concrete, specific, and achievable.

Including a Call to Action

Presentation storytelling differs from other types of storytelling in that it needs a *call to action* (CTA). Once you've taken the audience on the journey, help them understand what to do next so they have a happily-ever-after ending. CTAs may include the following:

- Setting up a meeting
- Clicking for a free trial
- Getting a price quote
- Signing a contract
- Downloading an e-book
- Joining a community
- Donating or volunteering
- Following on social media
- Reading the FAQs

TIP

You don't have to spell out the CTA. You can leave the interpretation up to the audience by tickling their imaginations and hinting at what might follow. Think of the story of *Snow White and the Seven Dwarfs*. It's resolved when she's kissed by the handsome prince and awakens from her eternal sleep. The unsaid CTA is, "Get a wedding planner ASAP." That's left to our imagination.

Embellishing your stories

Gandalf, a hero in *The Hobbit*, had a conversation with Bilbo Baggins. He told Bilbo that when he comes back from his adventure, he'll have many tales to tell, and he should embellish them. Gandalf was spot on! Don't hesitate to embellish your stories by adding decorative details, metaphors, humor, quotes, trivia, visuals, or whatever else will make it more memorable. It's like adding spice to a recipe. A little dab will do you! Even Mark Twain once said, "Never let the truth get in the way of a good story." It's your story, not a legal document which must be 100 percent factual.

SHERYL SAYS

I learned the art of embellishment from a master storyteller — my mother. Each time she shared a real-life story, elements of the story changed slightly. Even stories about going to her favorite department store changed with each telling. She jazzed up the most mundane incidents. They were always fun to hear, and the big picture was always truthful. We've all had relatives like that whom we enjoyed listening to. And many of their stories continue to be memorable.

Embellishing occurs in many areas of the arts. Musical arrangers edit musical scores, making them their own by adding trills, suspensions, retardations, passing tones, and more while remaining true to the original composition.

Choreographers adapt dance steps by adding gestures, stillness, and subtle movements that catch the audience's attention and evoke an emotional response. These adaptations make each choreographer's performance unique while remaining true to the original dance.

Movie script writers do the same thing by taking even greater liberties. You've watched movies or read books that are inspired by true stories. You enjoy them because they blur the line between the real and unreal, the possible and impossible. For instance, the ship *Titanic* really did sink. But the movie *Titanic* invented two characters, Jack and Rose, who didn't exist. They humanized the tragedy and made viewers empathize with the plight of the passengers.

Sometimes storytellers add a little bit extra to try to bring the moral of the story to the surface and make the story more memorable.

You can blur the lines to bring the moral of the story to the surface and make it more memorable. Use fanciful details or metaphors that speak directly to the imagination, include quotes, add a touch of humor, Your stories may have more reality than those of Hollywood, but you'd ultimately be doing the same thing — drawing conflict into sharper focus by paring back ancillary events or people, searching for conflict, and honing its edge. Embellishments that incite incidents, escalation, or resolution are just good storytelling. Understanding your audience gives you the creative freedom to play around with your story.

SHERYL SAYS

I appreciate that embellishing may be a controversial suggestion, and you may choose to stick to just the facts. That's personal choice. However, you can draw your audience into the story without compromising its integrity by embellishing small things, such as what a character was wearing or thinking.

WARNING

Embellishments are fine, provided they're grounded in honesty and reality, but you must know where to draw the line. Perhaps you recall Brian Williams, once a well-respected newscaster. He told a story on nationwide TV about a death-defying experience during the Iraq war in 2003, claiming he was shot down by enemy fire while on an NBC news assignment. The incident never happened, and Williams' illustrious career ended with a big Pinocchio. He was suspended for six months without pay and blemished what had been a sterling career.

STORYOPIA ARCHIVES: ADDING BELLS AND WHISTLES

I embellished this story for the Scribe Tribe mentioned earlier in this chapter. The story is authentic and sincere, but I elaborated a bit to add a bit of drama and suspense, making a boring story a more interesting one.

Actual events: One evening my husband and I neglected to check that our garage door was closed before we went to bed. Our next-door neighbor, Bradley, is a night owl and noticed the door was opened and got concerned. He tried calling and texting, but we were asleep and didn't hear either. He became worried that something was wrong and came over.

Section from my embellished version: . . . Suddenly, I was startled awake. The sound of a door squeaking open. The creaking of footsteps. No — this wasn't a Poe story. It wasn't a movie. It wasn't a dream. It was real — my life! Someone was lurking in my house. A chill spread from the nape of my neck to the base of my spine, like ice water cascading down my back. I started shaking Jon. "Get up, Jon. Get up. Someone's in our house. Get up. Get up." My heart was ticking like a time bomb.

Though just a few seconds, it seemed like an eternity before I was able to rouse him. Then, I heard the words, "Hello, hello" coming from the other end of our house. No one breaks into someone's house yelling, "Hello, hello." Was this a deranged mass murderer trying to lure us out of the bedroom? Was this a burglar trying to win our favor? Just who had broken into our house?"

Lesson learned: Add a little drama or embellishment to enhance your story. Remember, it's not historical text, and nobody will fact check.

Looking to others for inspiration

In addition to drawing from your own experiences, use the experiences of friends and colleagues. Check with your marketing and sales teams. They always have good stories to share. Focus on your intended outcome — what you want your audience to do, think, feel, or learn — and incorporate stories so they imagine themselves as heroes on the same journey. Here are some ideas:

- How you took on a challenge, overcame obstacles, and became the hero or antihero
- A time you experienced failure, started again, and what you learned along the way
- How the ideas of different people converged and were successful

» A dramatic, unforgettable event you build up to
» The mistakes and blunders of others or your own (if you're brave enough to share)
» A snippet of something unexpected, then backtracking to how you got there
» The status quo and path to a better way
» Something predictable with a surprising, unpredictable ending

STORYOPIA ARCHIVES: IMPACTING OTHERS

Many years ago I volunteered to tutor six high school students to help them improve their reading and writing skills, which they were shirking whenever possible. I related to that because when I was in high school, I didn't like reading or writing, and I shirked those assignments whenever I could. (That may be hard to believe given that I'm a former English teacher, author, and avid reader.) Practicing what I preach, however, I went through the process of identifying people, places, and things, as you saw earlier in this chapter. Here's what I arrived at:

Person: Mrs. Shaheen, English teacher

Place: High school

Thing: Books

Story: I had Mrs. Shaheen as my high school English teacher during my senior year. Her husband had lost his eyesight several years earlier. One of the things he missed most was reading, being able to read while enjoying the feel of pages in a book. Mrs. Shaheen often spoke about the heartfelt joy they shared, sitting side by side on the sofa with Mr. Shaheen holding the book in his hands and Mrs. Shaheen reading the narrative, making words came alive. She singlehandedly taught, inspired, and nurtured. She instilled in me a love of reading that continues to transport me from the world I'm in, to the worlds within the pages of each book I read.

I didn't realize the immeasurable impact she had on my life until many years later. It's amazing how someone, especially a teacher or mentor, can profoundly impact someone's life. Sadly, Mrs. Shaheen never did learn of her lasting contribution to me because she died shortly after I graduated. I truly believe that you must be a reader in order to be a writer, and I hoped to use this story as a springboard to help these students.

How and when I used it: I shared the story with these students. They listened attentively, but I wasn't sure of its impact. I asked each of them to read a fictional story (any story of their own choosing) and re-write the ending. I was amazed at how well they did and how much fun they had, despite the grumbling when I first presented the assignment. That was the start of many inventive reading and writing activities.

I don't know how most of them fared afterward, but I did hear from one of the young women. She had just graduated from college and had gotten a position as English teacher. She said I had inspired her. From Mrs. Shaheen, to me, to this young woman — a beautiful chain of stories that was passed forward.

Lesson learned: Tell your stories. Things you learn or teach aren't always apparent at the time. You don't know what impact your words or actions can have on people at any time.

Refining Your Stories

After you think your story is complete, revisit it for clarity and how it relates to your audience and the intended message. The following sections provide you with some guidance on how to effectively refine your stories.

Including sensory language for added depth

Adding depth isn't the same as embellishing. It's stating the facts as they relate to one or more of the five senses. Sensory language creates an immediate connection with your audience; their imaginations become engaged. It brings them viscerally into the situation. Plus, you have more fun telling the story. Here are a few examples:

- **Seeing:** Vivid, fiery, burnished, crystalline, craggy, velvety, radiant
- **Touching:** Crisp, grainy, woven, pebbly, slimy, oily, lukewarm, contoured
- **Tasting:** Buttery, creamy, alkaline, burnt, zesty, woody, citrusy, briny
- **Smelling:** Smoldering, piquant, pungent, rancid, savory, gamy, ambrosial
- **Hearing:** Dulcet, melodic, rich, pure, muffled, momentous percussive

TIP

Consider words that add sparkle: snazzy, pizzazz, intriguing, piquant, spellbinding, seductive, staggering, sassy, titillating, astonishing, outrageous, chilling, revved up, dramatic, vibrant, galvanizing, enthralling, stirring, monumental, and others. Well-placed visuals can also add spark to your story.

Replacing insensitivity with mindfulness

Words matter. Words can hurt more than sticks and stones and leave more lasting scars. Here's a very brief list of words to replace in your vernacular.

Primary or main (not master)

Native American (not Indian)

Work force (not manpower)

Liaison or mediator (not middleman)

Atypical (not abnormal)

Legacy or carryover (not grandfathered)

Quick check (not sanity check)

Revisiting the language of genders

In the following, which doesn't belong: aunt, brother, cousin, father, grandfather, grandmother, mother, nephew, niece, sister, uncle? The answer is "cousin" because it's the only gender-neutral term. Gender and inclusivity police are all around. Use language to minimize biases, avoid stereotypes, bridge communication gaps, and remove any expressions or phrases that might discriminate against others or make them feel unwelcome or unsafe.

The language of genders has evolved over the time. Many of us had become accustomed to using she/her/hers for females and he/his/him for males. As gender vocabulary continues to evolve, it's proper to address a singular person as they, them, *ze*, or *hir*. Many people now put their gender preferences in the signature blocks of emails. Inclusive language offers respect, safety, and belonging to all people.

Having said that, *The Chicago Manual of Style* (a staple reference for writers and editors since 1906) is watching the generic use of inclusive language, stating: "*They* and *their* have become common in informal usage, but neither is considered fully acceptable in formal writing." The bottom line is to use good judgment and always consider your audience.

Coining Your Own Word (Becoming a Neologist)

The English language is fluid and constantly evolving. Every word you use was coined by someone. New words express ideas to get points across in a new, refreshing way. But with millions of words at our disposal, why are we constantly making up new ones? Because they're fun, creative, and fill a gap in our ever-changing world.

People who coin new words are called *neologists.* Many of the words we use today were coined by authors, writers, critics, and journalists. Probably the best known is William Shakespeare who's credited with coining about 1,700 words we use in our everyday vocabularies. They include accommodate, apostrophe, bloody, countless, critical, dishearten, eventful, exposure, grateful, hurry, impartial, lapse, laughable, monumental, obscene, reliance, submerge, swagger, worthless, zany, and many more.

SHERYL SAYS

Of course you wouldn't coin a new word for every presentation, but you may think of one for a topic you present often.

Learning from a modern-day expert

Erin McKean, lexicographer, did an interesting broadcast on TED Talks titled "Go Ahead: Make Up New Words." (Check it out on YouTube at `https://www.ted.com/talks/erin_mckean_go_ahead_make_up_new_words`.) Eric speaks of the value of making up new words. Getting your meaning across, grabbing people's attention, focusing on what you're saying. When you make up a new word, people pay attention because they want to learn what it means. And what presenter wouldn't want to be a neologist to be remembered for a unique word? McKean uses examples of coined words that include:

Brunch (breakfast + lunch)

Motel (motor inn + hotel)

Electrocute (electric + execute)

Rising to the challenge

Create your own name-game-changing word. Get your meaning across. Grab people's attention. Every word you coin is a chance to put a focus on what you're saying and a novel way to get your idea across. Here are a few suggestions:

- **Start with a portmanteau.** That means putting two words together to form a new one.
  - Jeggings (jeans + leggings)
  - Glamping (glamor + camping)
  - Frenemy (friend + enemy)

- **Take from other languages.** Words we've stolen ("stolen" works better than "borrow" because we're not returning them) include *bon voyage, a la carte, modus operandi, pro bono, status quo, en masse, lasagna*, and countless others.
- **Turn an object (noun) into a verb.** You may recall that the word *friend* was always a noun before Facebook "verbed" it.

SHERYL SAYS

Storyopia is a word I coined for this book and its associated workshop. (Among my other credentials I can now call myself a *neologist.*) I wanted to create a word to blend *storytelling* with *seeing* or *vision.* I toyed with several permutations and stumbled upon *opia*, meaning "vision." I squished several thoughts together and ran them by trusted colleagues. They all agreed on *storyopia* — and so it is! It expresses a story that takes audiences on a hero's journey from what is to what can be — where they can see themselves as heroes along the same path . . . I also coined *slizedilla*: a cross between data-laden slides and Go*dzilla* (the monster).

TIP

Continue to Chapter 5 to find out how to create opening stories for a groundswell audience response.

STORYOPIA ARCHIVES: COINING WORDS

One of the world's most popular word games was discovered by a Welsh engineer, James Wardle. He originally created it for his partner who enjoyed word games. Then he expanded it and made it available to the public. The game became so popular he ultimately reached a seven-figure agreement with the *New York Times* where the game appears daily. In 2022 Google released its most popular search word, and (drum roll, please) it was "Wordle," the inventor's play on his own last name.

Lesson learned: With a little imagination, newly coined words can come from anywhere. Make sure the word you coin is snappy, easy to pronounce, and memorable. (Do you think the game would be as popular if Wardle's last name were **Gwynllyw?**)

IN THIS CHAPTER

» Getting the attention of the audience right away

» Using a story to open your presentation

» Exploring other opening grabbers

» Trying techniques to enhance your opening

Chapter 5
Starting Strong for a Groundswell Response

If you haven't struck oil in the first three minutes — stop boring.

—GEORGE JESSELL, AMERICAN COMEDIAN

Imagine this: You're in a foreign country. You walk into a restaurant but aren't too familiar with local foods. Something on the menu strikes your interest, so you order it. Your order comes. It looks delish and smells appetizing. You take the first bite and determine if the dish is grand or bland . . . your audience will make that same determination about you within the first 30 seconds. Stop and think about that. Will your opening be grand or bland?

Don't waste those first precious moments of your talk boring your audience with self-serving information all about yourself and/or your company. That's information they undoubtedly learned before showing up or they don't care about. A self-absorbed opening sets the tone for a "snore fest."

Whether you call your session a workshop, training, presentation, seminar, lecture, or anything else — don't be a talking head. From the outset, make the session immediate, personal, and interactive. Involve your audience. Engage them. Make your opening interesting, digestible, and chewy. (Your audience will also remember what you say at the end. Don't waste either of these two opportunities. You can find out more about endings in Chapter 6.)

Grabbing the Audience's Attention as They Enter

Grab the audience's attention immediately to establish your leadership, get your message across, and sustain interest — the keys to being a powerful speaker.

SHERYL SAYS

Take a look at Figure 5-1. This is a slide I project to grab people's attention as they're entering the room to attend my Storytelling and Storyboarding workshop. Although I use slides very sparsely throughout the presentation, this one gets attention and a chuckle. Why? It's lighthearted and expresses the fears of most attendees. It breaks the tension for them and for me. After the audience is seated — and before I start the presentation — I turn the projector off so there's no glaring screen to create a distraction. (Discover more about opening slides in Chapter 8.)

R.I.P.
According to most studies, people's number one fear is public speaking. Number two is death. Death is number two... Does that sound right?
This means to the average person, if you go to a funeral, you're better off in the casket than doing the eulogy.
— Jerry Seinfeld

FIGURE 5-1: This slide is on the light side, yet it gets the point across.

shockfactor.de / Adobe Stock

SHERYL SAYS

If you're looking for great opening quotes, check out `https://you.com` (or simply you.com). It's an Artificial Intelligence (AI) generator that can come up with all sorts of things, including quotes. Regardless of how you feel about AI and all its positives and negatives, this website is a valuable resource not only for opening quotes but also for all sorts of things. Check it out and have some fun.

TIP

Think of an icebreaking slide that may introduce your topic in an interesting or entertaining way as your audience is entering the room and getting situated.

Opening your Presentation with a Story

Storytelling is a powerful hook to get the audience's attention immediately because, as human beings, we have an innate interest in each other. Opening with a story helps you grab their attention. It shifts their emotional state to a more learning-friendly one, and it helps them bond to you. It tells them immediately that you have feelings, emotions, and reason.

The following sections take you on a journey so you can take your audience on a journey.

Conveying a hero's journey

Folk tales and fairy stories often use the hero-centered approach. Use the journey to show your audience how to overcome obstacles and become heroes (as you learned Chapters 1 and 2). Make your topic come alive by injecting human experiences involving trials and tribulations to take your audience on the same path, such as:

- Highlighting the success of a client/customer who uses your product or service.
- Relating how a salesperson went from being a low-level income generator to a high-income generator.
- Sharing how a workshop turned an employee into a major contributor (a hero).
- Discussing the rewards of philanthropy.

TIP

A story of failure also presents a brilliant opportunity for learning. Avoiding such stories may mean continuing to do things the way they've always been done, which in turn maintains the status quo. For example, how a client didn't take legal advice and wound up in a real jam. Was there a time you tried something new, and it didn't work? What did you do? How did you move forward?

STORYOPIA ARCHIVES: OPENING WITH A POWERFUL STATISTIC STORY

Jamie Oliver is an English chef, restaurateur, and cookbook author. He's known for his casual approach to cuisine, which has led him to front numerous television shows and open many restaurants. Oliver reached the public eye when his series "The Naked Chef" premiered in 1999. Oliver didn't appear in the show in his birthday suit, but he explained that the word "naked" referred to his food — simple and bare (naked) preparations of dishes rather than pretentious preparations. Twenty years later Italy awarded Oliver the Order of the Star, with the rank of Knight. What a prestigious honor from the land of foodies.

Oliver appeared on TED talks and hooked his audience with a very short, yet powerful opening story: "Sadly, in the next 18 minutes when I do our chat, four Americans that are alive will be dead from the food they eat." That powerful hook expressed the gravity of the talk and how quickly death can strike each time anyone sits down to eat.

Lesson learned: Although your topic may not be as profound, consider opening with a staggering statistic. You can find one for nearly every topic.

Putting the backstory up front

A backstory is a literary device that leads up to the main event. Many times it speaks of rags-to-riches scenarios. Imagine you're presenting to a group of aspiring entrepreneurs. Why not start the presentation with the story behind the story? What happened leading up to success? What failures did people encounter along the way? Here's how the narrative may play out:

> *How many of you would want to achieve the successes of people such as Elon Musk, Bill Gates, Oprah Winfrey, Steve Jobs, Jeff Bezos, Michael Jordon?* (All hands go up.) *Well, here are their backstories!* (You've grabbed their attention.)

- **Elon Musk** was ousted from PayPal while on vacation. Two of his companies were on the verge of bankruptcy: Tesla batteries had problems with spontaneous battery combustion, and SpaceX had been on the verge of bankruptcy when several of his rockets exploded.
- **Bill Gates** was a Harvard University dropout and co-owner of a failed business called Traf-O-Data. It was intended to read the raw data from roadway traffic counters, but Gates didn't do any market research and underestimated how hard it would be to get capital commitments from municipalities.

- **Oprah Winfrey** Shortly after studying speech communications and performing arts, Winfrey was offered a job as a co-anchor on Baltimore's WJZ-TV. Seven and a half months in, she was booted out being told she was unfit for TV news.
- **Steve Jobs** had many failures: Apple III, Pixar Image Computer, Next Computer, and Lisa.
- **Jeff Bezos** admits that Amazon lost huge amounts of money on the video game Crucible and on LivingSocial, which was meant to rival Groupon. And when the Amazon Fire smartphone was introduced in 2014, it was a colossal dud. Within months of its introduction, the price plummeted from $199 to 99 cents.
- **Michael Jordon** As a teenager, Michael was told he's not tall enough to play professional basketball and his high school coach cut him from the team.

Yes, failure can beat you up. It's plagued nearly every successful person at some time in some shape or form. The difference between success and failure is how you react to it and what you learn from it.

REMEMBER

Remember that not all endeavors are about making money; many are about making the world a better place. If you've ever wondered why you haven't come down with measles, mumps, or rubella, you can thank Maurice Hillerman, a Depression-era farm boy turned virologist who earned a microbiology and chemistry PhD from the University of Chicago in 1944. By the end of his career, he'd developed more than 40 vaccines. Or James Watson and James Crick who revolutionized the scientific world when they published their model of DNA.

Telling a future story

This type of story places the audience in the mindset of thinking about future possibilities in a motivational way. It focuses on a time when the problem had been (or will be solved) and the rewards achieved. You can tell it in two ways.

- How a positive future can be achieved.
- How a negative future can be avoided.

Either one is powerful. A positive story can be an investor pitch. You state the possibilities that can be achieved by investing in your product or services. A negative story can be a missed opportunity and what that would mean, such as a stock you didn't buy because it was risky, then it became a blockbuster and you had regrets.

Sharing converging strategies

Converging-idea openings can be used to show how different ideas come together and propel an idea forward. For example, you may discuss two scientists with similar ideas who joined forces to find a cure for a disease. Another strategy would be to discuss how you were speaking with a colleague about a particular topic and the seeds of an idea started to germinate.

Crafting a case study

Use a story from your repertoire to craft a case study for small groups. Think about the aim you determined on the Start-Up Brief (Chapter 3) and what you want the audience to learn, think, do, or feel. The case study/story should present a challenge — a challenge similar to what your audience faces so you highlight what you want them to learn, think, do, or feel (all leading to the eventual call to action). Remember that both positive and negative outcomes are learning experiences.

There are two types of case studies you can present:

- A challenge that *didn't* end well because the people involved made poor decisions.
- A challenge that *did* go well. In this instance . . . leave the ending off as to how the people involved resolved the challenge. Let your audience decide what approach they would have used.

TIP

Don't present a case study as a closing. This a great exercise at the beginning of the session or during the presentation. For the ending, you want to present a meaningful story, quote, statistic, or something that will impact the audience emotionally.

STORYOPIA ARCHIVES: CRAFTING A CASE STUDY FROM YOUR EXPERIENCES

Germaine was a low-level manager for a large project at a manufacturing company. If the project succeeded, Germaine's company stood to gain one of its largest customers. One morning, during a sample run, something happened to a piece of equipment that threatened the successful outcome of the project. Many of the company's leaders were attending a conference in another state, and Germaine had to act quickly.

In her panic, she sent an email to three high-level people in her chain of command letting them know that immediate action needed to be taken. She wasn't authorized to make such a decision. Germaine neglected to flag the message as urgent. As a result, none of these people read the email in a timely manner; therefore, no one acted. The lack of action caused the problem to escalate, and the company ultimately lost the customer's business.

This company asked me to deliver a session on ways to prevent situations like this one from happening again. I prepared a case study based on this event. It developed into a brainstorming session, as I had hoped. The audience was asked to detail how they would have handled the situation. (I'm not sure what happened to Germaine; she didn't attend the session.)

Lesson learned: Several critical lessons came to the forefront. When immediate action is needed, there are several options, which don't rely on email or on email alone:

- Use email (that's flagged "urgent") in addition to phoning decision makers.
- Text the decision makers; they probably have their phones on vibrate.
- Find any high-level person in the building with authority to act.
- If the crisis is severe, have a conference employee pull a key leader from the conference room.

Delivering the story pitch

The basic idea of "pitching" is tossing a story at your audience, hoping to score a hit, as in baseball. Every presentation is some sort of pitch. As you learned in Chapter 3, nearly all presentations are to persuade your audience to do, think, learn, or feel something. That's what you're pitching and the direction in which your stories should be crafted.

If you've ever watched the TV show *Shark Tank*, you're familiar with the story pitch. *Shark Tank* features self-made tycoons (called sharks) who made their own dreams a reality and turned their ideas into lucrative empires. They're looking to help others. This program gives entrepreneurs from all walks of life the opportunity to secure business deals that could make them millions.

REMEMBER

Budding entrepreneurs looking to pitch successfully to investors need to remember the main aspects of the *Shark Tank* formula, and this is true for any pitch you'll ever make:

- Share the story briefly, enthusiastically, and convincingly.
- Have a bullet-proof plan that includes definitive sales goals, manufacturing costs, expected investments, and so on.

» Share how you'll overcome hurdles along the way.

» Believe in the long-term potential for the product or business — beyond the financing.

Using visuals to complement opening stories

Keep in mind that opening stories can be oral and/or visual. Together, they work hand in hand to reinforce the narrative. I'm thinking of Ned who was employed by an architecture landscaping company. When he joined the firm, he was asked to sign a noncompete agreement saying that if he were to leave the firm he couldn't take any of their clients. Five years later, Ned left the firm and had to develop his own clientele.

As part of his marketing plan, Ned joined a nationally known networking group and was asked to give a 10-minute presentation. He developed a slideshow highlighting many of the projects he'd designed and managed. A building developer was in the group and was so impressed with Ned's portfolio (shown on the slides) that he gave Ned the contract for a landscaping project for a new building he was constructing. This slideshow helped to launch Ned's new business.

When slides will enhance your story, don't hesitate to accompany your talk with relevant ones. Head to Chapters 8 and 9 to find out more about using slides effectively.

WARNING

Don't open with a slide of your family for audiences to *ooh* and *aah* over your cute kids. We've all been subjected to that by egotistical presenters. It's a real turnoff. The reality is your audience doesn't care about you or your family; they care about themselves and how you can contribute to the reason they're attending your talk: to do, think, feel, or learn something.

It *is* appropriate to use a family photo *only* when it delivers a visual story that enhances your topic. In the following examples, notice how the photos tie directly into the scenarios to bring clear focus to each story.

Example 1: Enjoying early retirement with gusto

Lorenzo left one of the large financial planning companies to start his own business. He calls his company Retire Young Financial. To kick start his business, Lorenzo organizes lunch 'n learn seminars. His target audiences are people between the ages of 30 and 50. He opens his talk with the slide showing a couple on Segways near a beautiful body of water. Then he pauses briefly and asks, *I'd like to see a show of hands. How many of you would like to retire like my in-laws did? Here they are at age 60, full of gusto, on a trip to Saint Lucia.* All hands go up. Not only does Lorenzo show a photograph (shown in Figure 5-2) that tells a story, he gets the audience involved by asking them to raise their hands.

FIGURE 5-2: Enjoying early retirement with gusto.

Photo courtesy of author

Example 2: Fostering the love of music at a young age

Evie graduated from the Berkeley College of Music with a master's degree. She's always wanted to have her own business, so she started a music school in Boston called B♯ With Evie. (♯ is the musical notation for sharp.) She goes around giving talks to parents of young children to boost enrollment. Evie talks about enrolling children over the age of one year to foster their joy of music. She opens with this slide (shown in Figure 5-3) and the words, *Even if your child may not eventually perform with the Boston Symphony Orchestra, as you can see by my young niece, children are never too young to love music.* (This gets a chuckle every time as well as the audience's attention.)

TIP

Discover more about visual storytelling in Chapter 9.

STORYOPIA ARCHIVES: USING PROPS TO WOW

I attended a photography conference several years ago. Peter, the speaker, was a photographer from *National Geographic*, and I read his impressive resume beforehand. Photographers for this prestigious publication usually have five to ten years of photojournalism experience with other newspapers or magazines and have highly specialized skills in areas such as wildlife, underwater, landscape, portraiture, cultural, geopolitics, and aerial photography — all top-notch professionals.

Peter walked on the stage carrying his prop: a large box. He looked around without saying a word. Then, suddenly he tossed the contents (thousands of negatives) into the audience and said: *These are my rejects. Even I have to take hundreds of photos before I get the great one.* That powerful opening immediately got everyone's attention and respect, including mine, and we all listened to every word.

Lesson learned: When you use a prop that offers an element of surprise at the outset, you've nailed the presentation.

FIGURE 5-3: Making music at a young age.

Photo courtesy of author

Other opening attention grabbers

Open your talk with something to garner interest or hit them where it hurts — with their problem (the villain). People are motivated by two things: avoiding something bad happening or making something good happen. What keeps them up at night? What will happen if they don't take action? What will make them look good (be heroes)? Here are suggested openings (besides stories or visual aids) that will immediately engage:

Opening remarks:

- *Imagine this . . .*
- *Raise your hand if you've ever . . .*
- *Every once in a while, you come across a [XX] that . . .*
- *I'm going to let you in on a little secret.*
- *[XX] may determine the future of [XX] . . .*
- *Don't let [XX] keep you from . . .*
- *Here's something worth considering.*
- *If you want to become part of today's [XX], wait no longer.*

Opening ideas:

- Ask a rhetorical, thought-provoking question.
- State a shocking statistic or headline.
- Use a powerful quote (perhaps from a well-known person or movie).
- Show a gripping photo or short video.
- Create a brief activity people can do individually or with others.
- Give them a questionnaire to fill out.
- Display or handout an activity to show comparisons or options.
- Show a contrast. (As in the opening of the Clinton v. Dole presidential debate in the section, "Asking for volunteers," later in this chapter.)

WARNING

The exception would be when delivering an executive briefing to senior-level individuals. They'll expect you to open with the bottom line and the presentation to be as brief as possible. Learn about executive presentations in Chapter 20.

TIP Although you shouldn't memorize your talk, *do* memorize your opening lines. Once you start speaking, you'll build confidence. Many speakers find that the minute they've delivered their opening lines, confidence builds and nervousness abates. It may be wise to also memorize your closing lines, but less critical.

Introducing Yourself and the Program

After your attention-grabbing opening, continue with the topic's relevance to your audience, the structure of your presentation, their takeaways, how you'll handle questions and comments, when to expect breaks, and cell phone expectations. Mention these in whatever order seems appropriate. Comments may include:

- *This topic is of particular interest to those of you who . . .*
- *The presentation is divided into three main parts.*
- *By the end of this morning (afternoon), you'll be able to . . .*
- *If you have any questions or comments, please feel free to jump in at any time. We have a lot to learn from each other.*
- *We'll take official breaks about every 90 minutes. The first one will be at 10:30. But, of course, leave the room any time you need to.*
- *Please put your cell phones on vibrate (or silence them) and leave the room should you receive an important call.*

After you've gotten those details behind you, very briefly introduce yourself and perhaps your company. If you want to mention some of your accomplishments to show you're the best person to deliver the presentation, do it modestly so you don't sound like a braggart. Tie the introduction into your key issue.

> **Modest:** While completing my doctoral program at Harvard, I was involved in research that [relevant to your key issue].
>
> **Braggart:** I got my PhD from Harvard.

Appreciating the Power of the Pause

Pausing at the right moment gives the audience time to process what you say. This allows them to stay engaged and helps you to make them excited about what's to follow. Pausing is also important for emphasis. Consider opening your presentation with a long pause, which the audience won't be expecting, as the following speakers did:

- Golf Pro Aaron Beverly walked on stage to deliver a talk. After a 10-15 minute pause, he said: *Be honest. You enjoyed that, didn't you?* (Laughter) By walking on stage and saying nothing, he grabbed the audience's attention and followed it with something humorous.
- Dan Pink, American author, opened a presentation with the following remarks: *I need to make a confession at the outset here.* (Pause) *A little over 20 years ago, I did something that I regret. Something that I'm not particularly proud of. Something that in many ways I wish no one would ever know, but that here I feel kind of obliged to reveal.* Then he paused for 10 seconds. The audience listened attentively to hear his confession. They were hooked.

Taboo Openings

Here are things to avoid early in your presentation — unless you do so strategically.

- Forecasts of doom and gloom: They're an instant turnoff. If you must forecast doom and gloom, intersperse something positive or hopeful.
- Personal experiences not related to the topic.
- Too many metaphors, analogies, and idioms.
- Slidezillas (boring or data-laden slides).
- Overused phrases such as no-brainer, touching base, 24/7, at the end of the day, thinking outside the box, low-hanging fruit, giving 110 percent, win-win, or move the needle — you get the point.

Avoiding Openings that Lack Confidence

Your opening remarks are going to make a big impression on your audience and set the tone for what's to come. Within seconds, they'll decide if you're worth listening to. Avoid remarks such as the following:

- *Today I'll attempt to . . .*
- *I don't know why I was asked to speak here today.*

- *I won't take up too much of your time.*
- *My topic is . . .*
- *I'm going to tell a joke. (Just tell it.)*
- *I'm not used to giving presentations, and I'm a bit nervous.*

Regardless of the size of your audience — whether it's one person or an auditorium full of listeners — open with confidence. Lackluster or self-deprecating openings will make people wonder: *Why am I wasting my time with this deadbeat?*

Presenting an Opening Activity

Some presentations touch hearts. Some change minds. Others put you to sleep. When you involve your audience from the start, they know your presentation will be worthy of their time.

REMEMBER

Start by thanking them for attending (in addition to thanking them at the end). This starts off with making the presentation "about them" and establishes a sense of respect.

STORYOPIA ARCHIVES: KICKING IT OFF WITH A BANG

The way I kick off my Storytelling and Storyboarding workshop with a bang is by asking two volunteers to read the opening comments of Bob Dole and Bill Clinton when they faced off in a presidential debate in 1996. Although this debate took place many years ago, it emphasizes the contrast between a weak and strong opening. Try this yourself. Read the following text aloud.

Bob Dole's Opening Statements

Thank you. Thank you, Mr. President, for those kind words. Thanks to the people of Hartford, the Commission, and all those out here who may be listening and watching. It's an honor for me to be standing here as the Republican nominee. I'm very proud to be the Republican nominee reaching out to Democrats and Independents. I have three very special people with me tonight. My wife, Elizabeth, my daughter Robin, who has never let me down, and a fellow named Frank Cafara from New York, along with Ollie Manninen who helped me out in the mountains of Italy a few years back. I learned from them that people do have hard times. And sometimes you can't go it alone.

And that's what America is all about. I remember getting my future back from doctors and nurses and a doctor in Chicago named Dr. Kalikian. And ever since that time I've tried to give something back to my country . . .

Dole's opening remarks are *not* engaging. Dole was very humble and thanked people whom he wanted to honor. Yes, that was important to him and to those mentioned, but his words didn't resonate with the millions of viewers waiting to hear something profound. Now let's take a look at Bill Clinton's opening remarks. Read them aloud.

Bill Clinton's Opening Statements

Thank you, Jim. And thank you to all the people of Hartford, our hosts. I want to begin by saying how much I respect Senator Dole and his record of public service and how hard I will try to make this campaign and this debate one of ideas, not insults. Four years ago, I ran for president at a time of high unemployment and rising frustration. I wanted to turn this country around with a program of opportunity for all, responsibility for all, and an American community where everybody has a role to play.

Four years ago you took me on faith. Now there's a record. Ten and a half million more jobs, rising incomes, falling crime rates and welfare rolls, a strong America at peace. We are better off than we were four years ago. Let's keep going. We cut the deficit by 60 percent. Now, let's balance the budget and protect Medicare, Medicaid, education, and the environment. We cut taxes for 25 million working Americans . . .

Notice the difference in tone and content. Clinton's opening remarks are dynamic. In one sentence, he briefly thanked the host city and mentioned his respect for Dole. Then he launched right into his accomplishments, setting the stage for what the millions of viewers could expect from him in the future. Those weren't just bragging points. They were facts. Do you think a powerful speech such as this helped Clinton get reelected?

Lesson learned: Kick start your session with a bang to capture the audience's attention and engage them right from the start.

Starting with a group activity

SHERYL SAYS

One week prior to presenting my business/technical writing workshop "Write It So They'll Read It," I start strong. I send a workbook to each of the 12 participants. It contains a brief description of the program, worksheets, and my bio. At the very outset of the workshop, I introduce the audience to an activity in the form of a contest. I hand out the following documents face down. Participants on one side of the room (Team B) get the document labeled BEFORE; those on the other side (Team A) get a copy of the document labeled AFTER. They don't know they're looking at unalike documents — the same information presented much differently. I then prepare them for a series of questions, prefacing the questions with the following:

> *Sy Burnett* (my attempted humor at the term "cybernet") *is the HR director of a mid-sized company. There have been rumblings about EEO violations, but Sy has no specifics. Before the rumor mill takes over, Sy has called a meeting and the entire staff must attend.* (Pause) *Let's see which team has had more coffee this morning.*

BEFORE

Date: April 6, YEAR

To: All Employees

From: Sy Burnett, Human Relations Director

Re: Reaffirming EEO policy

As you know, it is illegal to discriminate against any employee or applicant for employment because of race, color, religion, sex, national origin, handicap, or veteran status. I've scheduled a meeting because we need to discuss these critical issues. It'll be in the new cafeteria on April 13 from 10:30 to 11:30, and everyone must attend. There are several questionable issues that have come to my attention, and we need to reaffirm our company's policy.

Here are some of the issues we need to discuss: We must ensure opportunities for all employees and applicants for employment in accordance with all applicable Equal Employment Opportunity/Affirmative Action laws, directives and regulations of federal, state, and local governing bodies or agencies. Promotion decisions must be in accord with the principles of equal employment opportunity. And we must ensure that all personnel actions such as compensation, benefits, transfers, layoffs, return from layoff, company-sponsored training, education, tuition assistance, and social and recreational programs will be administered fairly.

Because we've added so many members to our staff in recent months, I've hired Di Hartt as a new assistant. She will be responsible for equal employment opportunity issues. I'll be introducing Di to you at the meeting. Employees with suggestions, problems, or complaints with regard to equal employment opportunities should report their claims to their managers. If this is not comfortable for any reason, see Di. She will monitor the program and be responsible for making quarterly reports to us on the effectiveness of the program.

AFTER

Date: April 6, YEAR

To: All Employees

From: Sy Burnett, Human Relations Director

Re: Mandatory Meeting on April 13 to reaffirm EEO policy

There are several issues regarding potential Equal Employment Opportunity (EEO/Affirmative Action violations that have come to my attention. I've scheduled a meeting for the entire staff.

Date: April 13
Time: 10:30–11:30 AM
Place: Cafeteria

Agenda Issues

1. We must ensure opportunities for all employees and applicants in accordance with all applicable laws, directives and regulations of federal, state, and local governing bodies or agencies.
2. Promotion decisions must be in accord with the principles of equal employment opportunity.
3. We must ensure that all personnel actions such as compensation, benefits, transfers, layoffs, return from layoff, company-sponsored training, education, tuition assistance, and social and recreational programs will be administered fairly.

New EEO Coordinator: Di Hartt

I'll be introducing Di at the meeting. Employees with suggestions, problems, or complaints with regard to equal employment opportunities should report their claims to their managers first. If this is not comfortable for any reason, see Di. She will monitor the program and be responsible for making quarterly reports to us on the effectiveness of the program.

The questions are:

1. **How many items are on the agenda?**
2. **What's the date of the meeting?**
3. **Who's the new EEO coordinator?**

After each question I ask them to turn their papers face up, find the answer quickly, and raise their hands. Once a hand goes up, I instruct them all to turn their paper face down. Team A always finds the answers immediately; Team B doesn't understand why they can't. At the end of the three questions, I hand each team what the other was looking at and ask them to label them Before and After. We discuss why it was so much easier for Team A (with the After document) to find information so quickly. As they analyze the two side by side, they determine that Team A's document has the following:

- Lots of white space
- Headlines that tell the story
- Numbered list
- Fewer words
- Subject line (Re:) that gives key information at a glance
- Key items stand out at a glance

Ohs and ahs follow, setting the stage for what's to come — the value of the workshop. Then I briefly introduce myself with the following, letting them know what they can expect their takeaways to be. Notice the strategic pauses.

> *Good morning, I'm Sheryl Lindsell-Roberts, and I thank you so much for coming. At the conclusion of this workshop you'll be able to write strategic documents that command attention.* (Pause) *Documents that deliver information at a glance.* (Pause) *Documents that drive action.* (Pause) *And documents get the results you want — just like in the After document. Participants who've taken this workshop tell me that once they start using the process you'll be learning, they cut their writing time by 30 to 50 percent and get results!* (Pause) *30 to 50 percent — that's huge.*
>
> *I want to encourage each of you to participate throughout this workshop. Share your own relevant stories and experiences. Ask questions as they come to mind. Join the conversation. You have as much to learn from each other as you have to learn from me.* (Pause)
>
> *Now, please turn to page. . .*

TIP

This approach works well for virtual presentations as well as face to face. Check out Chapter 18 for more about transitioning from standup to virtual.

Previewing the Audience on Q&A Expectations

Q&A is an essential tool that can make your presentation conversational and form a connection with your audience. After you've wowed them with your attention-getting opening, let them how you'll handle questions and audience comments. Your choice depends on your comfort level and the length of time you have. Check out Chapter 15 for the advantages and disadvantages of fielding questions throughout the session, at the end of each section, or towards the end of the presentation.

TIP

Here's a trick I've learned for shy audiences: I ask audience members to turn to a person next to them and pose a question they'd like to ask. Then they can ask questions that aren't their own, allowing shy people to get their questions answered because they're not the ones asking.

TIP

Continue to Chapter 6 to find out all you can about ending memorably with a killer story. Why skip to the end? What about the middle? Think of your presentation as if it were a sandwich. The first thing you do is take out the bread for the top and bottom. Then you add goodies. Preparing for presentations is much the same.

IN THIS CHAPTER

» Calling the audience to action

» Announcing your wrap up

» Creating the perfect, timely ending

» Being memorable and building your network

Chapter 6
Ending Memorably

I do not object to people looking at their watches when I am speaking. But I strongly object to them shaking them [the watches] to make sure they are still going.

—LORD WILLIAN NORMAN BIRKETT, BRITISH LAWYER AND JUDGE

The end of your presentation ushers in a new beginning for your audience in terms of the actions they'll (hopefully) start to take. A great presentation followed by a memorable conclusion can spark added skills, new insights, and perhaps changed attitudes.

On the other hand, a dud closing can completely undermine an otherwise great presentation. That's why you must give your ending thoughtful consideration. Chapter 5 discusses great openings; now let's discuss equally great endings — the two most important parts of any presentation.

Letting Them Know You're Wrapping Up

Provide a clear indication that the presentation is coming to a close. Signaling the close prepares the audience for the ending, which ironically makes it more memorable. (It's like a parent giving a child a five-minute warning that you're about to leave. It makes their ears perk up and they savor those last few minutes.) This is your last chance to get your points across and emphasize your call to action. Lead-in expressions may include any of the following:

- *This nears the end of today's session, but before you leave, I'd like to . . .*
- *Before we end . . .*
- *To sum up . . .*
- *To conclude . . .*

WARNING

Don't make the mistake of wrapping it up by asking if there are any questions or comments — or worse yet, showing a slide that says "Questions" or "Comments." There are several reasons for this. You won't be in control of the ending. Q&A endings aren't memorable. And if you get negative questions or comments, you've dulled your entire presentation and the audience will leave on a sour note.

Combining a Call to Action with a Story

Your entire presentation is basically a prelude to the call to action. Think of some sales presentations you've attended. Salespeople are great storytellers. Throughout their presentations, they're telling stories about how their product can change lives. Their final story (the call to action) is generally a kicker, hoping everyone in the audience (or as many as possible) will heed their call to action, whether it be signing up for a trial package, buying their company's product, signing on the dotted line, or whatever. They know that once the audience leaves the room, their conversion rate drops precipitously. They must "get you" while you're there.

Lawyers also rely on a persuasive closing statements to win cases. (They don't just wing it and hope the judge or jury will find in their favor.) They spend copious amounts of time — often with teams of legal professionals — crafting stories that make their closing statements irrefutable, so judgments of guilt or innocence (depending on which side they're on) will be rendered in their client's favor. They don't want a hung jury with no decisive verdict.

START-UP BRIEF

When molding your conclusion, pay special attention to numbers 7 and 8 in the Start-Up Brief (Chapter 3):

- In number 7 you identified your purpose: what you want the audience to do, think, feel, or learn. Persuasive concluding stories should center around the journeys of people or companies who did, thought, felt, or learned the same things and the valuable lessons they learned along the way.

» In number 8 you identified questions the audience needs to have answered. You can address these answers in the form of stories. Here's an example: You expect the audience may ask for options to a certain issue. You can share stories of people or companies who exercised different options and what the outcomes were. Remember that positive and negative outcomes are valuable to heeding the call to action.

REMEMBER

Endings shouldn't be long; they should be memorable and impactful. Here are two examples to consider:

» **You're completing a session on climate change.** You may end by saying, *"I'm passionate about climate change; you are as well, and that's why you're here. Our planet is quickly running out of time* (reiterate a very short story or statistic). *Now is the time to take action. When you leave here today, please take up the challenge by doing* (a, b, and/or c) *for the future of our children and the generations to follow."*

» **You're completing a sales pitch.** Share a very brief story of a company that was successful because it purchased your product or service and company that suffered failure because it didn't make the purchase. A rhetorical closing question could then be: *"Which company do you want to be?"* (It doesn't call for an answer because the answer is obvious.) Then state the call to action: *"If you're interested in learning more, please fill out the form on the table in back of the room before you leave, and I'll be delighted to contact you to set up an appointment."*

STORYOPIA ARCHIVES: CIRCLING BACK TO A STORY YOU TOLD EARLIER

During each of my presentations (regardless of the topic) I ask each participant to share a particular challenge that brought them to the session and what they hope to do, think, feel, or learn as a result. I write each of their responses on a sticky note (that's on an easel) or white board in front of the room. The comments during the Storytelling and Storyboarding workshop are relatively consistent: Getting rid of jitters, not knowing how or where to start, and so on. Occasionally, there's an outlier with a unique issue, but most are the same. I open with a story to show I identify with the audience. It's about of one of my early presentations. Here's a condensed version:

"My hands were sweaty. I rushed through the whole 15-minute presentation in less than 10 minutes. I'm not sure the audience noticed my nervousness, but I could practically hear my knees knocking."

(continued)

(continued)

Then, I conclude the session by reminding them of that earlier story and how, just a year later, after lots of practice, I stood in front of more than 400 people to give an acceptance speech for an award. This time I was calm, and I used my humor to win over the audience. I nailed it.

Lesson learned: When you show the audience you identify with them at the outset, you create a bond. In this case, I concluded by giving the audience the confidence that their jitters will decrease as they gain experience.

Exploring Other Powerful Closings

It's not enough to assume your presentation will inspire the audience to take action. Reiterate the action. Cast it around what you set out for your audience to do, think, feel, or learn. Options may include the following:

- Summarize the key points.
- Echo the core message.
- Ask a thought-provoking or rhetorical question.
- Display a powerful quote or statistic.
- Make them laugh.
- Show a relevant visual image.
- Tell a short story.

SHERYL SAYS

I often end my Storytelling and Storyboarding workshop by showing a slide with George Burns' famous remark. "The secret to a good sermon [session] is to have a good beginning and ending, and the two should be as close together as possible."

Ending Gracefully and On Time

Here are three hard-and-fast presentation rules for ending your talk:

1. End on time.
2. End on time.
3. End on time.

Make sure to cover your content in the time allotted or with a few minutes to spare. It's good practice to plan your presentation for 90 – 95% of the allotted time. That means if your talk is scheduled for 60 minutes, plan to speak for 50 minutes.

WARNING

Running late is inconsiderate of your audience's time. Here's what may happen:

- » People start walking out. Once someone gets up to leave, others follow.
- » People start thinking about their next appointment and tune you out.
- » You miss the golden opportunity for your wrap-up and call to action.
- » You lose credibility.

Curtailing if you need to

People have tightly packed schedules, and it's inconsiderate to ask, *Can you stay for another [however many] minutes?* Decide in advance which part or parts you can omit if you become pressed for time. Time crunches may happen if there are lots of questions and comments from the audience during the session. However, that's a good thing because it means they're engaged and are learning from you and from each other.

Consider using the following tactics to cut out info on the fly without compromising your overall message:

- » **Use layers.** This is like dressing in layers for cold weather where you can take off one layer at a time as you warm up. With your presentation, break out the major points, minor points, and nice-to-know data. If pressed for time, start eliminating the nice-to-know data, then the minor points if necessary while still covering the major points.
- » **Make it modular.** If you invite friends for dinner and are running late for a show, you may opt to skip dessert. Decide which modules (sections) you can skip without affecting the integrity of your message. Not all information has the same importance. There may be sections you added to your presentation that wouldn't be missed if you eliminated them.

TIP

Here are a few ways to keep track of the time: If there's a clock in the room, that's the most basic indicator that you can view without being obvious. If not, use the countdown clock on your phone. Keep it muted so it will vibrate and not be obvious to the audience.

Thanking everyone for coming and relishing the applause

After your concluding story, quote, slide, or whatever ending you use, signal the end of your presentation by thanking your audience. Sound sincere by giving them an actual reason you're thanking them. Many presenters merely thank the audience for coming, suggesting they may have spent their time doing something more important.

Here are some suggestions for delivering a sincere thank you:

- *Thanks so much for coming and for your valuable participation. We surely learned a lot from each other.*
- *I sincerely appreciate your giving me the opportunity to share this morning [afternoon or evening] with you.*
- *I can see that our time is up, and I'd like to thank you so much for all your participation.*
- *It's been an honor to be among such accomplished individuals and be able to share my perspective. Thank you all and have a wonderful rest of the day (afternoon or evening).*
- *It's no secret that the success of today's session has been your active participation. Thanks to each of you.*
- *If there are any further questions or comments, I'll be around for a while and look forward to chatting with you. Thanks so much for coming.*

Then it's time for applause. When someone starts to applaud, look directly at that person, smile, and mouth the words *thank you*. Everyone will then join in (perhaps with a standing O as you see in Figure 6-1). Resist the temptation to start shuffling papers, packing up your computer, removing your mic, and such. Stand comfortably (not stiff like a post) and enjoy the accolades. Smile, look people in the eye, and nod your head to show your appreciation.

FIGURE 6-1: A very appreciative audience!

Studio Romantic / Adobe Stock

Giving Them Something to Remember You By

Add even more value to your presentation by giving each member of the audience a *leave piece* to make the event linger. If your audience has 15 participants or fewer, consider handing the piece to each person. If the audience is larger, leave the pieces on a table near the exit door and remind them to take one as they're leaving. Leave pieces can include but aren't limited to:

- Business cards (yours, of course)
- Brochures or flyers
- Relevant article (whether you or someone else wrote it)
- List of relevant reading material
- Tip sheet (nice if it's laminated)
- Trinket related to your topic

TIP

Make sure each leave piece includes your name and contact information. If the piece is of value, participants may share it with others — leading to additional presentations.

Staying in Touch to Build Your Network

Unless you're presenting to an audience within your company or to people you know well, this presentation is a good opportunity to build your network. Make sure to bring plenty of business cards to distribute. Also have a well-polished elevator pitch for networking before, during, or after the event. This is especially valuable when you're presenting at a conference and you'll mingle with people who haven't attended your presentation. (Check out Chapter 11 to find out more about elevator pitches.)

Here are some ways to stay in touch and expand your network:

- Suggest that people share their social media handles and/or Substack.
- Refer them to an online blog or newsletter, if you have one.

- Send a thank you note to each participant unless the audience is very large. Personalize the notes and call out something special about that person's participation.
- If you were unable to answer a question during the presentation, send an email to each attendee with the answer to that question.

WARNING

Think carefully before inviting people you don't know into your LinkedIn network. I recommend you take LinkedIn's advice and only connect with people you know personally and trust on a professional level. LinkedIn is most powerful when you connect with the right people, not the most people.

TIP

Continue to Chapter 7 where you discover how to use storyboarding to merge your narrative and visuals to see how your entire presentation will shake out and shine.

IN THIS CHAPTER

» Before you start storyboarding. . .

» Understanding the storyboarding process

» Different types of storyboards

» Creating heroes for sales presentations

Chapter 7

Storyboarding: Bringing Stories to Life Frame by Frame

Storyboarding is what I call an "idea landscape" — one that can help unleash creativity, improve communication, and identify practical solutions to complex problems. The beauty of storyboarding is that ideas from an entire team are harnessed, not just those from the extroverts or vocal members.

–BILL CAPODAGLI, *INTERNATIONALLY RECOGNIZED BUSINESS AUTHOR, CONSULTANT, AND KEYNOTE SPEAKER*

Storyboarding has a long history. In 1898, a Russian theatre practitioner, Konstantin Stanislavski, developed storyboards for his production plans for the performance of Chekhov's *The Seagull* at the Moscow Art Theatre. Yes, storyboarding dates back that far! Better known, however, is Disney's Webb Smith who's considered the father of modern-day storyboards. In 1933, he started to draw rough sketches to animate *Three Little Pigs*. He pasted the sketches up on a wall to show how a storyline comes together. In 1939, *Gone with the Wind* became the first movie to be completely drawn with a storyboard.

Storyboarding has evolved through the centuries and is now widely embraced by business communities.

In this chapter you discover critical storyboarding techniques that will make your next presentation a showstopper.

Storyboarding in Business

Storyboarding is the gold standard for presentation planning whether the sessions are face-to-face, virtual, or hybrid. It's also valuable for planning ad campaigns, training sessions, videos, commercials, proposals, and more.

Simply put, storyboarding is an outline of a presentation shown frame by frame. It's very helpful when you and/or your team have lots of ideas swirling around in your heads. The storyboard will help sequence these ideas into frames in order to convey the narrative and associated visuals. It lets you make umpteen revisions until you're satisfied that your presentation takes your audience on a journey from what is to what could be — storyopia. In essence, storyboarding is a simplified way to accomplish the following:

- Establish a narrative and conversational flow to your presentation (tell).
- Know which stories to relate.
- Focus on visuals that can *say* it louder than words (show).
- Pinpoint where details may be lacking.
- Allow teams to alternate between creative brainstorming and critical reviewing.

SHERYL SAYS

If you're new to storyboarding, no worries. I have you covered. This chapter guides you through what you need to know and what different types of storyboards can look like.

Before You Start Storyboarding. . .

START-UP BRIEF

Before you start your storyboard, make sure you have learned all you can about your audience by filling out the Start-Up Brief in Chapter 3. Doing so will ensure that your audience remembers your essential message amidst the supportive points. Your narrative and visuals will be the prelude that leads to your call to action.

The following is a memory aid to condense the key information captured from the Start-Up Brief. It will get you jump-started.

I'm presenting:

____

No. 1: Key issue for audience to remember

To:

____

No. 2: Primary audience

In order to:

____

No. 7: Call to action (purpose)

Considering Different Storyboarding Formats

Storyboards can take many different forms: comic book-style frames, sticky notes, wall-papering, or Tell and Show columns prepared in a word processing program. You see examples of each in this section. Storyboarding is appropriate for one person who'll deliver their own presentation, but it's often a team approach consisting of a writer and designer, at the very least. If you're preparing a storyboard for a video, it may also involve a director, cinematographer, narrator, and others.

Using comic strip frames

If you can't envision a storyboard, one way is to think of a comic strip. Each frame shows what's being said and who or what's in the scene, as you see in Figure 7-1. You can draw them by hand or use one of the popular apps: Canva, Paintstorm Studio, Manga, Comic Creator Studio, Pixton, or Toon Boom Studio to name a few.

FIGURE 7-1: You don't need to be this talented to create your own comic-style storyboard.

Framestock / Adobe Stock

Using sticky notes

This process can either be done on actual sticky notes or using apps such as Jamboard or Mural. Either way, it involves capturing one concept at a time. (A concept isn't the equivalent of a slide; it's a small chunk of information.)

This evokes a team approach of visual thinking and planning where a small team (perhaps two to four people) can brainstorm together, placing their ideas on notes, then putting them on the wall or any other flat surface for viewing. At this point, there's nothing permanent, just a flow of ideas. Teams can arrange and rearrange the notes until they're reasonably pleased with the structure and core message. Then it's time for a team member to transfer the narrative to the computer. (You'll see examples later in this chapter.)

Figure 7-2 shows the sticky note storyboarding technique. The left column is the Tell column — snippets of what to say. The right is the Show column — what to show.

Using "wall-paper" editing

Although this isn't a storyboard, it's part of the process. Some groups use collaborative word processing apps such as Slack, Trello, Asana, or Monday.com for this type of editing; others prefer wall-paper editing. This process has some similarity to the sticky notes process; however, it involves printing out draft pages of text and/or graphics and pasting them to a wall — hence, the name "wall-paper." This works well for larger teams when several people or groups will edit.

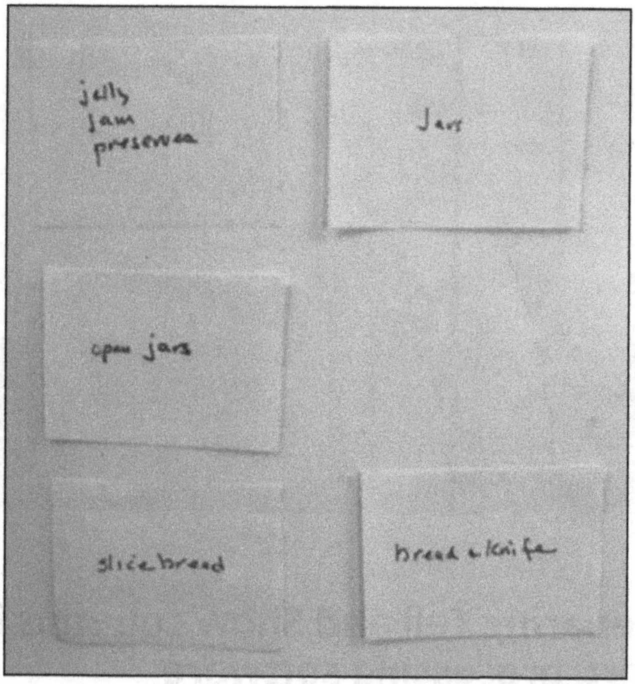

FIGURE 7-2: Sticky note storyboarding which can be stuck to any flat surface.

SHERYL SAYS

Wall-paper editing isn't an actual term, so you won't find it in a search. It's a term I coined for lack of a better one. (Alternatively, you may have heard the term "brown paper technique," which gets its name from taping brown paper to the wall before affixing the draft.) You get the gist of what this is in Figure 7-3. Here's how the process works:

1. **Print the document with text and/or images and tack each page to a wall in sequential order using easy-release tape.**

   You may do this one section at a time, one chapter at a time, or whatever works for the length of your document. You may also do this for each round of revisions. (If you double space the text pages, you allow room for people to make notes.)

2. **Schedule a date and time for each person or group to edit the document.**

   Ask people to place their initials near their edits to replicate Track Changes.

This process works well because it encourages people to commit to a time for this task or they lose their right to provide input. (This also prevents the all-too-common reviewer who ignores the document until "Someday," which isn't one of the seven days in a week.) All you have to do is post the document on a wall, generate a schedule for people to edit, and make sure they know the time and place. Build this process into the production schedule so people know you're serious.

FIGURE 7-3: Wall-paper editing.

Gorodenkoff / Adobe Stock

Preparing Tell and Show columns in word processing software

TIP

Before you start this process, get yourself in gear:

- Create a comfortable environment.
- Get all your stuff together.
- Set attainable goals.
- Stay focused.
- Work on one section at a time.
- Keep drafting for the time you allotted.

Create two columns: Tell and Show. They become your building blocks (or frames). It's much like show-and-tell from your early childhood days in school. You'd bring an object from home, show it, and then tell about it. For business presentations you reverse this: First note what to tell, then add what to show.

Tell	Show

You can populate the Tell column in one of the following ways depending on your comfort level:

- **Document your narrative verbatim.** This works well if you're more comfortable writing every word for a presentation you'll deliver, if you're preparing a presentation for someone else to deliver, or if someone else will be narrating for a video.
- **Use bullet points.** This maps key information in sequential order. You'll fill in the blanks as you deliver your talk.
- **Jot down notes.** If you tend to present extemporaneously and just need a few notes in the order in which you'll present them, this is for you.

Starting with the Tell column

At this early stage, you're creating a preliminary draft of what you want to tell your audience — your initial thoughts. This is your chance to express yourself without being critical of anything you write. You can censor yourself later. Your task right now is to document all those thoughts swirling around in your head. Avoid going back over what you wrote; save that for later. The most important thing is to keep moving forward.

If you can't think of the right word or words, here are a few things to try:

- Use another word or words and keep moving ahead.
- Leave a blank space and fill it in later.
- Put XXXXXXs (as many as you like) as a placeholder.

TIP

If you've already developed a groundswell opening (Chapter 5) and memorable closing (Chapter 6), go right to it and start filling in the Tell column. If you haven't solidified either, start with the section that's most comfortable. There's always a portion of the presentation you can jump right into. Then proceed to the next most comfortable section. Before you know it, you'll be on a roll, and your audience will never know where you started.

Table 7-1 shows a well-developed *draft* using bullet points for a 30-minute presentation to the Martians. This has gone through several iterations of sticky notes pasted to the wall until the level of detail that needed explaining was incorporated. (For example, an initial entry on the sticky note was "open the jar." But how? Anyone not familiar with opening a jar wouldn't know to turn the cap counterclockwise.) This storyboard includes three stories: one near the beginning, another in the middle, and the final one near the end. (There's an underscore at the point of each story.)

Table 7-1 Tell Column of Storyboard (Draft)

Tell	Show
• Welcome and brief intro. • Please feel free to jump in with any questions as we go along.	
Story of how PBJ& started and that it became so popular there's even a national celebration on April 2. (The actual story is in Chapter 1.)	
• Discuss how peanut better can be smooth or chunky. • Mention that oil in natural peanut butter separates and must be mixed. • Clarify the difference between jelly, jam, and preserves. • Describe what jars look like as opposed to cans that you can't see through. • Explain how to open jars. (Twist cap counterclockwise.)	
• Explain what a knife looks like and what it's intended to do. • Mention how to hold a knife so it's safe. **Story** of Clyde who didn't hold his knife correctly and got a bad gash.	
• Explain that some breads come as whole loaves and aren't pre-sliced. • Explain how to slice a whole loaf of bread that isn't pre-sliced.	
Story of how kids all over America pack their paper bag (or lunch box) with an easy-to-make-PB&J sandwich, an apple, and juice box, noting that the average child will eat 1,500 PB&J sandwiches before graduating from high school.	
Everyone is invited to come up and give it a try.	

TIP

After you've finished your draft, get some distance from what you wrote. It's hard to be objective when you've just completed it. In a perfect world, you could put your draft down and revisit it in a day or two, but this isn't a perfect world and you'll undoubtedly be working with deadlines. Get as much distance as time will allow. Grab a cup of coffee. Make a quick phone call. Go for a short walk. Pat yourself on the back.

Filling in the Show column

After you've completed a draft of the Tell column, it's time to pair it with what you'll show. (The Show column will contain anything that isn't part of your narrative, although not necessarily something visual, such as brainstorming.) Always determine what show is appropriate for your audience, purpose, and venue. Here are a variety of things you can include to enhance your story and sub-stories:

- Slides
- Photographs
- Audio and/or video clips
- Live demonstrations
- Handouts
- Whiteboard
- Brainstorming
- Individual or group activities
- Questions and answers
- Polls and chats (if virtual)
- Audience member speakers or guest speakers

REMEMBER

Also, think of physical props that may be relevant to your presentation. A prop can be a book, phone, gizmo, or whatever. (The word "prop" comes from the term *theatrical property*, referring to objects used by actors to add realism to a story to advance the narrative.) You can change the rhythm of your presentation with one or more props of visual interest.

Table 7-2 shows the final storyboard for the presentation to the Martians. Notice how smoothly it flows:

- To grab the audience's attention quickly, it opens with a short, entertaining YouTube video (prior to the welcoming remarks).
- It continues with how PB&J started. (Check out Chapter 1 for the full story that will be shared.) There are two accompanying slides: One showing the original recipe from 1901 and another representing National PB&J Day on April 2.
- Props are used for the demo.

STORYOPIA ARCHIVES: USING THE RIGHT PROPS AT THE RIGHT TIME

Bill Gates, not known as one of the most eloquent speakers, gave a TED talk titled "Mosquitoes, Malaria, and Education." Part way through the presentation he opened a glass jar and let mosquitoes loose in the lecture hall. His accompanying words were: *Now, malaria is of course transmitted by mosquitos. I brought some here, just so you could experience this. We'll let those roam around the auditorium a little bit.* (Laughter) *There's no reason only poor people should have the experience.* (Laughter and long pause) *These mosquitos are not infected.* (More laughter and applause) That prop was unexpected, memorable, and the story went viral. It was probably the most unforgettable talk Bill Gates has ever given.

Lesson learned: When you think of a prop, decide when to use it, explain its relevance to your topic, demonstrate it, and put it out of sight when you're finished. If your audience is large, make sure people in back of the room can see the prop. If not, include a photo of the prop projected on a screen. The right props used at the right time will enhance a presentation — even if the speaker is less than stellar.

» The presentation concludes with how children all over America take PB&J sandwiches to school for lunch. There will be a short video showing kids heading to school (fade out-fade in), then eating their sandwiches in the cafeteria.

» Then everyone is invited up to try making a PB&J.

SHERYL SAYS

In addition to what follows, please check out this storyboard as it appears in the color section. See how appetizing it is in full color — the contrast between the subdued color of peanut butter and the vibrancy of red jelly. It's eye popping! By using color to your advantage, you too can strengthen your message and make key elements jump out. (Chapter 9 goes into more detail about using black and white and color.)

Table 7-2 Final Storyboard

How to Make a PB&J Sandwich
30-minute Presentation for Martians

Tell	Show
	1-1/2 minute Video on YouTube 
• Welcome and brief intro. • Please feel free to jump in with any questions as we go along.	
Tell story of how PBJ& started. Boast of National PBJ& Day on April 2 for this all-American sandwich.	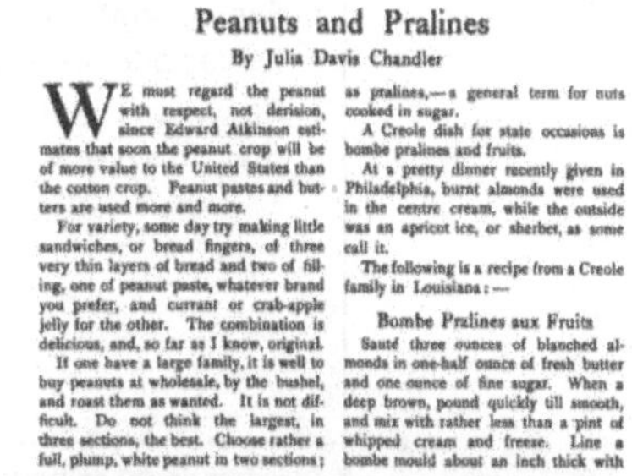 Peanuts and Pralines By Julia Davis Chandler WE must regard the peanut with respect, not derision, since Edward Atkinson estimates that soon the peanut crop will be of more value to the United States than the cotton crop. Peanut pastes and butters are used more and more. For variety, some day try making little sandwiches, or bread fingers, of three very thin layers of bread and two of filling, one of peanut paste, whatever brand you prefer, and currant or crab-apple jelly for the other. The combination is delicious, and, so far as I know, original. If one have a large family, it is well to buy peanuts at wholesale, by the bushel, and roast them as wanted. It is not difficult. Do not think the largest, in three sections, the best. Choose rather a full, plump, white peanut in two sections; as pralines,—a general term for nuts cooked in sugar. A Creole dish for state occasions is bombe pralines and fruits. At a pretty dinner recently given in Philadelphia, burnt almonds were used in the centre cream, while the outside was an apricot ice, or sherbet, as some call it. The following is a recipe from a Creole family in Louisiana: — Bombe Pralines aux Fruits Sauté three ounces of blanched almonds in one-half ounce of fresh butter and one ounce of fine sugar. When a deep brown, pound quickly till smooth, and mix with rather less than a pint of whipped cream and freeze. Line a bombe mould about an inch thick with 

(continued)

Table 7-2 (continued)

• Mention that oil in natural peanut butter separates and must be mixed. • Clarify the difference between jelly, jam, and preserves. • Describe what jars look like as opposed to cans that you can't see through. • Explain how to open jars. (Twist cap counterclockwise.)	
• Explain what a knife looks like and what it's intended to do. • Mention how to hold a knife so it's safe. Story of Clyde who didn't hold his knife correctly and got cut badly.	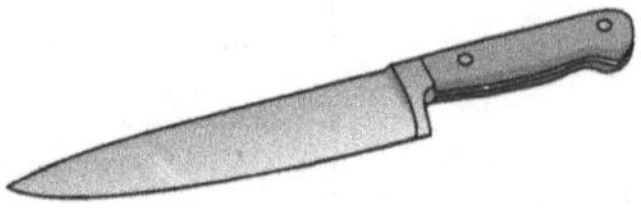
• Explain that some breads come as whole loaves and aren't pre-sliced. • Show how to slice a whole loaf of bread that isn't pre-sliced.	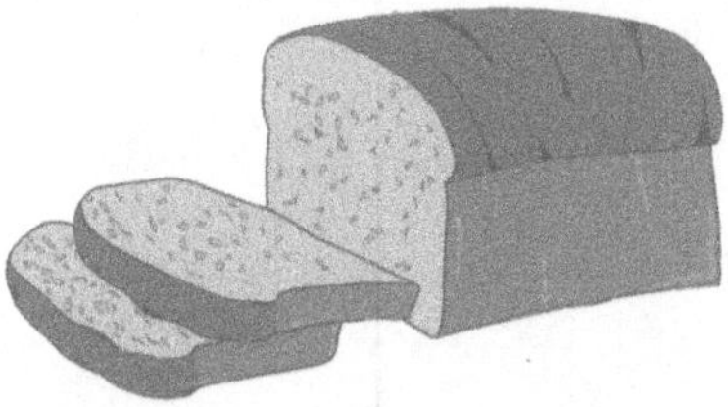
Closing story of how kids all over America trek to school with a paper bag (or lunch box) packed with a PB&J sandwich, an apple, and juice box. Note that the average child will eat 1,500 PB&J sandwiches before graduating from high school.	
Invite everyone to come up and make a PB&J sandwich.	

LIGHTFIELD STUDIOS / Adobe Stock

Using greeking when visuals drive the talk

There are instances when visuals drive the talk, and the Show column will be prepared before the Tell column. In such cases, storyboarders use *greeking* — also known as lorem ipsum — as a placeholder for the narrative. One instance may be a manufacturing plant that's showing its delivery process.

Lorem ipsum dolor sit amet, consectetur adipiscing elit, sed do eiusmod	Lorem ipsum dolor sit amet, consectetur adipiscing elit, sed do eiusmod tempor	Lorem ipsum dolor sit amet, consectetur adipiscing elit, sed do eiusmod tempor incididunt ut labore et dolore magna aliqua. Ut enim ad minim veniam, quis nostrud exercitation

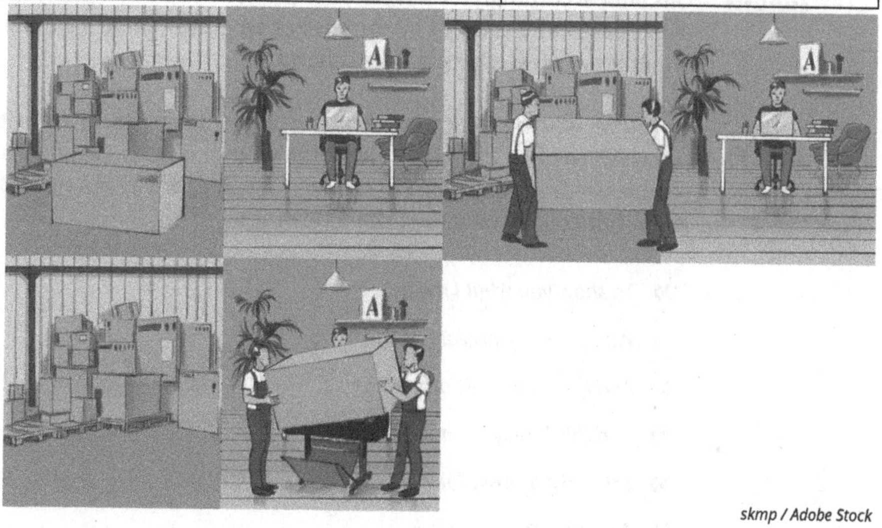

skmp / Adobe Stock

Building Transitions and Breaks into Your Storyboard

You have a natural adrenaline flow when you're presenting, but your audience's attention may be waning. Therefore, it's incumbent upon you to vary your program and build in variety. Write transitions and breaks into the storyboard. (Also, be prepared to transition on the fly if you hear any snoring.) Here are a few ideas to rejuvenate the audience:

- **Get them to participate.** Request questions or comments. Ask them to share their own stories. This presentation isn't about you; it's about your audience. Bring them into the conversation.

- **Give a demo.** Something as simple as a video of a customer (or mock customer) using your product or service adds a multimedia component to your presentation. It can even be a testimonial.
- **Introduce a prop.** Pull out an unexpected prop. Steve Jobs was the master of props. Like a magician, he pulled the first iPod out of his jeans pocket. He pulled the MacBook out of an envelope. Each prop was projected on a large screen behind him because his audience was massive.

REMEMBER

Be sensitive to the audience's biological needs. Although many people will discreetly leave to use the restroom as needed, others wait for an official break. Therefore, announce during your opening remarks when breaks will be so people can plan accordingly. It's recommended that you build into your storyboard official breaks at least every 90 minutes or wherever there's a natural pause or transition between sections in that timeframe.

TIP

If you're writing your narrative verbatim, incorporate transitional words and phrases. They're the glue that holds your thoughts together so they can move seamlessly from one point to another. Avoid expressions such as *um*, *like*, and *you know*, but consider some of the following:

- *To show you what I mean . . .*
- *With your permission, I'd like to . . .*
- *And that's just part of the story . . .*
- *And this is only a small sampling . . .*
- *Let's take a closer look at . . .*
- *And if that's not enough . . .*
- *Let's look at the record . . .*
- *I've saved the best for last!*

Stepping Back and Looking at the Big Picture

When you think your storyboard is complete and your team has given their input, step back and review the Tell and Show columns. Study how everything connects.

- Does each frame build a logical narrative to enhance your key message?
- Do the visuals enhance your narrative?
- Are the points you make supporting your argument?
- Are there relevant stories, sub-stories, metaphors, or analogies incorporated?
- Can your audience see themselves in your scenario?

TIP

Check out the section of the online Cheat Sheet titled "Summing It Up: Rock Your Next Presentation." (To access the Cheat Sheet, simply go to dummies.com and type Storytelling in Presentations For Dummies Cheat Sheet in the search box.)

Outsourcing to the Pros

There are times you may need a premium production for social media, corporate promotions, commercials, high-end training, and the like. Most companies don't have the in-house capabilities and aren't savvy in video production or video marketing. So finding the right vendor can be daunting. This section offers a few pointers.

Knowing your needs

First, consider whether you want a local company or national company. For a local search, check the Internet for "video production companies [city];" ask your network; get referrals from your local Chamber of Commerce; check the Better Business Bureau; or Google Yelp and UpCity. For a national search, check the Internet for "video production companies." You'll find loads of them.

Then, narrow your search to the type of services you need:

- **Feature film productions:** Covers all the bases from pre-production to production to post-production. Services can include scripting, storyboarding, location scouting, hiring directors and crew, and more.
- **Commercial productions:** Produces stock footage, training videos, and short corporate videos.
- **Animation and SFX productions:** Offers special effects that may be unique to your idea.

» **Post-production:** Offers video editing, special effects, color correction, sound mixing and editing — the magical parts. This is after the upfront work of storyboarding, which they or you can do.

» **Niche production:** Represents a niche market which could be music videos, TV commercials, and the like.

Vetting vendors

With any provider, it's important to "see the proof in the pudding." Here are some things to ask:

» Request links to three or more videos in their portfolio that are similar to the type of video you want to produce.

» Confirm what their timetable typically is: How long it will take to get the first round (rough cut) of your video after the film shoot, and so forth.

» Find out what value-added tips they offer to maximize your budget.

WARNING

Caveat emptor, "Let the buyer beware." Here are a few things to be aware of:

» When a production company gives you a referral, they're not going to give you the names of dissatisfied customers. So check that their website looks good, has a modern logo, and has samples of their work that matches what you're looking for.

» If a company calls itself "award-winning" and it's an award you've never heard of, chances are they're boasting a paid-for award. Any company can get an award by paying a fee.

REMEMBER

Make sure you and your entire team approve the storyboard before going into production. Although the pros are there to give you guidance and provide the skills and services you don't have in-house, it's your presentation and you have the final say!

Storyboarding for Sales Presentations

Now let's focus on the millions (yes millions) of sales presentations delivered each year. They run the gamut from teaching salespeople how to sell to vendors incentivizing prospective customers to buy.

Is the presenter the hero — the courageous knight in shining armor who shows up on the gallant steed to free the prospect from inefficiency, help them slay the (dragon) competition, and recover the treasure chest full of gold? No. The problem with this scenario is that it leaves the audience (prospect) out of the story. The hero must be the prospect, the audience — the knight in shining armor.

Making the audience the heroes of every sales presentation

Seth Godin, American author and former .com business executive says: "Marketing is no longer about the stuff that you make, but about the stories you tell." In sales and marketing there's nothing more convincing than a compelling story that relates to people's emotions, especially to their lives, finances, jobs, and companies.

START-UP BRIEF

Make sure to fill out the Start-Up Brief in Chapter 3. It will help you paint a picture of your audience as the glorious knights who save the corporate township from the fierce (dragon) competitors.

Everyone likes to be the center of attention and hear stories about themselves. It puts them in the powerful position of being the heroes to their managers, co-workers, and stakeholders. You must know their obstacles and goals and tie one or more success stories into the presentation. Your sales and marketing teams can be of great help in gathering success stories. These stories will demonstrate how your audience can see themselves in the same position and will strengthen your call to action.

- What worries them in a personal way?
- What would make them look good to their managers, co-workers, and stakeholders?
- What would earn the company greater profits?
- What could help them earn larger commissions?

You want them to leave armed with the tools to help them shine! Your storyboard is the perfect way to plan and prepare a winning presentation. The initial draft can flow something like the one in Table 7-3, leading to a call to action. Only one show has been determined so far; more will be filled in as the storyboard gets developed.

Table 7-3 Storyboard for a 30-minute Sales Presentation (Draft)

Tell	Show
Opening: Hook with a story Appeal to emotions. Persuade to attract attention, inspire interest, and capture the imagination.	
Relate the opening to the audience: "Bob. I know your company has been grappling with . . . . "	
Share the main features and benefits of your product or service as they relate to their needs.	Table, chart, video, or live demo
Create a sense of urgency: "Bob will happen if you continue on your current path?"	
Call to action: • Action on your ideas. • Action for a follow-up meeting. • Action on your proposal. • Action to buy your product or services.	

TIP

Now that you've completed the Nuts n Bolts, head to Chapters 8 and 9 to discover how to create slides that will round out your brilliant presentation.

3

Adding Flourishes

IN THIS PART . . .

Recognize which slideware is best for your needs, figure out how to sidestep slidezillas, know the power of the opening slide, and create presentations with accessibility for all.

Tell stories with slides, discover what makes a good slide, create slide titles, incorporate videos and graphics, and avoid the seven deadly sins.

Kick your handouts and workbooks up a notch, write the copy, print and bind, and know when to distribute them.

Establish instant credibility with a brilliant bio, let your personality shine, be introduced, and introduce yourself.

Prepare open- and close-ended questions, value feedback, and do a self-assessment.

IN THIS CHAPTER

» Getting to know some slide software players

» Understanding the power of an opening slide

» Formatting text and using bulleted and numbered lists

» Being inclusive

» Editing yourself

Chapter 8
Slideware: Buying and Applying

PowerPoint doesn't kill meetings. People kill meetings.

—*PETER NORVIG*, GOOGLE DIRECTOR OF RESEARCH

The problem with shoddy presentations isn't the fault of the slides any more than shoddy carpentry is the fault of the hammer. It's the fault of presenters who prepare and deliver Death by PowerPoint. Too many presenters think of slides as "The Presentation" as opposed to tools to enhance the presentation. Slideshows are often poorly designed, lack relevance, have distracting transitions, or contain way too many bullets on way to many slides, among other blunders.

Like anything in life, excess yields negative results. Two aspirin tablets may help your headache, but a hundred may result in acute aspirin poisoning. Your time is valuable, and so is your audience's. Don't waste it inundating them with slidezillas. Rather, make sure each slide serves a purpose that will enhance, not distract.

As you go through this chapter, you'll discover how to enthuse your audiences by meshing narratives with meaningful and purposeful slides and other visuals.

TIP

Please check out Chapter 9 next. It works in concert with this chapter to share what does and doesn't make a good slide.

Life Before Death (by PowerPoint)

Before jumping further into this chapter, step back several centuries for a little history that highlights the evolution of visual communication techniques:

- **Chalkboards:** The first purpose of presentations was for education. The credit of inventing the first blackboard goes to James Pillans, a geography teacher at the Old High School in Edinburgh, Scotland in 1801. Teachers continued using chalkboards with chalk that often made the blood-curdling sounds. (I cringe as I write this, recalling that sound.) For decades, scientists and mathematicians continued using chalkboards to present complicated calculations. They filled large boards with equations and pointed at different sections with a long stick.
- **Whiteboards:** The whiteboard was invented in the 1950s but it didn't earn its place in the presentation arena until the 1970s. Early whiteboards were difficult to clean and required a wet cloth to remove the ink. Then markers became erasable and whiteboards started appearing on walls at presentation venues. At the turn of the millennium, the advancement of technology pushed whiteboards to the next level and made them electronic. Many of these have the capability to carry meetings across the country and the world.
- **Flip charts:** The earliest known patent of a flip chart dates from May 8, 1913, but they became popular for business presentations when a newer version was introduced by Peter Kent. They were paper flip charts that clipped to a stand. Flip charts are still widely used.
- **Transparencies:** In the early 1960s the overhead projector paved the way for page-sized sheets of transparent plastic film (also known as foils) where the image was projected. The foils were taped to cardboard or plastic frames for easier handling. Transparencies allowed for addressing on-the-fly needs of an audience, as the presenter could take a marker and write on the transparency.
- **PowerPoints:** This software was developed by Robert Gaskins and Dennis Austin for the American computer software company Forethought, Inc. The program, initially named Presenter, was released for the Apple Macintosh in 1987. Microsoft released its first official version in 1990. PowerPoints and other slide presentation software offer a collaborative solution. They're highly customizable and can be used virtually anywhere. The slides can be exported in different formats and can have multimedia inserts.

- **Slide decks:** It's a term derived from the early days of presentations when slides were transparencies, as mentioned earlier. The term is still used today to represent slides produced by presentation apps. Think of each slide as a card in a deck with its own meaning, value, and structure.

Buying: Meeting the Cast of Presentation Players

Today's presentation apps accommodate text, images, animation, audio, and video. PowerPoint remains the most prominent name in slideware and has become synonymous with slides in general. But there are many other choices. (It's for that reason, I use the term "slide" generically.) Some offer a free version, others are cloud-based, and many offer collaboration features. It all comes down to knowing your needs and finding an app that fit those needs.

Knowing your needs

Here are some things to consider when looking for the right app:

- What's the pricing like? Are there hidden costs?
- Is the software easy to learn?
- Can you add audio, video, and animation?
- Is there a built-in library of templates?
- Does it offer the ability to collaborate with your team on the design and delivery?
- Will it integrate with other existing apps in the company?
- Can you track analytics?
- Does it allow you to deliver your presentation on multiple devices?
- Can your presentations be uploaded to the cloud privately with password protection?
- Can the finished presentation be shared online straight from the app?
- Is it desktop and/or cloud based?
- Is a free trial available?

Finding the app that fits

When trying to decide on which app would be best for you, use the Goldilocks theory: *Don't pay too much. Don't pay too little. Pay what's just right for the features you need and your budget.* A free app may be all you need. Check the Internet for "best presentation tools." You'll find many, including the following (listed in their order of popularity):

- PowerPoint (Comes with Microsoft Office Suite)
- Visme
- Canva
- Prezi
- Google Slides
- Keynote (for Macs only)
- Pitcherific
- Haiku Deck

Using and Sharing Slideware During Virtual Meetings

By sharing slideware, you can keep all your participants on the same page (literally) and enable them to stay connected and be part of the conversation or problem-solving at hand. Here are a few suggestions:

- **Use the screen-sharing feature:** Both Zoom and Teams (the most commonly used programs) have a screen-sharing feature that enables you to share your presentation with other participants in the call. Before you start your call, make sure you know how to share your screen.
- **Share only the slide window:** Make sure you share only the slide window, not your entire desktop.
- **Use the presenter view:** Most slide apps have a feature called "presenter view" so you can see your notes, next slide, and timing on your screen while

your audience sees only the slideshow. Make sure you know how to use this feature before your presentation.

- **Test your Internet connection:** Slow or unstable connections can cause delays and interruptions during your presentation. Well in advance of your call, test your Internet connection to ensure that it's fast and stable. If yours isn't, limit background programs and/or switch to a wired Ethernet connection.
- **Use a headset or microphone:** To ensure your audience can hear you clearly, use a headset or microphone. This will also help to reduce background noises and echoes.
- **Record your presentation:** Both Zoom and Teams allow you to record your presentation. This is a great option to share your presentation later or if some participants are unable to attend the live presentation.
- **Send your presentation beforehand:** If you're presenting to a larger group, it's a good idea to send your presentation beforehand. Doing so allows participants to review your content before the call and also helps to ensure everyone is prepared to participate.

TIP

Chapter 18 offers loads of tips and tricks for delivering virtually.

Giving Your Presentation an Enticing Title

Just as every movie and documentary needs an enticing title, your presentation does as well. You don't have to think of one title early on. Start with a working title (a place holder). For the Martians, it could be something as simple as, *How to Make a Peanut Butter and Jelly Sandwich.* As you go through the process of creating your presentation, different ideas will come to you. Here are a few iterations for the presentation to the Martians:

PB&J Made Easy

Do you want to eat?

PB&J — Make Your Day!

Staving Off Hunger the American Way

Not needing to reinvent the wheel

If the name of your presentation is boring, your intended audience may think your presentation will be boring as well. There are a number of tried-and-tested tips professional writers and journalists use to fashion headlines. They go to a swipe-file and pull out which headline works best for the current topic. (A *swipefile* is a collection of examples that journalists and other writers use as inspiration and reference when creating their own content. It can include headlines, ledes, story structure, quotes, and other writing techniques. With slight variations, they make them their own.)

TIP

The next time you pick up a magazine or read a headline in a news app, notice how many enticing headlines (titles) seem to appear again and again. Go online and search for "title generators." There are several. Then create your own swipefile.

To title a presentation, think of the many you've attended and note what did and didn't appeal to you. Here are a few tips from the pros:

- **Include a tempting benefit:** How to . . .
- **Tell a story:** Go From . . . to . . .
- **Use the number three or any odd number:** Three Sure Ways to . . .
- **Inject curiosity:** New Research Reveals . . . How to Improve Your . . .
- **Start with an *-ing* verb:** Propelling Your . . . Becoming a . . .
- **Use alliterations:** Seven Simple Steps . . .
- **Rhyme:** Meet and Repeat
- **Pose a question:** Why do . . .? Are you still . . .?

Knowing your audience's inner monologue

If you've attended a conference recently, you probably had to decide which break-out sessions you wanted to attend. You scanned the titles and presenters. If the presenter was someone you've heard before and found interesting, your inner monologue told you that's the session to choose. If not, you scanned the titles and your inner monologue said, *Nope. Nah. Hmmmmmm. Sounds boring. That'll be a yawn.* But one, with an appealing title, may have enticed you.

Table 8-1 shows some weak and strong titles and possible reactions.

TABLE 8-1 Examples of Weak and Strong Titles

Titles	Reactions
Weak: Plan for Your Retirement NOW!	Oh no. Not another snoozer.
Strong: Three Ways to Ensure Financial Independence in Retirement	Hmm! Ensure? Just three ways . . . May be worth checking out.
Weak: Fourth Quarter Update	Vague. Couldn't they just send the report?
Strong: Fourth Quarter Exceeds Expectations	Great news. Waiting to hear if we get end-year bonuses.
Weak: Latest Software Update	What is it this time?
Strong: Long-Awaited Software Update to Close Security Risks	Finally! Let's find out how to make this happen.
Weak: Diversity Training	Yawn!!!
Strong: Multicultural *Mélange*	Hmm? Sounds exotic. Maybe I'll go.
Weak: Shed Pounds During Lunchtime	Yeah, sure!
Strong: Lunch Crunch	Catchy name? I can spare an hour.
Weak: Networking 101	What's this, high school?
Strong: Mingle Makers	Hmm! I'll give mingling a try.

STORYOPIA ARCHIVES: BRAINSTORMING FOR IDEAS

When I first started delivering my workshop titled "Business/Technical Writing Workshop," the name wasn't very inspiring and drew small audiences, no matter how much I advertised and marketed. When people did attend, many thought the focus would be on punctuation and grammar, rather than on process and outcome. The name I had selected was missing something, and I couldn't figure out what it was.

I attended a networking event that had a breakout session on naming businesses, and we each were allowed a five- to ten-minute brainstorming opportunity. I chose to focus on renaming my workshop. The group generated lots of great ideas, which resulted in renaming the workshop, *Write It So They'll Read It!*™ (It ties the name with the value proposition.) That new title was the springboard for those workshops. With the new branding, I started working with several companies, and there was always a waiting list.

Also, I renamed my "Grammar & Punctuation" workshop (another boring name), *What I Forgot From Ms. Grump's English Class.* That, too, became a hit!

Lesson learned: Brainstorm with others to round out your ideas. What's in a name? A lot!

Appreciating the Power of an Opening Slide

Presentations are intended to persuade your audience to do, think, feel, or learn something. Whether you're an entrepreneur pitching investors, a small business owner selling a product to a retailer or potential customer, a startup presenting a new initiative, or a low-level manager asking senior management for budget or staffing resources, what you put on your opening slide is important and serves as a prelude to your call to action. It should set the tone for what's to come.

Although this section is about opening slides, it's not suggesting that you open your presentation with a slide. Although it's certainly one option, there are many other engaging ways to open a presentation. Check out Chapter 5 for more info.

Understanding how not to open

This section refers to the initial slide you'll show, such as the one you may have on the screen as the audience enters. Most of them are big yawns. We've all seen them, and they may have looked something like this:

Title of Presentation

Presenter's Name and Title

Presenter's Company

Name of Sponsoring Organization

Date (optional)

Everyone knew all that before they entered the room. Don't waste this opportunity to capture your audience's attention and imagination.

START-UP BRIEF

Be sure to fill out the Start-Up Brief in Chapter 3. It will help you to understand your audience so you can prepare a presentation with a narration, visuals, and stories that will make them the heroes.

Designing an engaging opening slide

An opening slide should capture the audience's attention. It can include any of the following:

- A great photo (not of yourself or your family)
- A powerful quote
- A thought-provoking question
- A startling statistic
- A brief quiz
- A 3- to 4-line story
- A challenge
- Something humorous

Figure 8-1 is the opening slide architects at 2M Architecture use as a wow factor to kick off their presentations to builders and/or potential clients. This dramatic home showcases one of the firm's recent projects and demonstrates the scope of their creativity. What builder wouldn't want to partner with this team for an astonishing construction project? What potential clients couldn't see themselves living in a home like his one?

FIGURE 8-1: A home with wow appeal!

Photo courtesy of 2M Architecture

Knowing How and When to Use Bullets and Numbers

There's nothing more narcolepsy-inducing than slidezillas (one after another) heaped with data-laden bullet points. It's like putting the audience in front of a firing squad and blasting away. Whether you're trying to convince managers to support a new campaign, talking with a prospect to close a deal, or building a new piece of marketing collateral, you need to craft a presentation that wows. You can use lists in an engaging way, as you'll see in this section. It offers an explanation of when to use a bulleted list or a numbered list, how to present your lists, and how to avoid the dreaded laundry list.

Using bulleted lists

Use bulleted lists when rank and sequence aren't important. Bullets give everything on the list equal value. Always head the list with a descriptive sentence. For example:

Following are the fabrication methods for stencils:

- Laser cutting
- Chemical etching
- Electroforming

Using numbered lists

If you ever believed in Santa Claus, you know all about making lists. When you prepared your Christmas wish list, you wrote the hottest item as number one; the second hottest as number two; and so on. If you didn't use numbers, you wouldn't have given Santa any visual clue as to what was most important. Santa may have just picked a few things you asked for, and then you'd be disappointed on Christmas morning when your shiny red Jaguar wasn't waiting in the driveway.

The items that follow show you when to use a numbered list.

» **Show items in order of priority.** Doing so gives the reader a visual clue that the items on the list are in the order of importance.

Example:

Please take care of these issues in the morning:

1. Call the ABC Agency to arrange for a consultant for the week of May 15.
2. Ask Jim to prepare his R&D report.
3. Schedule a meeting with everyone involved in the Diamus project.

» **List steps in a procedure.** When you describe steps in a procedure, start each numbered item with an *action word* (a verb) something the reader should do.

Example:

Following are the requirements for formulated water printing:

1. Use a squeegee action to deliver all the stencil aperture contents in the UBM surface.
2. Remove any remaining solder beads with the automated wiping process.
3. Eliminate oxides from the solder beads during the reflow process.
4. Remove flux residues after the reflow with mild chemistries.

» **Quantify items.** If you don't number a long list, people count the listed items in their heads to make sure the number of items is correct. When you number the list, you let readers reserve their brain power for more important things.

Example:

Following are the ten people in the room:

1. John Allen
2. Janice Teisch
3. Ali Arshad
4. Maureen Hines
5. Farhana Zia
6. Jim Pollock
7. Barbara Geller
8. Uri Zimmer
9. Pete Sandler
10. Arlene Karp

Using parallel structure

Whether you use a bulleted or numbered list, items should be parallel in structure. That means all elements that function alike must be treated alike. For example, in the parallel bulleted list that follows, all the bulleted items are gerunds — they end with *-ing*. In the nonparallel bulleted list, the first two items end with *-ing*, making the last item (*specify*) stick out like a wart at the end of a witch's nose. (Notice there's no colon to introduce the list because the lead-in word is a verb, as you'll see in the next section.)

Example (parallel structure):

Effective measures should involve

- Designing and maintaining the facility
- Training the operators and other people in the field
- Specifying security personnel and procedures

Example (nonparallel structure):

Effective measures should involve

- Designing and maintaining the facility
- Training the operators and other people in the field
- Specifying security personnel and procedures

Punctuating a list

People often get confused as to when to use a colon to introduce a list and when to use a period to end a list. The following demystifies these pesky punctuation problems. (I just love alliterations.)

» **Colon:** Use a colon to introduce a list when the words *the following, as follows, here are,* or *here is* are stated or implied. For example:

- Please consider the following ideas:
- Please consider these ideas: (*The following* is implied.)

» **No colon:** Don't use a colon to introduce a list that ends in a verb. A list such as this is actually a sentence with bullets used instead of commas. Put a period at the end of the last bullet because it ends the sentence. (Capitalizing the first word in each bullet is your choice.) For example:

The three reasons are

- The check has been mailed.
- All deadlines have passed.
- No further considerations will be extended.

» **Periods and question marks:** Use a period after each item in a list when the items on the list are complete sentences. The same holds true for a question mark. For example:

I have the following two questions:

- Which would you prefer?
- When would you like delivery?

Avoiding laundry lists

When you have too many items on a list, you create a laundry list and readers may just gloss over everything you worked so hard to emphasize. Instead of creating a long list of bulleted or numbered items, consider breaking the items into categories. Take a look at what follows. On the left you see one long list. On the right you see how the list was divided into two logical chunks of information each with a heading.

Our global expansion takes in the following countries: Austria China Hong Kong Indonesia Malaysia Portugal Spain Sweden Thailand	Our global expansion takes in the following countries: Asia China Hong Kong Indonesia Malaysia Thailand Europe Austria Portugal Spain Sweden

Formatting Text

Formatting is a critical element in making your slides visually appealing. That includes design elements, color, proper alignment, font sizes, and more. They all work towards giving your presentation a spiffy look.

Formatting do's for text

The following will help to make your presentation appealing:

- Use a 36-point font. Much of what you read tells you to use a 24-point font for headlines and 18-for text. That, however, leads to slidezillas (packing each slide with too much text).
- Use uppercase and lowercase letters — never all caps (even for headlines).
- Limit each visual to five to seven lines of text, not counting the title.
- Use bulleted or numbered lists, sparingly.
- Left justify bullets and numbers.
- Limit bullets to one line of text when possible.
- Consider a sans serif font (such as Arial) for the headlines and a serif (such as Times New Roman) for the text.
- Use black text on a light-colored background for the best readability.

Formatting don'ts for text

Here are some things to avoid entirely or use very sparingly:

- **Animation and sound effects:** Use them sparingly, and only when they add value. An example would be the brief PB&J video in the storyboard in Chapter 7.
- **Overused bullets with layers of sub-bullets:** They pack too much info into one slide and lose everyone's attention.

Preparing graphs, charts, and tables

If your presentation is data driven, include simplified graphs, charts, and tables.

- Limit data to what's absolutely necessary.
- Stick to one dataset per slide.
- Label axes, data lines, and charts for easy understanding.
- Create a legend when you need to explain a graphic.
- Use an array of colors to emphasize certain information (for example to differentiate between percentages on a pie chart).

TIP

Check out Chapter 4 for great ideas on crafting data stories.

Adding transitions and animations

You can transform a boring presentation into a fun, interesting, or dramatic one by adding a limited number of special effects such as transitions and animations. (The key word here is *limited*.) One advantage to special effects is that if your audience is daydreaming, any slight movement will snatch their attention right back.

- **Transitions:** A transition can be as simple as pressing the clicker and having the next slide appear. For added interest, you can control the speed or add a pleasing sound. However, avoid dissolves, fade-ins and fade-outs, wipes, and other such stuff.
- **Animations:** This is a great tool to capture your audience's attention for a specific purpose. For example, to show a multistep process or to overlay a graph or chart. Just don't overuse animations or use too many consecutively. That would undermine your message and give your audience a collective migraine.

Incorporating videos

People like to be entertained, so (depending on your content and audience) consider changing it up. The right videos at the right time will invigorate audiences. Here are a few reasons to add a video or two (depending on the content and length of the presentation):

- **Enhanced engagement:** When you vary the media, it helps to maintain the audience's interest.

- **Says more, shows less:** Videos can explain complex topics that may be difficult to explain otherwise.
- **Helps with retention:** People have better recall when they're immersed in multi-sensory environments.

TIP

For stock videos, check out YouTube, Storyblocks, Adobe, Shutterstock, Vimeo, to name a few. Or you can create your own. For example, let's assume you're presenting to an audience of potential donors. A great way to get them to dig into their pockets is to show a video testimonial from one or more recipients whose lives have been changed because of past donations. Or if you're trying to sell a product or service, video testimonials from delighted customers may be just enough to seal the deal.

Adding Sizzle to Your Presentations

There are several cloud-based, interactive audience-engagement platforms that can bring your presentations to an entirely new level whether your presentation is face-to-face, virtual, or hybrid. Your audience can join a presentation by using a smartphone to scan the presentation's QR code or on the Internet device used to join the presentation.

Unlike typical slide software, these platforms allow for an interactive experience in many of the following ways and can create engagement:

- Crafting an insightful icebreaker
- Taking polls and quizzes
- Creating graphs, charts, or word clouds (aka tag clouds)
- Letting everyone vote, ask questions, and interact
- Getting feedback (shared with everyone or for the presenter only)
- Tracking learning by asking questions and downloading results

Finding popular platforms

Check out the three most popular platforms: `https://www.mentimeter.com`, `https://ahaslides.com`, and `https://kahoot.com/`. You can use them to create ice breakers, to open a presentation, or create interaction anytime during the presentation. The results can appear as pie charts, bar graphs, word clouds, or more. Or you can use this activity as an assessment of your presentation, and the results are for your eyes only.

Visualizing in the cloud

Word clouds have recently become a staple of data visualization and are especially popular when analyzing text. Among other things, they can facilitate brainstorming new concepts, identify new topics important to the audience, depict what audiences think, summarize their view on a topic, measure understanding of a topic, and more.

SHERYL SAYS

Figure 8-2 is a word cloud that depicts a little fun I had with a few colleagues using one of these platforms. We were inputting our favorite snacks. (Some of us were on laptops; others on smartphones.) The word cloud created a cluster of our words depicted in different sizes and directions. As you can see, chocolate is biggest and boldest because it was input most often. (No surprise there.) When you create an activity such as this related to your topic, it creates a fun opening and everyone gets involved.

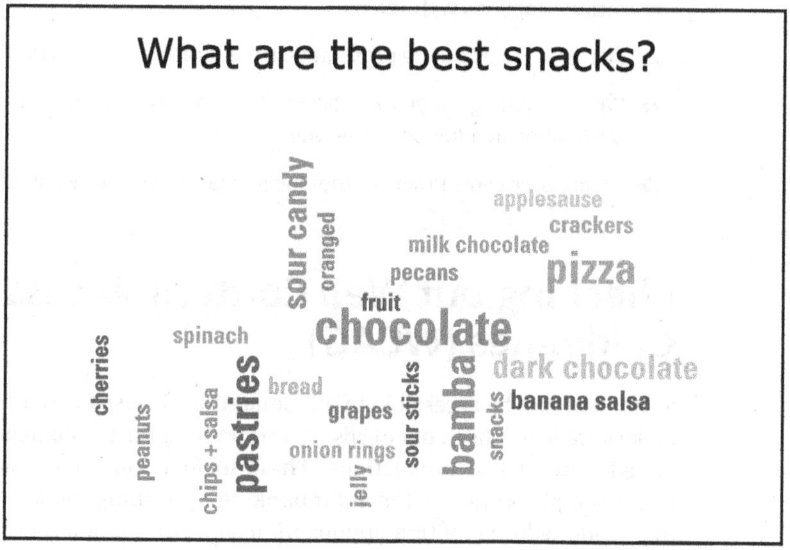

FIGURE 8-2: Word cloud rating chocolate as the best snack. Do you agree?

Creating Slide Accessibility for All

People in your audience may have various levels of visual, auditory, motor, and/or cognitive abilities. It's estimated that up to 4 percent of the population relies on some sort of Assistive Technology (AT). They may have trouble with certain layouts, colors, fonts, links, charts, and tables. This is especially problematic when the slide show will be delivered electronically. Most (if not all) major presentation software apps have accessibility checkers to address many of the problems, so find out how to tackle these issues before creating presentations.

Here are a few general guidelines that work for everyone, regardless of abilities:

- Minimize the amount of text on each slide.
- If consecutive slides have the same title, include numbers to distinguish between them.
- Avoid distracting animations and transitions.
- Provide high color contrast.
- If you embed an audio file, include a transcript.
- Include captions with videos.
- Decide if tables can be presented as paragraphs with descriptive headings.
- When including hyperlinks, convey clear and accurate information about the destination in addition to the URL.
- Create accessible PDFs or other file formats of your presentation.

Checking out Web Content Accessibility Guidelines (WCAG)

Animation can be accessible to all. Sometimes it just takes a little extra effort to make sure it is. Check out `https://www.w3.org` for recommendations about animated content and interactions. These include guidelines for when to provide pause and play controls, limits for blinking or flashing the screen, advice on when to provide reduced motion options for users with motion sensitivities, and more.

Preparing slides for colorblind audience members

Statistically, nearly 10 percent of the population is colorblind. Here are a few tips for preparing slides/visuals with that audience in mind:

- **Don't use the combination of red and green.** Use magenta (purple) and green instead. (And really, this isn't about Christmas.)
- **Label graph elements.** If showing graphs and line drawings, label elements of the graph on the graph itself rather than making a separate color-coded key because matching colors in distant places is extremely difficult for colorblind people.
- **Think outside the color box.** Don't convey information in color only. For example, use solid and dotted lines, different symbols, various hatching, and so on.
- **Consider the color of the text.** Avoid using red characters on a dark background.

Proofreading Until Your Eyes Hurt

Can you read the following? *Eye cant' impres upon ewe enough the importence of spel cheking end poofreading.* Of course, this is an exaggeration, but make sure your words are clearly represented.

TIP

Your audience will be reading and proofreading your slides as you present them. Despite your best efforts, however, an error may slip by and an audience member may call it to your attention. If that happens and someone mentions it in front of the group, simply say: *Thanks, I'm going to change that right now.* Then go into edit mode and make the change immediately. How graciously you acknowledge your mistakes separates you, the professional, from the amateurs. Here are some specific things to check on your slides and handouts beforehand:

- [ ] Verify all names, including middle initials, titles, and company distinctions.
- [ ] Make sure all numbers are correct.
- [ ] Look for omissions of who, what, when, where, why, or how.
- [ ] Check for consistency of indentations, font sizes and styles, and line spacing.
- [ ] Print out the slides and read the hardcopy.
- [ ] Read from bottom to top and/or from right to left.

REMEMBER

Spelling and grammar checkers can be helpful, but don't turn on your computer and turn off your brain. These technical helpers won't pick up misspelled names, correctly spelled words used incorrectly (like writing "you client" instead of "your client"), transposed numbers, or incorrect data. People often don't see their own mistakes, so it's prudent to have someone else proofread.

STORYOPIA ARCHIVES: DESTROYING CREDIBILITY

My husband and I attended a seminar offered by Sidney, a financial planner. He was hoping to win the business of people in the audience. I recall Sidney to be an Ivy League type, with an expensive suit and highly polished black leather shoes. He gave a nice welcome and provided everyone with lunch. During dessert, Sidney got down to business. He put up his first slide. Oops! It had a typo. No matter what he said, my eye kept returning to the typo. Thereafter, each time Sidney put up a new slide, I kept looking for another typo. That typo completely distracted me from his message. Later in the presentation he showed a statistic and apologized that the numbers were old. He excused himself by saying he didn't have the current numbers. Hmm!

As we were approaching our car, my husband asked: *Did you notice the typo on his opening slide? Yes, I did,* I answered. He then said, *I was ready to walk out after that because the guy's presentation was sloppy. He lost all credibility. And then,* my husband continued, *the guy didn't even show us the respect of using current numbers. Sidney's a real jerk. That was a total waste of time.*

Lesson learned: Proofread very carefully because even one typo can destroy your credibility. And always respect your audience by making sure your information is correct and current.

WARNING

Never think it's okay to simply apologize for any known errors in your slides (or handouts). If you know something isn't correct or current, *change it* or *don't use it.* Take a peek at the Storyopia Archives to see what happened to "Sloppy Sidney."

IN THIS CHAPTER

- » Crafting the story with slides
- » Maximizing the use of each slide
- » Incorporating titles, statistics, and images

Chapter 9

Slide Sense: Using Slides Effectually

Perfection is attained, not when there is nothing more to add, but when there is nothing more to take away.

—ANTOINE DE SAINT-EXUPERY, AUTHOR
(BEST KNOWN FOR THE LITTLE PRINCE)

Although you may never achieve perfection, if you strip away all that's unnecessary, you come as close as you can get. The old expression "less is more" couldn't be more relevant when it comes to slides — less information provides more value. Strive for the following:

- » Turn paragraphs into sentences.
- » Turn sentences into strong bullet points.
- » Use fewer words (and bullets) per slide.
- » Show a visual when it will enhance or replace a slide.
- » Show fewer slides.

While there's no magic number when it comes to how many slides to use, the fewer the better. (Discard the archaic rule of one slide per minute.)

SHERYL SAYS

You've undoubtedly heard of KISS (Keep it Simple Stupid — or as I prefer Keep it Short and Simple). But have you ever heard of a "weight weenie"? It's a road bike enthusiast who obsesses about the weight of the bike. The cyclist is in pursuit of the lightest frame, the lightest seat, even the lightest water bottle. I ride for pleasure, so I'm not overly concerned about the weight of my bike. But I'm a "word weenie" and obsess about the weight of too many words, too many slides, and too much information.

In this chapter you discover how to be a "word weenie" by telling stories with slides, understanding what does and doesn't work, and keeping 'em short and simple to provide more value.

START-UP BRIEF

Until you've completed the Start-Up Brief (see Chapter 3) and created a storyboard (see Chapter 7), don't even think about creating slides. Start with your main message, the narrative, and the stories to make the topic come alive. The narrative part of your presentation needs to stand on its own. When you use slides (or any other props), they should support the narrative.

Don't Lambaste Slides

Despite all the negativity about "Death by PowerPoint," slides aren't inherently evil. When you use them to tell a story and convey important information — not deliver lots of yawn-inducing slidezillas — they serve a valuable purpose. It's not the slides that are the culprits; it's the heedless people who prepare them. Imagine this scenario: You're driving down the highway during a rainstorm, and there's a car racing along at a dangerously high speed, weaving in and out of lanes. A few miles down the road you see that car involved in a pile-up. You wouldn't blame the car. You'd blame the reckless driver. For the same reason, don't blame slidezillas for a poor presentation. They're nothing more than a "vehicle" for delivery.

TIP

Get yourself a good clicker. Here are two good ones:

- **Targus remote:** This is my favorite. I use very few slides, and it's important to turn OFF the presentation when you're not displaying a slide. Not all offer this feature. If you don't turn off the presentation, people are staring at a big white screen, distracted from the message.
- **Logitech Spotlight Presentation Remote:** Clicking remotely means you can stand anywhere in the room and click through the slides from 100 feet away. You don't have to hold the clicker out and point. This offers universal compatibility and can magnify areas on the screen in pixel-perfect detail.

Getting the Most from Your Slide Real Estate

When you have the option of selecting a template, think of what you'd wear to deliver the presentation. Formal? Conservative? Casual? Key to your consideration is your audience and the message you want to deliver. Does your choice represent you and your industry well? Is it too subdued or flashy? Is it too abstract or concrete? Does it add or detract from your message? You can design your own template or choose from the many that are available with your software. If your company has a template it standardly uses, you're stuck with it. But you can still simplify the content and add pleasing visuals.

TIP

White text on a black background provides high-value contrast, but it's not very readable and causes greater eye fatigue faster than black text on a white background. Consider using a charcoal grey, dark green, dark blue, or a dark color other than black with off-white text.

In this section, you take a look at a variety of slides to learn what does and doesn't work effectually.

Slides that are not effectual

Instead of giving a killer presentation, slidezillas such as the following will kill a presentation:

Figure 9-1 is an image I show during my Storyteling and Storyboarding workshop. I ask, *What would you think if you walked into someone's office and saw this desktop with piles of unsorted papers and folders?* This slide gets several chuckles and witty comments. I continue, *This is the equivalent of a slidezilla that has too many bullets, sub-bullets, or charts and tables which can be messy, disorganized, and off putting.*

Following that, I show the slide in Figure 9-2 and say: *This is an actual slidezilla prepared by NASA. It's much like that messy desktop — waaaay beyond information overload.*

Figure 9-3 shows another disasterous slidezilla produced by the United States Air Force. Someone circled the word "simplification." Too bad they didn't take their own advice and simplify.

The slide in Figure 9-4 has far too much information, and the person who prepared it certainly wasn't a "word weenie." There are several options, however, to making the slide valuable. The best option would depend on what you determined the audience needs to know.

FIGURE 9-1: Think of a slidezilla as an overly cluttered desk — too much stuff to be useful.

stokkete / Adobe Stock

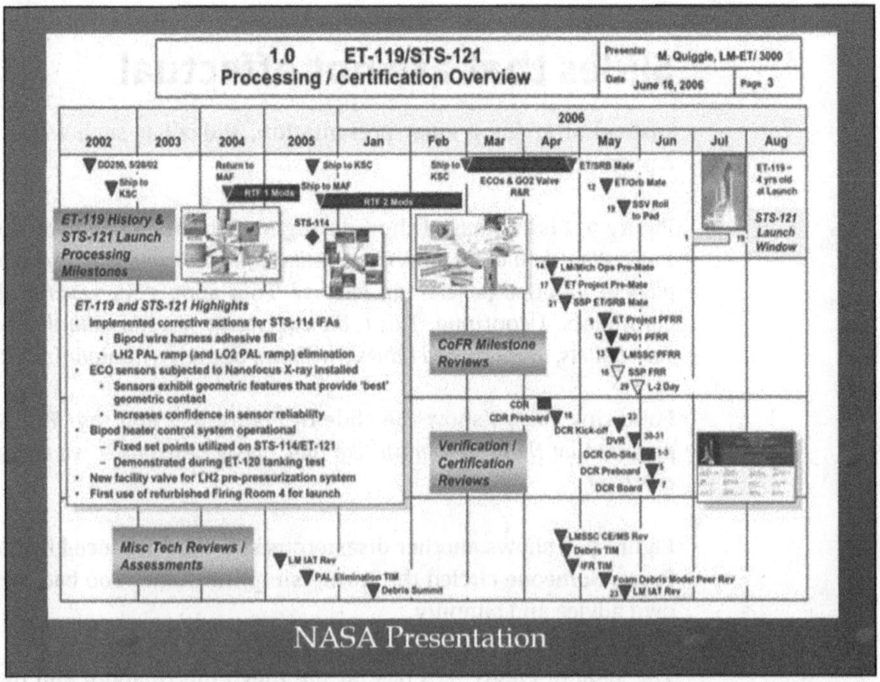

FIGURE 9-2: How can anyone get useful information from this slide?

NASA

US Air Force

FIGURE 9-3: Simplification is definitely not the first thing that comes to mind here.

Stencil-Printer Wafer Bumps

- **Electroforming process needs updating**
  - Stencil cleaning
  - Lithography
  - Pattern effects limit uniformity
- **Classroom and other facilities need updating**
  - Stencil handling
  - Airborne particles
  - Air conditioning
- **Quality system needs updating**
  - PM program
  - SPC

FIGURE 9-4: You need to pare this down so it's readable and useful.

Option 1: Expand the headline to read (Need Updating) so it's not repeated in each bullet. Also, include just the three primary bullets and speak to the additional information in the sub-bullets.

Option 2: Break each of the primary bulleted items into a separate slide and make each one the heading. The sub-bullets become primary bullets. Here's an example of breaking out the second bulleted item. You'd do the same for each of the three primary bullets.

Although many presenters will put up a "Questions?" slide, such as the one in Figure 9-5, or display a big question mark, I advise against either. It adds no value to put up a slide like this. It only distracts from questions (and answers) because eyes will be on the screen. Instead of a slide that asks for questions, turn the projector off and ask, *Are there any questions?* The same holds true for a slide that reads "Comments."

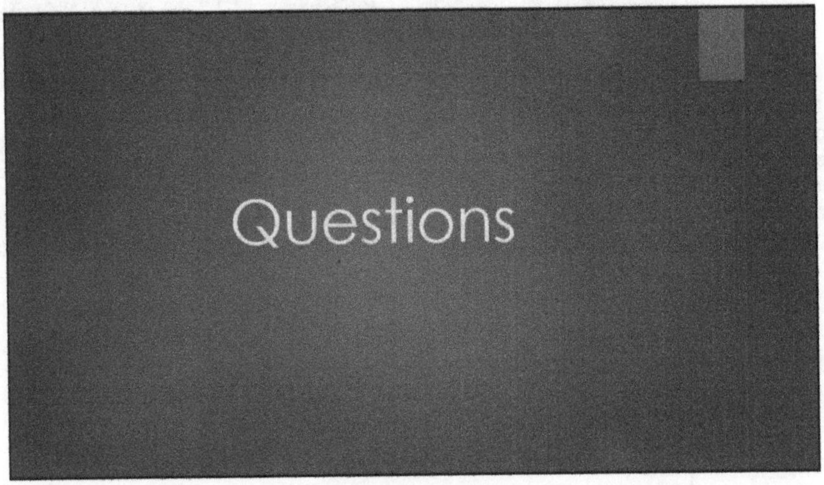

FIGURE 9-5: Rather than use a slide like this one, just turn off the projector and ask if there are any questions or comments.

Slides that are effectual

The most engaging slides are the ones that support your message to illustrate your main points — but they must be brief, visually appealing, interesting, and informative.

This section shows some slides that add value and attract rather than distract.

Figure 9-6 is a great example of what to do when it's important to show the size of an object. Scale it so viewers can clearly envision it. In this slide, you see the size of the object relative to a person's hand.

Showing a list of benefits, as you see in Figure 9-7, is a crucial part of a presentation. You want people to focus on the benefits — seeing them as well as hearing about them. Telling and Showing will drive the point home and make a strong case for the audience to heed the call to action (which you'll deliver near the end).

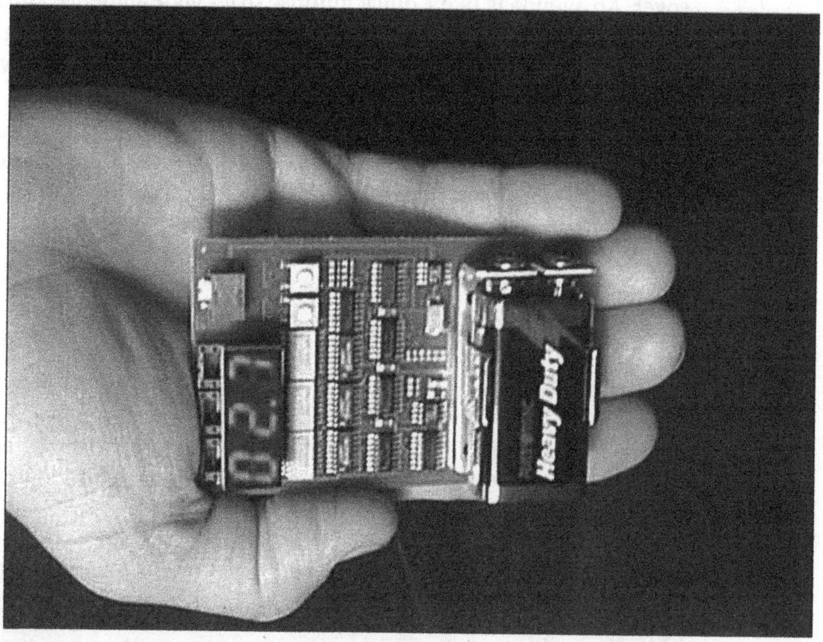

FIGURE 9-6: This simple image gives you a clear picture of the object's size.

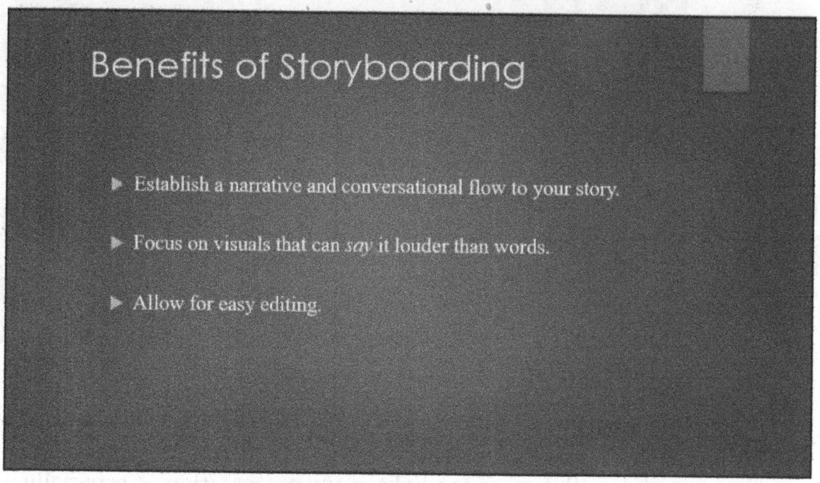
Benefits of Storyboarding
Establish a narrative and conversational flow to your story.
Focus on visuals that can *say* it louder than words.
Allow for easy editing.

FIGURE 9-7: It's always a good idea to let the audience "see" the benefits as well as "hear" them.

TIP

If you highlight several strong benefits, create one slide for each and discuss them at length. A benefits slide can be a testimonial or visual of someone using the product.

As for agendas, suppose you're delivering a presentation with many topics to cover. An agenda is like a quick glimpse to let your audience know that interesting topics are coming. This lets them orient their thoughts and stick with you until the end. If your presentation is short or focuses on one or two topics, skip an agenda slide.

WARNING

What's important to learn from this slide, is more than when to open with an agenda. It's about not starting each bullet by repeating articles such as *to*, *the*, *a*, *an*, and others. Therefore, *don't* say:

- To elect
- To discuss
- To approve

Notice how each of the bullets in Figure 9-8 starts with the action item — the verb. This is true for *any* list you prepare for any presentation or document.

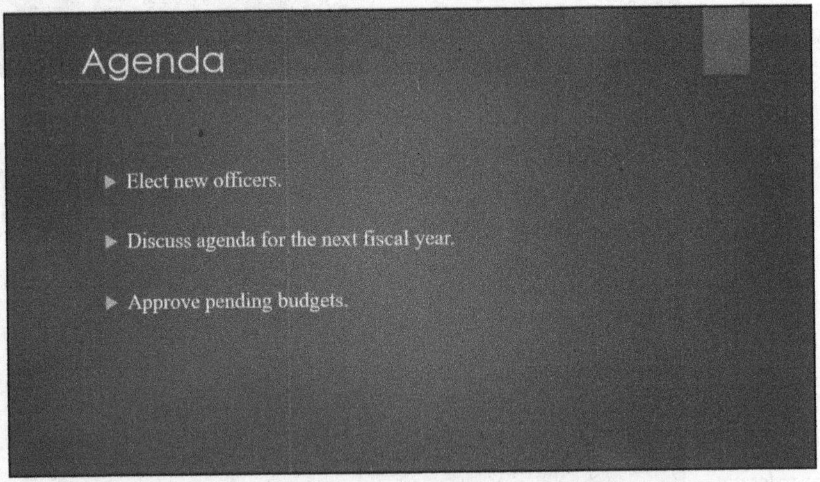

FIGURE 9-8: When you include an agenda at the beginning of a meeting, start each action item with a verb.

TIP

Making your audience laugh or chuckle is a good way to engage them.

A slide with humor can lighten any presentation — especially if the presenter has a difficult time being humorous. Figure 9-9 shows a slide for a sales presentation with banter between a manager and salesperson. Notice that it's simple and easy to read.

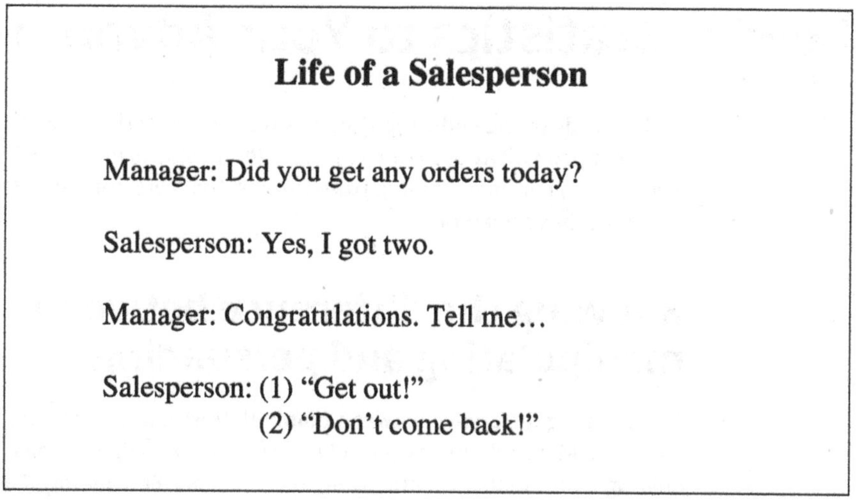

FIGURE 9-9: It's fun to insert some humor into your slides! Why not?

In Figure 9-10 you see a word cloud (aka tag cloud, word collage, or text cloud) that can make otherwise boring data sizzle. It's an attractive design method for conveying key concepts within a single slide. These clouds simplify data visualization by displaying key words in various angles, sizes, and colors at a glance. The bigger and bolder words signify the most important ones or the most times they were mentioned.

REMEMBER

A word cloud can work well as an icebreaker. If you're presentation is about motivation, you may show a word cloud such as in Figure 9-10 and challenge the audience to select two or three words that reaonate with them and explain why. Or have them prepare a word cloud as you see in Chapter 8 incorporating their own words. Mentimeter (`https://www.mentimeter.com/`) is one of the most popular tools for generating word clouds.

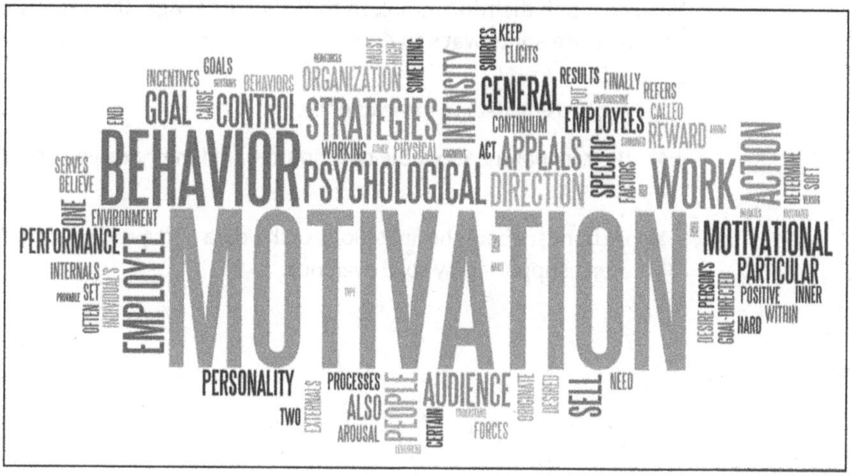

FIGURE 9-10: Word clouds can simplify data in a witty way.

Showing Statistics to Your Advantage

In the words of the enduring Homer Simpson, from the long-running TV program "The Simpsons," *Aw, you can come up with statistics to prove anything . . . Forty percent of all people know that.* Coming from Homer, that certainly sounds innocent enough. But is it really? Read on.

Knowing the difference between manipulating and persuading

There's a big difference between manipulating and persuading, mainly intent and outcome. Manipulating is morally wrong and breeds mistrust. It involves withholding truth, malicious intention, and coercion. Persuading is an attempt to positively guide the audience in accepting the truth or point of view by presenting relevant, insights, and arguments. Credible presenters persuade — they don't manipulate.

Here's an example: I read an article a while back about a small town in the Midwest that had experienced a 50 percent rise in unemployment in just two months. *OMG*, I thought. *That's devastating.* My mind immediately wandered to the hardships the community must be suffering. As I read further (down near the bottom), the article gave real numbers. Ten people had previously been unemployed, and now there were 15. Yes, it's a 50 percent rise, but it doesn't elevate to the level of OMG or devastating. Manipulation or persuasion? You decide.

Remaining ethical

With so much disinformation in today's digital age, it's important to remain ethical. Here are some ways to do so:

- Avoid using data to mislead or lie.
- Be transparent about the data sources and methods you use to obtain the statistics.
- Be honest about the limitations of the data and avoid making claims that aren't supported by solid evidence.

Incorporating Images

Although actions speak louder than words, well-placed images can speak even louder. Too many slides without images are like sleeping pills; they can have a soporific effect on the audience that can lead to disengagement, boredom, and even cause people to fall asleep.

Our brains process images more easily than words, and good images can significantly increase engagement. Images allow people to join in the moment, bringing the moment to life.

There's a wide variety of online imagery. Some are free; others require a fee. Check your company's website and your presentation software for images. Here are some of the popular apps listed in random order:

- Adobe Images
- Unsplash
- Pexels
- Pixabary
- Freepick
- Fotosearch
- Freerange
- Shutterstock
- iStock

Using photos

Whether you opt to use stock photography or your own, you can harmoniously combine text with a photo to convey your message successfully. Photos compel viewers to form a dramatic, emotional connection with the slide.

Overlaying text

Figure 9-11 shows a photo I took and used to help a realtor prepare for a presentation. The realtor wanted to entice the audience to purchase a timeshare or rent a place along the beach. The text embellishes the photo. (I gave my permission for the photo but (sadly) couldn't wangle a free timeshare or week at a beachfront resort.)

FIGURE 9-11: Overlying text on a photo can call out what you want the audience to remember.

Photo courtesy of author

Applying the rule of thirds

When including photographs, apply the *rule of thirds* — a photographic composition breaking the images into thirds horizontally or vertically, putting the point(s) of interest off center. Notice the difference between Figures 9-12 and 9-13. In Figure 9-12 you see a beautiful Balinese pagoda that's centered. Figure 9-13 show the same pagoda moved to the right-hand third of the scene, creating a more dramatic effect.

FIGURE 9-12: Point of interest is centered and not very dramatic.

Photo courtesy of author

FIGURE 9-13: Point of interest is to the right third, creating a more dramatic photograph.

Photo courtesy of author

Using clipart

Clipart has gotten a bad rap. Naysayers claim it's outdated, cheap, overused, and unprofessional. However, that doesn't mean you should avoid it like the middle seat on an airplane. Much like emojis, clipart draws from a universal language everyone relates to. Growing up, we were inspired by surrealists, cartoonists, and graffiti artists. And many of us even doodled our way through high school.

Anyone questioning the validity of this art form should visit the Museum of Comic and Cartoon Art in New York City, the Cartoon Art Museum in San Francisco, and the Hall of Heroes in Washington, DC (a superhero and comic book collection preserving and covering 80 years of superheroes in comics, toys, film, and animation). Who wouldn't relate to one of the graphics in Figure 9-14 that can deliver a punchy message?

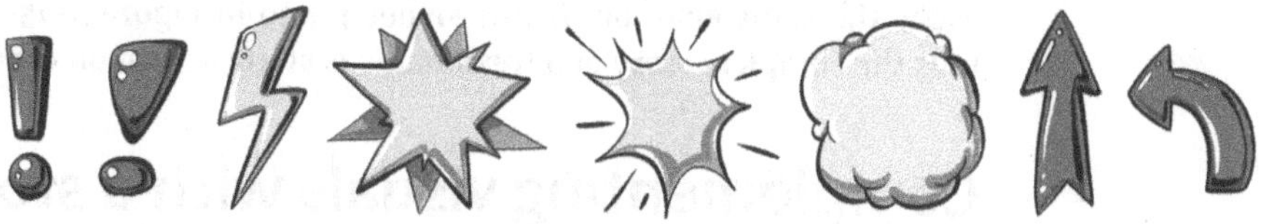

FIGURE 9-14: Sometimes, clipart says it all!

Bartosz Ostrowski / Adobe Stock

Clipart in moderation can make a slide presentation more pleasing. Just be sure to pay for what you use or, if it's free, make sure it's not copyright protected. Search "clipart" or "clip art" for a wide variety of websites. Also, check out the clipart that included with MS Office or other apps you use.

TIP

Keep a library of clipart that relates to your industry. Make sure your selections are consistent with the look of your presentation regarding colors, style, and overall feeling.

Living in a Visual World

We live in a robust *visual* world. Highway billboards. TV commercials. Social media. Newsfeeds. Pop-up ads. They're all sending us messages. These visuals aren't designed merely to be colorful or pretty; they're designed for strategic purposes — to get us to *notice* and *see what could be*. This can be described in one word: *Neuroscience*. Neuroscientists have discovered that an idea expressed in visual form is processed 60,000 times faster than the same information either printed or spoken.

Visuals can come in a variety of forms. In addition to what we've discussed in this chapter, don't discount the visual appeal of text — the most commonly used visual. You can jazz up your text with contrasting font sizes, colors, and styles. Be careful, however, to use them sparingly because you don't want to make your slides look like circus posters.

Using visuals to tell an entire story

Storytelling inspires audiences. There are times a picture or video can tell the story that a million words can't. (The expression used to be "a picture is worth a thousand words," but that was before inflation.) A visual can express specific emotions, feelings, moods, or things that are nearly impossible to convey with words. If the presenter from a college recruitment department tried to explain in words that a freshman "jumped for joy" (a cliché) on the day of arrival, would that evoke the same emotion as this joyous photo in Figure 9-15? Never. This photo tells the complete story of a freshman's ecstatic arrival on campus.

Complementing visuals with a story

A story can be brought to life in the storyboard when the Tell and Show align, which creates a stronger emotional connection with your audience. To accomplish this, your visuals must be relevant. So be aware of what's happening in the world

FIGURE 9-15: This photo says it all — "jumping for joy" isn't just a cliché.

Photo courtesy of author

around you because your topic doesn't exist in a bubble. Use images that are relevant not only to the topic, but to the time and the culture. Also use images that engage the senses. For example, macro shots and close-ups can show textures. Long shots offer a wide perspective so your audience can immerse themselves into the scene. Here are some visual storytelling approaches:

- **Use actual photos.** Opt for candid shots and look for images that convey what your presentation represents. Styled feeds and flawless images are beautiful, but they don't work as well to connect with audiences.
- **Consider stock photos.** If you don't have your own photos, stock photos offer a wide variety of options. Some are free, others charge a fee. Check for some of the popular names in the section, "Incorporating Images," earlier in this chapter. (Find more online with the search words "websites of images" or "images of . . . .")
- **Add video clips.** They provide a nice change of pace and can enhance your story with a different perspective. YouTube is one of the best resources, and many of the videos are free. Keep the video brief and embedded into the slide deck. To ensure good flow to your visuals, it's important that any change of medium (such as video) is seamlessly integrated.

» **Include infographics.** This is an artistic representation of data and information that can tell a story, such as you see in Figure 9-16. It's much more interesting than showing a slide with the heading "Design Template," then presenting a list numbered 1-5 with the details.

Infographics can be used to make comparisons, represent survey results, explain a complex idea, raise awareness, or share a fact. If you don't have in-house graphic designers, look into Adobe Creative Cloud Express, Canva, Venngage, or Snappa. (Find more online with the search words "infographic vendors.")

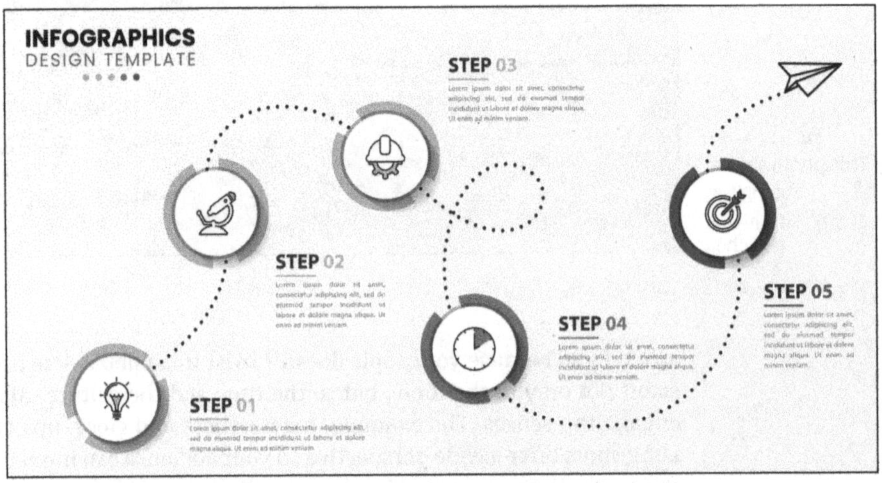

FIGURE 9-16: Artistic infographic that tells a story, step by step.

kuliperko / Adobe Stock

Turning data and tables to into a story

Whether you're delivering a business pitch or assessing the results of a project, it's likely your slides may need some data. After all, hard facts and stats can show that your company (or project) is moving in the right direction. However, rather than overwhelm your audience with too many data points they're not likely to remember, convert basic data sets to simple charts and graphs. Elements, such as line charts, bar charts, and others, can translate flat data into effective visual presentations.

TIP

Check out Chapter 4 to discover how to create data stories.

IN THIS CHAPTER

» Creating useful handouts and workbooks

» Elevating your takeaways with excellent copy

» Polishing it off with printing and binding

Chapter 10

Handouts and Workbooks: Kick 'Em Up a Notch

Handbooks are the bridge between theory and practice, offering guidance and instruction on how to turn knowledge into action.

—AI GENERATED (ON YOU.COM)

A well-designed handout or workbook can make the difference between a mediocre event and a memorable one. And, yes, it's the bridge between theory and practice. Studies show that people retain very little information several days after an event. So handbooks or workbooks give audiences something to use during the event and something to review (and share) after the event. They offer one more chance audiences to be reminded of you and your key message. You want these materials to enhance the perception your audience has of you and your business. And you want them to leave with something memorable.

SHERYL SAYS

I couldn't find a strong opening quote for this chapter in my book of quotes or on Google, so I turned to you.com, an AI generator. It came up the one you see above. That quote says it all! This is just a small example of how staying current and using the latest technology can help you up your game when it comes to storytelling and presentations. At the end of Chapter 19 you'll find a discussion of AI generators — the good, the bad, and the ugly. Take a peek.

What's the difference between handouts and workbooks? Handouts can be anything from flyers, articles, charts, or tables to more comprehensive contents. Workbooks can contain any of those things in addition to instructions and exercises pertaining to a particular learning event.

This chapter is divided into four parts:

- Preparing handouts
- Crafting workbooks
- Writing copy
- Printing and binding

Preparing Handouts

To provide handouts or not? This is a very good question that many presenters ask. Some feel adamantly that a good presentation doesn't need a handout; others feel just the opposite. (I'm in the "give-them-out" camp.) A handout can be something as simple as an article you wrote, regardless of whether it got published. It can be a tip sheet, worksheets, copy of slides with note-taking sections, relevant articles (with permission to use), or anything that will extend the value of your presentation.

Consider what handouts can offer:

- **Benefits for the presenter:** A common conundrum is having a colossal amount of content you absolutely need to share during a presentation, but you have a limited span of time. That's one benefit of a handout. Here are a few more:
  - You can reduce the amount of material you cover, thereby cutting information overload.
  - You leave the audience with a concrete reminder to make you and your presentation more memorable.
  - Audience members can contact you later because your handout is a reminder of the event.
  - You have an opportunity to promote your brand.

» **Benefits for the audience:** People like takeaways. If you've ever been to a tradeshow, you've noticed how attendees grab shopping bags and stuff them with literature, pens, pads, key chains, and any other goodies on the tables. Most of these things get thrown away, but the important items are kept and shared. Audiences like to leave presentations with takeaways as well.

- Inspiring topics will give added information.
- They'll have memory refreshers after the event.
- When attendees take notes, they'll include them where applicable and needed.

Presenting handouts of your slides

SHERYL SAYS

I always had an unbending rule that you should never create a handout of your slides. If you're one of those put-everything-on-a-slide-and-stand-there-and-read Neanderthals, that still holds true. You'd only be turning a dreadful presentation into a dreadful handout. However, as more and more savvy presenters are using slides to enhance their themes and stories, I've become more flexible. I now suggest that you include a few key slides that may relate to stories you tell, analogies, anecdotes, quotes, statistics, graphics, and anything else you want to be memorable.

TIP

If you're presenting to a large group, it's a good idea to send your presentation beforehand. Doing so allows participants to review your content before the meeting and also helps to ensure everyone is on the same page (literally).

Leaving room for notetaking

If you do include slides, leave a notes section so people can jot down information they want to recall later. If you customize your talk for each audience, leave several blank pages so people can take lots of notes. This will keep you from having to create new handouts with each iteration. Figure 10-1 shows an example of a slide with notes someone found relevant.

Knowing what to include

You may want your handout to extend beyond your presentation for people who didn't attend. Or you may want to use it as a recall for people who did attend and may have forgotten some salient points. Either way, kick your handout up a notch. The following sections show you how.

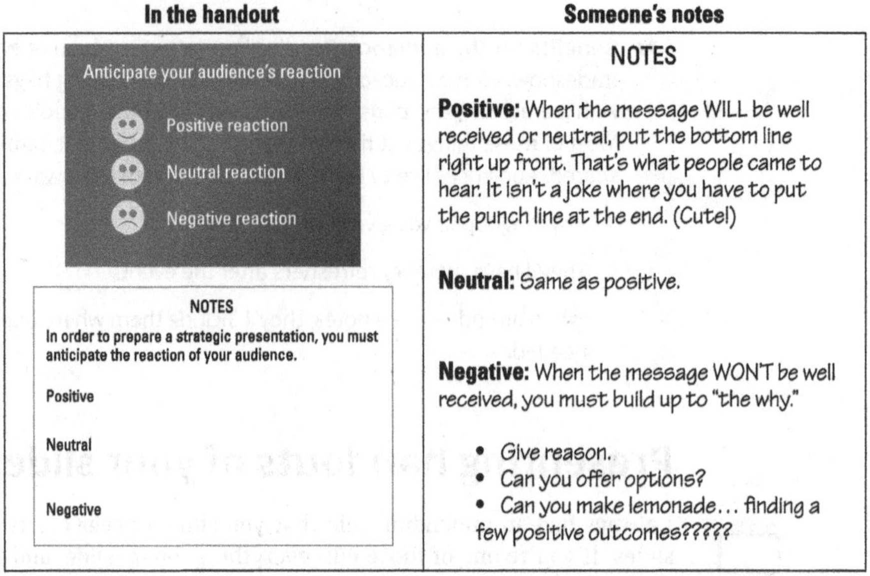
In the handout
Someone's notes
Anticipate your audience's reaction
Positive reaction
Neutral reaction
Negative reaction
NOTES
In order to prepare a strategic presentation, you must anticipate the reaction of your audience.
Positive
Neutral
Negative
NOTES
Positive: When the message WILL be well received or neutral, put the bottom line right up front. That's what people came to hear. It isn't a joke where you have to put the punch line at the end. (Cute!)
Neutral: Same as positive.
Negative: When the message WON'T be well received, you must build up to "the why."
• Give reason.
• Can you offer options?
• Can you make lemonade… finding a few positive outcomes?????

FIGURE 10-1: Leaving space to take notes makes your handout useful to your audience.

Making lists

Love lists or hate them, they display a sense of order. Lists have a sense of mastery, amplifying clutter-free knowledge that's easy to understand. Numbered lists indicate the order in which things should be done, such as in procedures or priority of items. Anyone who's ever believed in Santa, knows the value of prioritizing lists. If they'd written Santa pages of paragraphs, they may not have gotten their wishes because the items considered a priority would have been lost in the clutter.

The same holds true for lists in handbooks. Lists increase readability, keep people focused, and drive action. However, don't use too many lists because too much of a good thing is counterproductive. Check out Chapter 8 to learn more about preparing bulleted and numbered lists.

Including content not in your presentation

A handout is a wonderful way to add even more value to your presentation. Add credence to your topic with stories, articles, quotes, analogies, and other content. Here are some things to consider adding:

- Simplified charts, tables, and diagrams
- Case studies to show working examples of your message
- Relevant websites and blogs

- Magazine, journal, and newspaper articles
- Your brief biography (see Chapter 11)

REMEMBER

Be sure to include your name, contact information, and copyright notice on each handout. If it's just a page or two, staple your business card.

Adding a list of references

Handouts are rarely meant to impart massive amounts of information. However, they're good for sharing high-level information and inspiring people to learn more. There's a ton of information you can include for additional reference: websites, blogs, articles, books, journals, whitepapers, and anything else that will enhance the audience's experience.

Deciding when to distribute handouts

There's a long-standing debate as to when to distribute handouts. It boils down to the situation and your level of comfort.

- **Before:** If you pass out handouts before a presentation, your audience will likely spend more time reading through your handout than actually listening to you. Also, they know what to expect and what comes next. This can divide their attention and make the presentation less interesting. (Workbooks, of course, need to be distributed beforehand.)

  REMEMBER

  If you opt to distribute handouts beforehand, you can minimize distractions by asking them to take a moment to flick through the material, then asking them to put it aside and engage in the discussion.
- **During:** Distributing handouts at an appropriate time during the session supports key points and emphasizes your argument. For example, if you want everyone to have a copy of a chart or table to discuss, hand it out at the point of discussion. These can be separate from handouts being distributed before or after and can replace a slide so attendees can mark it up.
- **After:** When you distribute your handouts at the end, it serves as a summary of your presentation and won't accidentally ruin any surprises or exciting moments you've planned. Let your audience know at the beginning of your presentation that you'll be distributing handouts at the end. This is a great way to recap the session and have it shared with others who couldn't attend.

STORYOPIA ARCHIVES: TALKING WITH YOUR AUDIENCE, NOT AT THEM

I was called by my client, Emile, to help develop a slide presentation for a very big customer his company was hoping to land. I went to Emile's office and learned he was going to make the presentation to four representatives in Emile's conference room on the twentieth floor. The room had large windows with a sweeping view of Times Square. The blue walls "brought in" the sky, and the atmosphere was very organic. A round, mahogany table sat in the center of the room, and warm paneling flanked the walls. It was a perfect place for conversation. Rather than talking *at* your guests, I stressed to Emile the importance of talking *with* them.

That meant instead of preparing slides, I prepared a handbook. Each visitor had something valuable to take back their superiors — the final decision makers. The handbooks included a welcome letter, testimonials from several delighted customers with well-known names, benefits of working together, and forms that would need to be filled out. On the cover were two logos: the logo of the visitor's company largely displayed and the logo of Emile's company in half the size. As hoped, the meeting went well. I also suggested that Emile order coffee and pastries because people always like to be fed. After an informal getting-to-know-you discussion over coffee and pastries, the meeting ensued. **Emile's company won the contract!**

Lesson learned: A narrative approach to presenting (rather than using slides) lets you talk *with* people, rather than talking *at* them.

Crafting Workbooks

A well-crafted, activity-based workbook can be a constructive teaching-learning tool for audiences to solve a problem or learn a new skill in addition to being a valuable business asset for the presenter.

REMEMBER

Here are some general guidelines for workbooks:

- **Write the workbook in a conversational style.**
  - Talk directly to your audience, using the word "you."
  - Write in the active voice.
  - Use contractions.
  - Vary sentence lengths.

- Choose simple, easy-to-understand words.
- Cut the gobbledygook.

» **Create strong visual appeal for easy reading.**

- Use lots of white space with 1 or 1-1/2" margins on the top, bottom, and sides.
- Use informative headlines and subheads.
- Chunk information into bite-sized bits.
- Incorporate graphics and images.
- Use bulleted and numbered lists.

The following sections provide additional guidance for what to include in your workbooks to make them valuable to your audience.

Giving step-by-step instructions

Write instructions with clarity and keen attention to detail. Never assume your audience will read between the lines or read your mind. The step-action table on the following page is a powerful tool. Here are some guidelines followed by a sample:

STORYOPIA ARCHIVES: CREATING WORKBOOKS FOR INTERACTIVITY

Several years ago, I made a presentation to about 250 salespeople on how to write effectively for marketing and closing deals. It was held in a large lecture hall with a pitched floor and tiered, semi-circular seating. Instead of a lecture, I turned the presentation into a mini-workshop, and each attendee received a five-page workbook. The presentation was very interactive, people were fully engaged, and I got rave reviews. Now, several years later I'm still being contacted by some of the attendees asking me to present the full workshop at their companies. The workbooks turned into an excellent marketing tool and brought me lots of residual business.

Lesson learned: Even a presentation before a large audience can be interactive when you use workbooks to keep them engaged. And the results can live well beyond the event.

- Create a title for each process or procedure.
- Start each step with a verb, representing something the reader should do.
- Use clear, understandable language.
- Include in the Action column any notes, results, screenshots, graphics, photos, if-then tables, or anything else to further clarify the action.

PROCEDURE FOR GETTING STARTED

Step	Action
1	Go to https://www.abcdcompany.com to fill out the Contractor Sign-Up form. [Screenshot of the form]
2	Enter your company's information and be sure to check the subcontractors and suppliers you want in your database. *Note:* When done, press [ENTER].
3	Place a checkmark next to one of the two standardized letters you would like us to send to your database.

TIP

To make this useful beyond the instructions, include in the workbook story testimonials from delighted customers who gained business by learning [whatever]. In the case of this procedure, it would be testimonials from delighted customers who were part of the subcontractor/supplier database.

Including Before-and-After examples

When appropriate, I suggest you include Before-and-After examples in your workbooks so your audiences can make comparisons. Often, the before is what they're currently doing, and the after signals what they should be doing.

The following are Before-and-After examples I show as I open my Write It So They'll Read It workshop. Pay close attention to the difference in readability between the two.

This Before is an outline form that's loaded with numbers and indentations that add no value. The document is downright confusing.

BEFORE
Johnson Space Center Handbook Chapter

101.1 Policy

It is the basic policy of JSC to take all practical steps to avoid loss of life, personnel injury or illness, property loss or damage, or environmental loss or damage.

101.2 Goals and Objectives

101.2.1 Goals

JSC's goals are

a. To achieve a successful and unified occupational safety and health program while accomplishing ISC's objective for excellence in human space flight.
b. Of equal importance, to become a nationally recognized center of excellence for occupational safety and health. This excellence will also be a prominent feature of JSC's environmental protection and emergency preparedness program.

101.2.2 Objectives

JSC shall comply with applicable regulations and standards, including those of the Occupational Safety and Health Administration (OSHA) and the Environmental Protection Agency (EPA). By exercising flexibility and creativity in in striving for excellence, JSC will go beyond the minimum requirements of the regulations and standards to provide the best feasible protection for workers at JSC and the environment within the constraints of available resources.

JSC further recognizes that environmental protection and emergency preparedness are natural adjuncts to its occupational safety and health programs. This handbook documents these programs as well.

This After document gets right to the point. It tells immediately the value of reading the document and who should follow the handbook. It details information in chart form, which is easy to read, giving key information at a glance.

AFTER
Johnson Space Center Handbook Chapter

This could be you … A hypergol technician didn't follow requirements and caused a major fuel spill and was burned.

A person using a tool didn't follow the requirement to have it tethered. The tool fell 16 stories to the floor. Fortunately no one was hurt. Two employees spilled a caustic battery electrolyte on their hands. The batteries hadn't been through qualification testing. There were no requirements to prevent the technicians from working with unqualified batteries.

1. Who must follow this handbook?

This handbook applies to anyone at JSC or JSC field sites, unless exempted in a specific chapter. For this handbook, "JSC" includes all JSC sites in the Houston, Texas, area such as Ellington Field and the Sonny Carter Training Facility. The handbook applies to operations involving JSC personnel or equipment at non-JSC locations, including Foreign countries. See Chapter 113, Paragraph 5, for more information on following standards at on-JSC locations. The following tells you who must follow this handbook:

If you…	Then you must follow…
Are a federal employee	This handbook unless you work at a site that involves unique military equipment and operations
Are a JSC contractor	This handbook as called out in your contract's statement of work
Work at a JSC remote site (such as White Sands Test Facility) as a civil service employee or contractor employee	All chapters that don't exempt you and local requirements that meet the intent of any chapter that exempts you
Are a non NASA or non contract employee	This handbook while on JSC property

Incorporating stories

You're the subject matter expert (SME) for the workshop you're facilitating. Therefore, you have lots of stories from your own experiences, the experiences of past attendees, and stories you've heard about. As you've learned throughout this book, stories are the most valuable teaching tools. In addition to telling the stories during the workshop, include a few in the workbook for audiences to take with them and share with others.

Adding practice exercises

Include practice exercises to reinforce what you expect the audience to learn. For example, if your goal is to teach the active voice, have exercises for attendees to turn passive-voice sentences into active-voice sentences. Or if you're teaching how to use positive words and phrases, have exercises for the audience to turn negative words and phrases into positive words and phrases.

SHERYL SAYS

Don't include answers in the workbook, especially if you're sending it in advance. It's too tempting to peek. Here's how I use the workbook, which I send out beforehand: After we discuss a section, I ask them to write down answers to the related questions. When they're finished, I request volunteers to share what they wrote. It's amazing how many correct ways there are to say the same thing.

TIP

Include a table of contents (TOC) if the workbook is more than ten pages. For a PDF, provide hyperlinks to help audiences navigate to specific pages. For ease of interactivity, have fillable fields, embedded media, links to external resources, and social media share buttons.

Remembering your bio and contact information

Write a one- or two-paragraph bio so your audience can see why you're the best-qualified person to facilitate the workshop. Include the name of your company, other services offered, and contact information. Some people put their bios at the end; I prefer to put mine at the beginning. This establishes credibility as soon as attendees open the workbook. (Check out Chapter 11 to learn more.)

Writing the Copy

START-UP BRIEF

Check out Chapter 3 and fill up the Start-Up Brief. It's critical that you understand your audience whether you're preparing handouts or workbooks. Who are they? What's in it for them? How will they apply the information? What's the key issue for them to remember? What questions will they need answered?

Here some tips for preparing copy for handouts and workbooks:

- Use a readable font such as Times 12 or Calibri 11.
- Leave 1 or 1½-inch margins on the top, bottom, and sides for notetaking.

- Include bold headings and subheadings for easy reference.
- Limit paragraphs to eight lines of text and sentences to 20 words or less.
- Make sure the materials are in the same order as your presentation.
- Number the pages for easy reference.
- Use graphics when visuals can "speak" louder than words.
- Include your name and contact information on each page.
- Include a copyright notation by using the symbol ©, the year first published, and your name as copyright owner. Even if your work hasn't been copyrighted, it may dissuade people from claiming it as their own.

WARNING

Never claim someone else's work as your own. If you're copying information or using any material from someone else, make sure you get written permission and give credit to the author and publication.

Printing and Binding

Your goal is to have professional-looking pages that are easy to read, easy to turn, and easy to write on. This section covers some suggestions for printing and affixing.

Printing options

Print your materials on 24 lb. white bond paper. This is thicker than regular 20 lb. bond paper and will make your materials appear more authoritative and credible. (Paper weight is measured in pounds per 500 sheets, which is a ream.) Brick-and-mortar stores such as Staples and local print shops offer walk-in as well as online printing and binding services. Popular online options include such as VistaPrint, GotPrint, Snapfish, and Zazzle, to name a few.

Binding options

There are several ways to bind. Your choice should depend on the number of pages and how the materials will be used.

Stapling

If you have ten pages or fewer, staple them together at a 45-degree angle on the upper-left side about an inch from the edge. (Any closer can cause the pages to fray.) Don't use paper clips because the document can come apart too easily. (Your cover sheet can be the same paper stock. A back cover probably isn't necessary.)

Saddle stitching

This is an economical binding for booklets up to about 50 pages. Figure 10-2 shows what a saddle stitched handbook will look like. It's called saddle stitching because the pages will be folded in half and placed over an apparatus (stapler) that looks like a saddle. One disadvantage of saddle stitching is the pages don't fold flat so it's not as easy to write notes on the pages as with other bindings. (Your front and back cover sheets should be a thicker paper stock, as shown in Figure 10-2.)

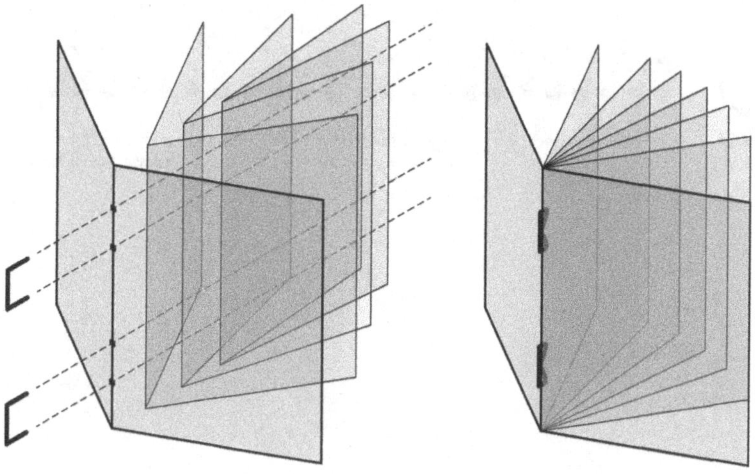

Zern Liew / Adobe Stock

FIGURE 10-2: Saddle stitching.

Binding

Wire-O Coil binding or Sprial Coil bindings will allow participants to fully open the pages to a full 360 degrees and lay flat. This is great for workbooks. There are a variety of bindings to choose from as you can see in Figure 10-3. (Your front and back cover sheets should be a thicker paper stock.)

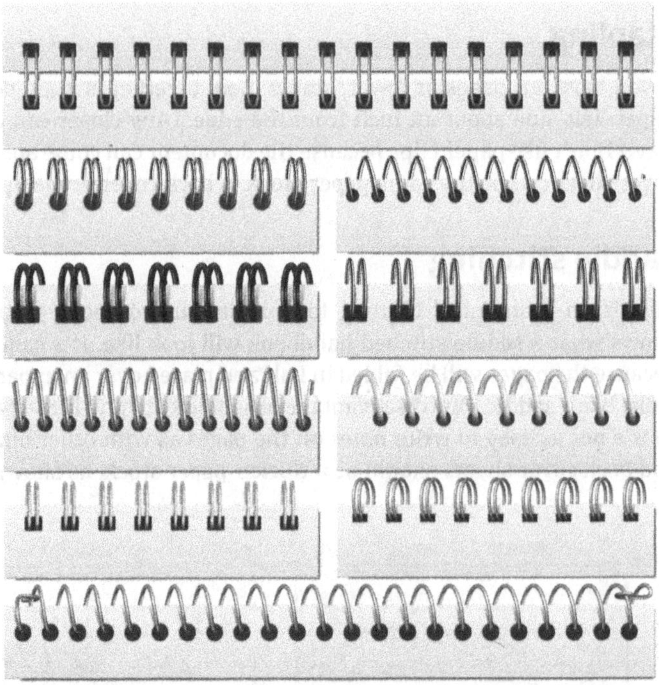

FIGURE 10-3: Variety of wire bindings.

WinWin / Adobe Stock

IN THIS CHAPTER

- » Using search engine optimization
- » Knowing what's out there about you
- » Letting your personality shine
- » Writing your infomercial
- » Putting your bio together for introductions

Chapter 11

Your Bio: The Story of You

The road to success is always under construction.

—LILY TOMLIN

Just as the road to success is always under construction, so is your life — personal and professional. By virtue of being alive, you're always involved in new things. Perhaps you learned a new language, took an interesting course, acquired a new skill, engaged in a new hobby, or wrote an article. These things should be in your bio.

Think of your bio as a snapshot of the story behind — you — the person. Your infomercial. Your advertisement. Your personality. Of course, your bio should contain your name, current job title, company or personal brand statement, relevant achievements, education, personal and professional goals, skills, and areas of expertise. Beyond that, make it your own. You never know when someone in the audience will relate to something that interests you.

SHERYL SAYS

Here's a great example: For 25 years I owned a 30-foot sailboat and listed sailing under activities I enjoy. At the conclusion of a workshop I facilitated, Jeremiah came up and told me he too was a sailor. We started chatting. To make a long story short, not only did Jeremiah bring me into his company to facilitate several workshops, we became friends and shared many wonderful sailing adventures. I've since sold my boat, but my husband and I continue to sail with Jeremiah and his partner.

Your bio is one the most important pieces of copy you'll ever write about yourself: It's the story of who you are as a person, personally and professionally. Whether you're writing an elevator pitch with a few pithy lines, a two-paragraph profile, or a one pager, a bio goes beyond a standard resume or curriculum vitae (CV). It should tell your story that aligns with your values, goals, and aspirations.

In this chapter, you find out how to showcase your personal and professional self, whether it's for delivering an elevator pitch, a two-paragraph profile, a single pager, or promoting yourself on social media.

Showing You Have a Personality, Not Just a Pulse

If you look at bios of people from certain professional groups, you'll notice they typically sound alike. For example: Certified Financial Planners all have CFP after their names. They all boast of helping clients to create diversified portfolios, plan for the future, save for children's education, yadda, yadda, yadda. Finding a financial advisor can dictate the path of your financial future for decades, so you must select one carefully. What makes them different? How do you find one who's right for you?

SHERYL SAYS

When I was looking for a financial planner, I looked beyond the basics that make them all alike. I wanted a snapshot of the story behind the person. Here are just a few things I checked out on social media sites, followed by a phone call to those who looked interesting. I asked each one the same questions:

- Are they fiduciaries? If they are, they must act in my best interests, offering the lowest cost financial solutions to fit my needs. (Not all financial advisors are fiduciaries.)
- Are they fee-based, commission-only, or fee-only?
- Will they listen carefully to my goals and needs?
- Are they comfortable being asked and answering all of my questions?
- Do they have good communication skills and explain concepts at my level of understanding?
- Are they committed to ongoing education for themselves to stay current with the latest financial trends and tools?

STORYOPIA ARCHIVES: SHINING ABOVE THE COMPETITION

When my former PCP retired, I started the search for a new doctor. After checking with friends, I learned that their doctors weren't accepting new patients. *This isn't going to be easy,* I recall thinking — especially finding a doctor who believes in a holistic approach, not one who just dispenses prescriptions.

I scoured the Internet and found many doctors who were accepting new patients. I viewed their credentials, and most sounded alike. Of course, they graduated from different medical schools, did their internships and residencies in different hospitals, but what made them unique? Many even said they come from medical families or they'd wanted to be doctors all their lives. So what? None of them gave me any insights as to the way they view patient care.

Then I came across the doctor I ultimately chose. His bio jumped out from the rest. First of all, next to his photo he had a large headline indicating that he values patients who want to collaborate and work together on improving their health. *My philosophy exactly!* So, I read on. This doctor further states that if patients come in and ask for medication, he tries to understand their needs beyond medication. What are their lifestyles? And how do these lifestyle choices impact their health? *Another check mark.* His hope is to work with patients toward healthier lives, minimizing the need for medications. *That's my kind of doctor; I knew that immediately.* And, at the time, he was accepting new patients. I've been using this wonderful doctor for several years and am delighted with his approach to my health care.

Lesson learned: Use your bio to state what makes you different from others in your field. Whatever it is, shout it out and the right people will listen!

Establishing bragging rights

Your bio should sound as though it were written objectively . . . yet it's anything but objective. Many people find it difficult to "brag" about themselves. If you're one of those people, think of your life as though you were someone else peering in. What would you say about "that" person. Give this serious thought and present the information interestingly:

> **Interesting:** Six years ago Sam followed his dream, leaving the safety net of his six-figure salary to start his own coaching business.
>
> **Uninspiring:** Sam left his job six years ago to pursue his own coaching business.

TIP

Add a recent photo to your bio. (Remember this isn't a resume or CV.) When people know what you look like, it adds a sense of trust and familiarity. That's why people put photos of themselves on websites, social media sites, business cards, and more. Realtors, short of plastering their faces and phone number on their children's fore-heads, display their pictures everywhere. It's all about personal branding.

Breaking from the pack

Convey what makes you different. Interesting. Relatable. Consider the following questions to ask yourself as you're crafting your bio:

- What do I enjoy doing when I'm not working?
- Was I raised in another part of the country or world?
- Do I have a rare pet?
- Do I have an interesting hobby or unique collection?
- What projects am I currently working on at work or play?
- What's my vision for myself, my company, the world?
- What volunteer activities am involved in?
- What am I passionate about?
- Where do I see myself five or ten years from now?

Choosing your voice

When introducing yourself or writing a bio for a social media site, write in the first person. It makes readers identify with you. Otherwise, write in the third person, as if someone else wrote (or said) all the wonderful things about you.

First person: I first entered . . .

Third person: Bob first entered . . .

Third person: He first entered . . .

Creating Your Infomercial

You're a product. A commodity. Create an infomercial to sell yourself modestly, succinctly, and clearly. A well-prepared bio can be a powerful tool to boost your credibility, whether at a speaking engagement or any other function.

TIP

Here are a few tips:

- Catch the reader's attention with a hook.
- Add flavor, perhaps something fun or interesting about yourself.
- Be humble, but confident.
- Include contact information.

This section helps you prepare your bio, whether it's an elevator pitch, a two-paragraph bio, a one pager, or social media content.

REMEMBER

If you don't have a bio or you have an old one that's been languishing in your computer or gathering dust in a file folder, it's time to create or update. Imagine being asked to fill a last-minute spot as a presenter. You know that opportunity would be a big career boost, but you don't have a current bio, and they want one submitted by the end of the day. So, you scramble to put one together, but it doesn't make you shine. You can avoid the rush by always having a current bio ready to go.

Crafting a pithy elevator pitch

A 30-second elevator pitch, as you see in Figure 11-1, is a short infomercial about you that's quickly shared with people you may be interested in forming a connection with. The elevator pitch got its name because it typically takes 30 seconds to ride in an elevator from the top to the bottom of a building (of course, without stopping at every floor). That's approximately how long you have to introduce yourself.

REMEMBER

Although the pitch is about you, people want to know you're interested in them as well, so pay attention to that last bullet. For example, at the end of your short spiel, you may say, *Please tell me about yourself and how I may be able to help you.* When putting together your elevator pitch, be sure to do the following:

- State your name and company.
- Present the problem.
- Offer a solution.
- Mention your value proposition.
- Hand your business card.
- Stress that you'd like to learn about the person you're speaking with.

Andrey Popov / Adobe Stock

FIGURE 11-1: My bio with hook, humor, accomplishments, and interests.

TIP

There are many uses for a bio of this length in written form. You can use it for an article you write, a media profile, a blog you publish, a company directory, or any other place where you need a brief introduction. In cases such as these, use the third person, so it sounds as if someone else is bragging about you. Here's the difference between the first and third person:

> **Example in the first person:** *Hi, I'm [Name]. When I started my journey to fitness, I was anything but the picture of health. I was overweight, had high blood pressure, and wasn't eating well or exercising. I developed a program that has worked for me and hundreds of others, several of whom started running marathons. I'd love to tell you more about my program and learn more about you and what you do. Perhaps we could set a time to meet for coffee? (Hand your business card and get one in exchange.)*
>
> **Example in the third person:** *When Tony started his journey to fitness, he was anything but the picture of health. He was overweight, had high blood pressure, and wasn't eating well or exercising. Tony developed a program that has worked for him and hundreds of others — several of whom started running marathons. Tony would love to tell you more about his program and learn more about you and what you do. You can contact Tony at [contact information].*

STORYOPIA ARCHIVES: NETWORKING SKILLFULLY

Networking has been incredibly productive for me. Most of my business has come from networking that started with my elevator pitch. I've acquired new clients, created strategic partnerships, and made lasting friendships. You must network skillfully, however, because there are many personality types you'll want to shun. Here are a few examples:

- **Ned the Narcissist:** This type of person is boisterous — the one you hear when you first walk into a room. They swarm all over you, broadcasting who they are, what they've accomplished, and how you can help them.
- **Micki the Marauder:** This type seems pretty decent at first. Then you realize they're asking you so many questions they're trying to glean your secrets to success.
- **Carlo the Card Slinger:** You've having a great conversation with someone you just met, and this person interrupts with, "Can I give you one of these?" They thrust a card into your hand and move to the next victim.
- **Beatrix the Beggar:** This type of person goes to every event expecting to ask for favors in the way of introductions to people in your network.
- **Nell the Newbie:** This type of person goes around telling everyone (usually whispering from the corner of their mouths), "I'm new at this. I've never been to one of these things. How does this work?"

Lesson learned: As much as you don't want to meet these people, don't be one of them yourself. Prepare a brief elevator pitch and present it with confidence and competence, always showing interest in the person you're speaking with.

Creating a two-paragraph profile

A two-paragraph profile is an abbreviated version of a longer bio. The main difference is the level of detail. A two-paragraph profile is usually more concise and focuses on the most important aspects of a person's professional or personal life, while a one-page bio can provide more context and detail. (More about a one pager in the next section.)

This type of profile is useful for social media or a quick introduction in a professional setting. You'll need two versions for introductions: one where you'll introduce yourself and another when someone else will introduce you.

Preparing for a self-introduction

Think about what your audience expects from your presentation. Why should they want to spend their time listening to you? What will be their valuable takeaway?

Why are you the best person to make this presentation? This is a make-it-or-break-it opportunity. Here's an accountant who didn't miss the opportunity.

> **Strong start:** *Hello everyone, I'm Jack Miller. I've had more than 20 years' experience in the financial world and help small businesses avoid IRS audits. In fact, throughout my career, I've processed thousands of tax returns without a single audit. This morning you'll learn how you can avoid IRS audits.*
>
> **Weak start:** *Hi, my name is Jack Miller and I am the VP of ABS Finance Company just outside of Boston. My background includes . . .* (When I hear introductions like that, I always think: *Hit the road, Jack.* I could have gathered that from your business card or bio. What's in it for me?)

When you introduce yourself, write in the first person and be as succinct as possible. Here's an example of what you may prepare. It's written in the first person from a presenter who teaches that laughing is the best medicine.

> *Hello, I'm Bruce Adams. I firmly believe that laughter is a bonding force. It has no cultural, social, or spiritual exceptions. Laughter is the sweetest human music. The medicine of the soul. The sound of healing. I'm the founder of A Dose of Laughter, and an experienced laughter therapist. I've spent the last 15 years helping people use laughter to relieve stress, reduce pain, improve a sense of well-being, and manage career and personal pressures.*
>
> *This highly interactive two-hour workshop includes laughter exercises, books, games, and puzzles. It's helped hundreds of people cope with the loss of loved ones, serious illnesses, career stresses, and personal setbacks. Experience all the health benefits of a good belly laugh to last you a lifetime. See for yourself. This is no joke.*

Preparing for someone else to introduce you

When someone else will be introducing you, write in the third person. Using the same example just mentioned, here's what you may prepare:

> *I'm delighted to introduce Bruce Adams. He firmly believes that laughter is a bonding force. It has no cultural, social or spiritual exceptions. Laughter is the sweetest human music. The medicine of the soul. The sound of healing. Bruce is the founder of A Dose of Laughter, and an experienced laughter therapist. He's spent the last 15 years helping people use laughter to relieve stress, reduce pain, improve a sense of well-being, and manage career and personal pressures.*
>
> *His highly interactive two-hour workshop includes laughter exercises, books, games, and puzzles. It's helped hundreds of people cope with the loss of loved ones, serious illnesses, career stresses, and personal setbacks. Experience all the health benefits of a good belly laugh to last you a lifetime. See for yourself. This is no joke. And now . . . here's Bruce.*

STORYOPIA ARCHIVES: HAVING A SENSE OF HUMOR ON HAND

I asked Patrick, a colleague, to introduce me to the large audience for a presentation I was asked to make. I always prefer to have others introduce me so I don't sound boastful. I chose Patrick because he has a wonderful sense of humor and a delightful way with words. I knew he'd warm up the audience. In addition to reading the two paragraphs I had prepared, Patrick embellished the introduction quite a bit. He added several of his own glowing comments which surprised (and delighted) me. Now I had to live up to them.

After thanking Patrick for the glowing introduction, I lightened up his boasting by walking on stage, looking at the audience, and spontaneously saying: *Thanks. My mother wrote that.* The audience found my remark very amusing, and it immediately broke the ice.

Lesson learned: Always keep your sense of humor!

WARNING

When introducing someone else, avoid trite expressions such as:

- Bruce needs no introduction.
- You can read Bruce's bio in the program book.
- Let me read to you what's in Bruce's bio.
- I've never met Bruce, but I hear he's awesome.

Crafting a one-page bio

A one-page bio may be used in more formal or professional settings, such as in a portfolio, a grant application, social media site, or a conference program. In a bio of this length you have more space to include details about your education, work experience, achievements, professional affiliations, volunteer activities, and personal interests. However, the exact length and content of your bio will also depend on the requirements or guidelines provided by the specific context or organization or site you're submitting it to.

The format, style, and content are typically up to you. Perhaps you have a personal motto, style, or philosophy that permeates everything you do. Your bio is the place to communicate that.

Make sure your bio is easy to read and entices people to want to meet you and learn more about you and what you offer. Here are some things to include:

- Name, title, contact information
- Professional associations and affiliations
- Published works (articles or books—even if self-published)
- Notable media appearances or mentions
- Professional awards
- Public speaking achievements
- Community involvement
- Family (adds a personal touch)
- Hobbies, passions, and special interests

SHERYL SAYS

I've included the one-page bio I use as Figure 11-2, so you can see how a finished one pager may appear. The style was my personal choice. I typically place it in training workbooks so the audience can see that I have the background to share valuable insights with them. (I didn't follow the advice earlier about including a photo. Instead I show covers of a few of the books I've written. They're better looking than I am. *Wink, wink.*)

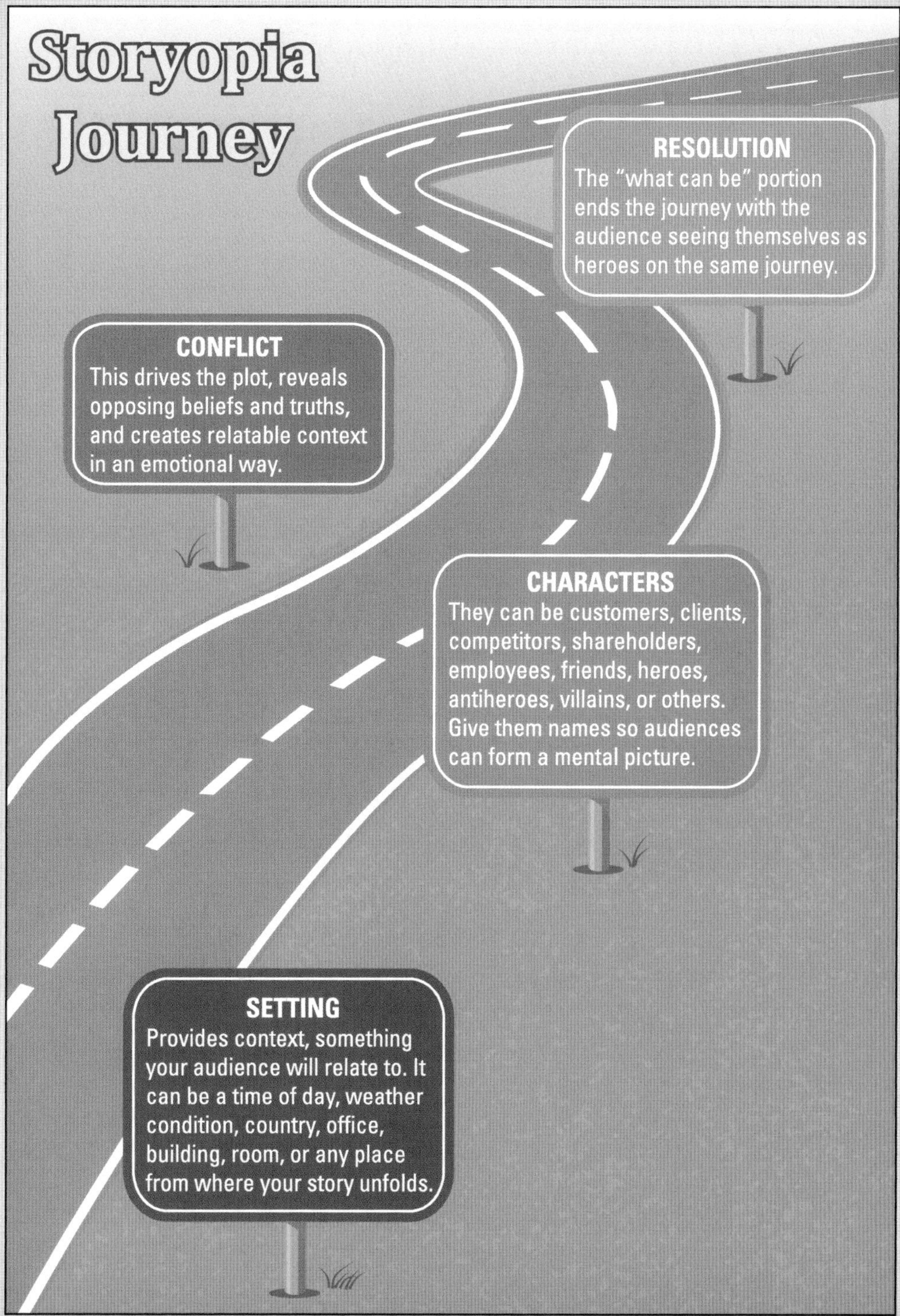
Storyopia Journey
RESOLUTION
The "what can be" portion ends the journey with the audience seeing themselves as heroes on the same journey.
CONFLICT
This drives the plot, reveals opposing beliefs and truths, and creates relatable context in an emotional way.
CHARACTERS
They can be customers, clients, competitors, shareholders, employees, friends, heroes, antiheroes, villains, or others. Give them names so audiences can form a mental picture.
SETTING
Provides context, something your audience will relate to. It can be a time of day, weather condition, country, office, building, room, or any place from where your story unfolds.

Storyboarding: Frame by Frame

A storyboard is basically an outline for a presentation — the sequencing of frames to convey the narrative a associated visuals. A preliminary storyboard is commonly done with cartoon-like sketches, sticky notes, greeking. Get on the road to storyopia and find out more about storyboarding in Chapter 7.

Oleksandr / Adobe Stock

Preparing comic strips lets you experiment with chronological sequencing and layouts.

Using sticky notes allows you to capture one concept at a time so you can reflow the narrative.

Images submitted by author

Greeking (aka *lorem ipsum*) is used as a placeholder when your narrative hasn't been determined.

ke your audience on a visual journey with images that convey critical information clearly and interestingly. ld habits die hard, but resist the urge to default to sleep-inducing, data-laden slide presentations. Delve into hapter 9 for lots of handy tips on using slides effectually.

Add a spot of color to a black and white image to make an element pop.

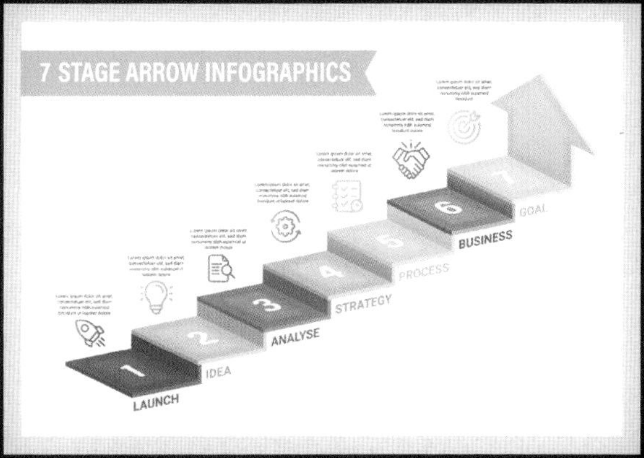

INKEYE STUDIO / ADOBE STOCK

Use an infographic to show steps in a process or procedure.

Combine text with an image to express a message succinctly.

LAUFER / ADOBE STOCK

Create a word cloud to identify important themes, patterns, and findings.

A Single Image Can Speak Louder than Words

Our brains process images more easily than words, and the right image can significantly increase an audienc engagement and understanding. Check out Chapter 9 to discover more about bringing stories to life with image

What do you think of when you see these images?
What emotional responses do they evoke?

GUY / ADOBE STOCK

Why is gaiety a state of mind regardless of age?

What pleasures do you derive from a sweet child in your life?

UNGVAR / ADOBE STOCK

Which encounters or storms (real or metaphotical) have caught you off guard?

What does a carefree sense of joyfulness mean to you?

Which event has caught you blindsided or surprised?

When was the last time you carried (or stood by) someone through thick and thin?

What's your most memorable high-five moment?

How does this majesty of nature make you feel?

Finalizing the Storyboard

This is the completed storyboard for making a PB&J sandwich for the Martians. It's a comprehensive visual accoun that will bring the presentation to life — expressing what to tell (in the left-column frames) accompanied by wha to show (in the right-column frames). To dive deeper into completing a storyboard, flip to Chapter 7.

<table>
<tr><th colspan="2">How to Make a PB&J Sandwich
30-minute Presentation for Martians</th></tr>
<tr><th>Tell</th><th>Show</th></tr>
<tr><td></td><td>1-1/2 minute Video on YouTube
</td></tr>
<tr><td>• Welcome and brief intro.
• Please feel free to jump in with any questions as we go along.</td><td></td></tr>
<tr><td>Tell story of how PBJ& started.

Boast of National PBJ& Day on April 2 for this all-American sandwich.</td><td>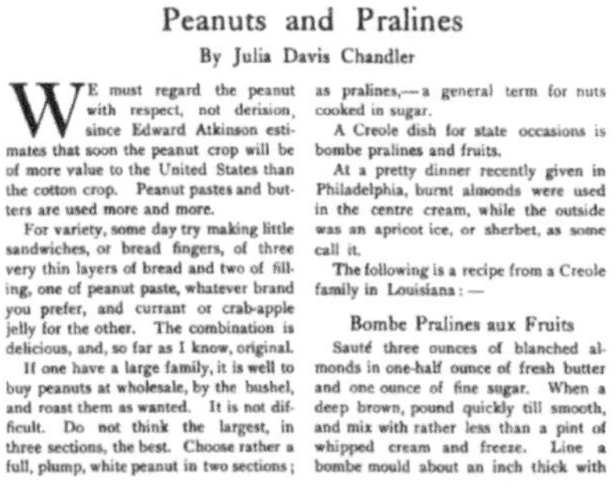
Peanuts and Pralines
By Julia Davis Chandler
WE must regard the peanut with respect, not derision, since Edward Atkinson estimates that soon the peanut crop will be of more value to the United States than the cotton crop. Peanut pastes and butters are used more and more.
For variety, some day try making little sandwiches, or bread fingers, of three very thin layers of bread and two of filling, one of peanut paste, whatever brand you prefer, and currant or crab-apple jelly for the other. The combination is delicious, and, so far as I know, original.
If one have a large family, it is well to buy peanuts at wholesale, by the bushel, and roast them as wanted. It is not difficult. Do not think the largest, in three sections, the best. Choose rather a full, plump, white peanut in two sections; as pralines,—a general term for nuts cooked in sugar.
A Creole dish for state occasions is bombe pralines and fruits.
At a pretty dinner recently given in Philadelphia, burnt almonds were used in the centre cream, while the outside was an apricot ice, or sherbet, as some call it.
The following is a recipe from a Creole family in Louisiana: —
Bombe Pralines aux Fruits
Sauté three ounces of blanched almonds in one-half ounce of fresh butter and one ounce of fine sugar. When a deep brown, pound quickly till smooth, and mix with rather less than a pint of whipped cream and freeze. Line a bombe mould about an inch thick with

</td></tr>
</table>

• Mention that oil in natural peanut butter separates and must be mixed. • Clarify the difference between jelly, jam, and preserves. • Describe what jars look like as opposed to cans that you can't see through. • Explain how to open jars. (Twist cap counterclockwise.)	
• Explain what a knife looks like and what it's intended to do. • Mention how to hold a knife so it's safe. Story of Clyde who didn't hold his knife correctly and got cut badly.	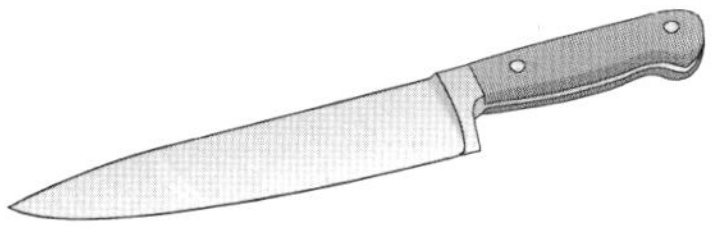
• Explain that some breads come as whole loaves and aren't pre-sliced. • Show how to slice a whole loaf of bread that isn't pre-sliced.	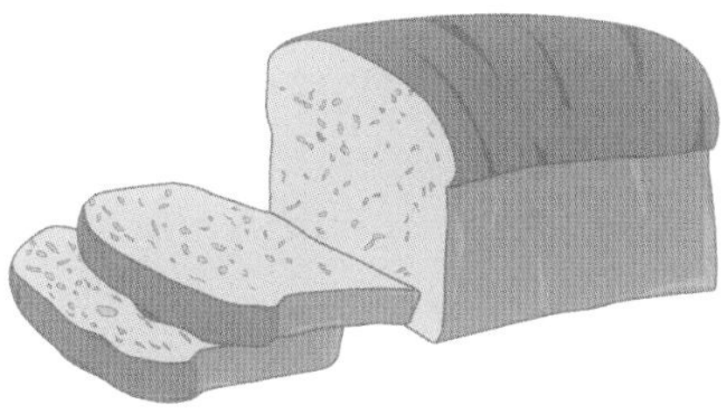
Closing story of how kids all over America trek to school with a paper bag (or lunch box) packed with a PB&J sandwich, an apple, and juice box. Note that the average child will eat 1,500 PB&J sandwiches before graduating from high school.	
Invite everyone to come up and make a PB&J sandwich.	

Most people look at data and don't understand their relevance without an explanation. When you create a stor around the data, you humanize the concepts. Data storytelling is a savvy way to illustrate trends or patterns or t explain complex concepts to give your audiences memorable *aha!* moments. Find out more about data storytellin in Chapter 4.

LunaKate / Adobe Stock

Creating Your Own Story

Be curious. Look about. Observe with all your senses. Everyday life offers a plethora of experiences — all of whi are potential stories to make your presentation memorable, leading to the call to action. Chapter 4 abounds wi guidance for morphing experiences into stories that take your audience on a storyopia journey from what *is* to wh *could be.*

gustavofrazao / Adobe Stock

Sheryl Lindsell-Roberts

You make more dollars when you make more sense.™

Having grown up in New York City, Sheryl still bears traces of her accent, which is very apparent when she says the word "coffee" (or as she pronounces it, *cough-ee.*) Sheryl stayed in New York with her husband and two sons, then moved to the Boston area of Massachusetts.

Communication is key to achievement

Sheryl became an expert communicator because she was raised by a mother who was a stickler for communicating well. That has resulted in Sheryl's stunning 25-year career as a business communications expert and principal of Sheryl Lindsell-Roberts & Associates. She's fiercely committed to helping people engage their readers and audiences in the following ways:

- Cut writing time by 30-50% and get dramatically improved results.
- Make electrifying connections with audiences by using a storyboard approach.
- Create emails with subject lines that shout "read me" and get meaningful responses.
- Communicate crisply with a multi-cultural and multi-generational workforce.
- Deliver key messages a glance with strong visual impact.

Books and media credits

Television and radio networks throughout the United States have interviewed Sheryl, and she's been featured and quoted in *The New York Times* and in magazines such as *Training Magazine, Profit, Home Business, CIO*, and others. Following are a few of the 25 books Sheryl has written:

Ideal clients — large and small and from a wide variety of industries — are those that believe powerful communication is the key to higher productivity and profitability. Join the thousands who have learned the art of written communication from a professional who has made a lifelong commitment to sharing best practices.

Passions and successes

Writing is one of Sheryl's passions. One day she hopes to write the "great American novel." But in the meantime, she and her team have produced proposals, brochures, websites, videos, manuals, technical papers, and more that have helped companies to close multi-million-dollar contracts. The biggest success was writing a proposal that helped an architectural firm close a $70 million school contract.

When Sheryl isn't writing, she enjoys reading, sailing, kayaking, cross-country skiing, snowshoeing, gardening, painting (pictures, not walls), creating pottery, going to the gym, or traveling around the world.

https://www.linkedin.com/in/sherylwrites/

FIGURE 11-2: My bio with hook, humor, accomplishments, and interests.

Developing Your Online Persona

Developing a strong bio for your online persona can be useful for branding, networking, and even job searches. Use your two-paragraph profile or one-page bio and tweak it as needed, depending on the site's word limitation.

It's important to consider your audience. For example, are you looking for consulting or freelance assignments or part-time or full-time placements? The key is to be intentional and strategic about the image you want to present and ensure that the image aligns with your personal and professional goals.

REMEMBER

Make sure to keep your profile current. Here are a few tips:

- If you posted a photo, does it look like you appear now (not 25 years ago)?
- Has your contact information changed?
- Has your name changed?
- Have you changed jobs?
- Have you gotten additional degrees or certifications?
- Have you included links to your website, blog, publications, or anything else online that tells of your uniqueness?
- Have you acquired any other bragging rights?

WARNING

Be honest and think before you post; there's always someone watching. Don't put anything online that's false or that you wouldn't want your parents, grandparents, kids, current or future employer, colleagues, or anyone else you value to see or read.

Including keywords for SEO

It's all about *search engine optimization* (SEO). Keywords relevant to your brand or industry help people find you when they search for those terms. Keywords may include **men's leather jackets, children's apparel, parenting, Zumba, seasonal rentals, email workshops,** or anything germane to you and your business. Using the correct terms will increase your visibility, attract the right audiences, and set you apart from the competition.

TIP

Free SEO tools include Google Keyword Planner, Ubersuggest, Keyword Surfer, and Moz Keyword Explorers, to name a few. For more, do a search for "keyword generator" and you'll find loads more for free and for fee.

Knowing your character-count limits

When you're posting your bio on a social media site and are pulling from the two-paragraph profile or your one pager, be aware of the site's character limitation. Here are a few as of this writing. Double-check each one before you post to make sure they haven't changed.

- **Twitter:** 160 characters for your bio (also known as "Twitter bio") and 280 characters for your tweets

- **LinkedIn:** 2,000 characters for your summary section, 120 characters for your headline, and 50 for your name
- **Facebook:** 101 characters for the intro section of your profile
- **Instagram:** 150 characters for your bio (called "Instagram bio")

Responding to comments

Social media is one of the most valuable tools for speaking directly to — and with — your audience, receiving feedback, and building trust and loyalty. After all, that's why you're on social media. When people leave comments or send you messages, respond in a timely manner to show you're active, engaged, and interested. Here are some tips for responding:

- **Respond promptly.** A quick response helps build trust.
- **Respond to everything.** It's good practice to respond to all comments, even if you answer with a simple "thank you."
- **Apologize and sympathize.** Keep a respectful and professional tone, even when comments are negative. Try to learn how you can resolve the issue.
- **Take it offline.** If someone has a complex or sensitive issue, offer to continue the conversation via email, phone, or whatever is appropriate.

Knowing What's Out There About You

Your online persona can impact your personal and professional life. This includes your social media profiles, online activity, credit rating, and other public records. And know that a majority of employers use online media to screen job candidates.

Checking for accuracy

Make it a habit to check regularly to see what information is available about you and take steps to control the information that's visible to others. This may include removing or modifying content, setting privacy settings, or creating content that presents you in a positive light. Here are some ways to do it:

- **Google yourself:** A simple search of your name, business name, email address, or username can give you an idea of what information others see. You may also want to try different variations of your name or nickname.

- **Check privacy settings:** Review your privacy settings on all your social media platforms to manage who can see your profile information, posts, and photos.
- **Use online reputation management tools:** Tools such as Statusbrew, BrandYourself, Birdseye, or Trustpilot are several of many that can provide an analysis of your digital footprint. This may include social media profiles, reviews, and mentions of your name or business. Search for **reputation management tools** to find more.
- **Check your credit report:** The three main credit reporting companies are Equifax, TransUnion, and Experian. They may contain different information such as your addresses (current and former), employment history, your credit limit, or outstanding debts. Prospective employers sometimes check a candidate's credit to get signs of financial distress that might risk theft or fraud.

Dealing with social media defamation

If you discover inaccuracies or, even worse, false statements or damaging information, you'll want to rectify them immediately. Terms for this *include libel*, *cyber defamation*, *disparagement*, *character assassination*, *cyberbullying*, and *cyber harassment*. There are bad actors out there who use their social media accounts to harass and defame others online. Although this can be challenging and time-consuming, here are some actions to try:

- **Respond.** If you see something untrue and you think it was innocently posted, respond immediately by leaving a comment or sending a direct message to the person who posted the statement. Provide the accurate information and ask that the post be corrected.
- **Report it.** Social media platforms have mechanisms for reporting false or misleading information. (Check what's available for each site.) If what you find seems beyond an innocent mistake, report it and provide the correct information.
- **Preserve the content.** If you've been defamed, don't respond to the defamer, but save the content. Without evidence of the defamation, you don't have a case.
- **Seek legal counsel.** If you find false information that can damage your reputation, seek legal counsel. A lawyer can advise you of your rights and take legal action, if necessary.

IN THIS CHAPTER

» Crafting evaluation forms

» Asking the right questions

» Conducting a self-assessment

Chapter 12

Requesting Feedback: Evaluation Forms

I like to listen. I have learned a great deal from listening carefully. Most people never listen.

—ERNEST HEMINGWAY, AMERICAN WRITER AND JOURNALIST

Always "listen" to evaluations from your audiences and take heed. Feedback is a critical tool to help you identify areas where you may need to improve. Whether you're a newbie or an experienced pro, whether you're giving a speech or a training session, whether you're speaking to a dozen people or hundreds, everyone can benefit from constructive input. Use it to improve your skills.

The word *evaluation* comes from the French word *évaluation*, which is the noun form of the verb *évaluer*, meaning "to appraise or value." How you interpret feedback and respond to it with your actions can weigh heavily on future sessions. After a training session, for example, the trainer may ask participants to rate the value or usefulness of various aspects of the training. That can be quality of the materials, relevance of the content, effectiveness of the delivery, knowledge of the trainer, and more. The resulting data can identify areas for improvement and to sway decisions about future training or performance management strategies.

This chapter covers several types of evaluations, including the following:

- On-the-spot visual assessments of your audience
- Audience evaluations at the end of the session
- Facilitator's self-assessments after the session

Making On-the-Spot Visual Assessments of Your Audience

Ed Koch, former Mayor of New York City, was noted for greeting people in the street and asking, *How am I doing?* He valued their opinions on his performance regarding city issues. In addition to their words, he noted their degree of enthusiasm and their body language. Koch recognized the importance of feedback in politics and used it to his advantage to improve his performance as a mayor. Use your audience's feedback to fine-tune and improve your performance.

TIP

Don't wait for evaluation forms at the end to find out how you're doing. Get ongoing feedback by looking around during the presentation. You can gauge the audience's interest, level of engagement, and understanding of the content by observing their body language:

- **Eye contact:** Are they making eye contact with you, or are they looking down or appearing distracted?
- **Posture:** Are they sitting straight up, leaning forward, or slouching and leaning back?
- **Facial expressions:** Are they smiling, nodding, raising eyebrows, or showing other signs of interest or disinterest?
- **Fidgeting:** Are they acting restless indicating they may be tuning out?

By observing their body language, you can make on-the-spot adjustments. For example, if several audience members seem to be getting sluggish or are checking their phones, perhaps it's time for a break, an interactive exercise, or brief video. If they look confused, consider introducing more stories and examples or pausing and asking for questions. On the other hand, if they're smiling, nodding, asking questions, and sharing their own stories, they're probably right there with you.

Audience Evaluation Forms

After you complete the session, evaluation forms help you "listen" to how you're doing, know what's working and what's not, learn what needs improvement, and determine the overall relevance of your program. If an organization is sponsoring your talk, they'll learn what worked, what didn't work, and other programs that may be of future interest.

Following are some suggestions to keep in mind for audience evaluation forms:

- Have the audience fill out the form as close to the event as possible.
- Keep the form brief, no more than one or two pages.
- Tie your questions to the objective of the session.
- Learn what you could have been changed or done better.
- Include open- and closed-ended questions.
- Ask what actions people will take as a result of having attended.
- Ask what other topics would be of interest.
- Thank them for their participation.

TIP

Some people are comfortable including their names on evaluation forms, while others are not. Give each person the option. Something as simple as "Your name (optional)" makes it clear they can choose whether to include their name. (And don't just write "Name," because some people may think you mean your name, the presenter.)

TIP

Check out `https://www.qualtrics.com/experience-management/customer/net-promoter-score/` to learn about Net Promotor Score (NPS). It's being used to evaluate presentations to show stakeholders and decision makers how their organizations are performing in terms of satisfaction and areas that need to be improved.

Asking closed-ended questions

This section talks about closed-ended questions — those that can be answered quickly. They're often listed as a scale (from 1 – 5, for example) or questions with a "yes" or "no" response. These are in contrast to open-ended questions that allow for more varied and subjective responses.

STORYOPIA ARCHIVES: MAKING SURE CHOICES ARE CLEAR

Writing this chapter made me reflect back to early in my career when I started facilitating business writing workshops. I told stories, engaged the audience, and was feeling pretty confident. At the end of each session I distributed short-answer answer evaluations with ratings from one to five, with five being the best. At the conclusion of what I thought was one of my best presentations, I looked at the first evaluation from Shelia, who had been one of the most enthusiastic participants. All the ones were circled. With the subtlety of a sledgehammer, my heart dropped down my knees. OMG! Had I been fooling myself? Was I too egotistical? As a new facilitator, I was devastated. However, I continued to read the comments and the rest were nearly all fives with a few fours. Where did I miss the mark with Sheila, I wondered? That niggled at me.

Several days later, Sheila sent me an email letting me how much she learned and how her writing had been getting great results. I got the courage to respond and asked why she'd given me all ones. She apologized profusely for not having read my evaluation scale and thought she was giving me the best rating — A-1 ratings for everything. I realized that my numbering system may have been clear to me, but it wasn't clear to everyone, and certainly not to Sheila.

Lesson learned: When you prepare an evaluation form, make sure the choices are clear. Also, provide for short and long answers so attendees can write in their own assessments. Long answers tend to offer the best insights. Pay attention to them — both the negative and positive.

Figure 12-1 shows some common closed-ended evaluation questions. It clearly identifies the range from strong agreement to strong disagreement. If you're using a sliding scale, make sure you clearly define which numbers are high and which are low.

Going for more detail with open-ended questions

Open-ended questions are intended to encourage respondents to provide detailed and thoughtful feedback that can provide valuable insights into the strengths and weaknesses of a course, program, or instructor. Be sure to allow ample space for answers, and mention that participants can use the back of the form if they need additional space.

	Strongly Agree	Agree	Neutral	Disagree	Strongly Disagree
1. The objectives of the training were clearly defined.	○	○	○	○	○
2. Participation and interaction were encouraged.	○	○	○	○	○
3. The topics covered were relevant to me.	○	○	○	○	○
4. The content was organized and easy to follow.	○	○	○	○	○
5. The materials distributed were helpful.	○	○	○	○	○
6. This training experience will be useful in my work.	○	○	○	○	○
7. The trainer was knowledgeable about the training topics.	○	○	○	○	○
8. The trainer was well prepared.	○	○	○	○	○
9. The training objectives were met.	○	○	○	○	○
10. The time allotted for the training was sufficient.	○	○	○	○	○

FIGURE 12-1: Common closed-ended evaluation questions.

Following are some examples of open-ended questions to consider in your evaluation form:

- What did you like most about this session?
- What aspects of the session could be improved?
- Were the visuals relevant and relatable?
- As a result of the session, what will you apply immediately to make a difference in your [be specific]?
- What other programs would you like to see offered?
- Do you have any suggestions for how the content or organization could be improved in the future?
- Please list any comments you have about the presenter.
- Any other comments?

STORYOPIA ARCHIVES: PAYING ATTENTION TO FEEDBACK

I've learned much from paying close attention to evaluation forms and have made many changes to my programs. Even after all these years, I'm still learning, growing, and changing.

I recall the very first time I made a formal presentation. I was well prepared and walked on stage with great energy. Nervous, yes, but it made me appear enthusiastic. Everything seemed to be going well. People were engaged and interactive. I expected the evaluation form to show rave reviews. Most of them were, but one person included a comment that made me sit up and take notice. She said, *I found your information to be very valuable, but you talk soooo fast, I missed some of what you were saying.* I paid attention to that! Thereafter, I slowed my speech waaaay down.

Lesson learned: Listen to the feedback from your audience; there's so much you can learn from them.

Putting it together

Figure 12-2 is an evaluation form I use. I've put it all together with easy-to-identify categories, allowing space for comments. I'm a consultant and additionally ask for referrals. That's gotten me lots of additional work. If that's appropriate for your situation, consider including it.

Check out Chapter 8 to find out how you can get instant feedback for virtual sessions from interactive engagement apps such as: `https://www.mentimeter.com`, `https://ahaslides.com`, and `https://kahoot.com/`. For post evaluation results, take a peek at Chapter 19.

Laser Sharp Technical Writing!™

Your name and title: (optional) ______________________ Phone No: __________

Workshop Content *I got the tools to:*	**Excellent**	**Good**	**Fair**	**Poor**
1. Write documents that get attention				
2. Help my reader find the key issues quickly				
3. Express my ideas more clearly and concisely				
4. Get started more easily				

Instructor	**Excellent**	**Good**	**Fair**	**Poor**
1. Knowledge of subject				
2. Confidence				
3. Enthusiasm				
4. Overall performance				

Productivity results: As a result of this workshop, I expect to cut my writing time. **Yes** **No**
If yes, by how much? **50%** **40%** **30%** **20%** **10%**

Based on what you learned on during the workshop and the coaching session, please write down some of your goals. What will you apply to your writing immediately? ______________________

____

____

What would you tell other people about this program? ______________________

____

____

Added value: The following are services that employees from other companies count on for the continued superior quality of their business documents. Please rank them in the order of importance to you, with **1** being the most important.

___ Follow-up coaching to help you stay on track and bring your documents to the next level.
___ Collaborating with you to write your critical documents in order to influence your reader's reaction.
___ Editing services to ensure consistency, strong visual impact, and a reader-focused tone.
___ Other ______________________

Referrals: If you know of someone in another company who can benefit from this experience as you have, I'd appreciate the referral. Thanks!

Person's name and title: ______________________ Phone No: __________

Company: __________ Address: ______________________

Sheryl Lindsell-Roberts & Associates
https://www.linkedin.com/in/sherylwrites/

FIGURE 12-2: One-page evaluation form.

Mirror, Mirror on the Wall

Big breath. You just delivered an important presentation. You tidied up the room and removed anything attendees left behind. You replayed the last few of the minutes over in your mind. Before running your victory lap, however, think back to your on-the-spot observations. Did the audience participate? Were they actively engaged? Then take a moment to look at the audience's evaluations to make sure you earned a victory lap. If you get favorable reviews, do a self-assessment. If the audience's assessment and yours align, then run your victory lap. If they don't align, take a look in the mirror to see where the discrepancies might be (see in Figure 12-3).

FIGURE 12-3: Do others see you as you see yourself?

EwaStudio / Adobe Stock

Doing a self-assessment

Honing your skills as a presenter never ends. Every skilled presenter should do a self-assessment at the end of each session to reflect what did and didn't work. Each audience offers a different experience, so there's always something to learn and improve. The following are self-assessment questions to consider:

Presence

- ❑ Did I grab the audience's attention with a powerful introduction?
- ❑ Did I appear confident and relaxed?

- ❑ Did I build rapport?
- ❑ Did I move around with purpose?
- ❑ Did I use pauses for emphasis?
- ❑ Did the audience seem engrossed overall?

Props

- ❑ Did I share stories that added value to the topic?
- ❑ Did I have sufficient interactive materials?
- ❑ Were my slides engaging or disengaging?
- ❑ Were there too many?
- ❑ Were the handouts clear?

Other stuff

- ❑ Did I effectively manage the Q&A?
- ❑ Did I include the audience in my language: more *you* and *we* than *I* and *me*?
- ❑ Did I end on time?
- ❑ Did members of the audience make verbal comments after the presentation?

Next steps

- ❑ What worked well?
- ❑ What didn't?
- ❑ What can I do differently and why?

Once you've made your self-assessment, go back and compare it with the audience's evaluations. In addition to the short answers, pay special attention to the written comments. For example, did more than one person mention they felt you rushed through the presentation? Or that you didn't allow enough time for questions?

If either is the case, perhaps you need to cut some of your second- or third-tier materials, slow down your pace, and allow more time for questions. Check out Chapter 6 to learn how to modify your presentation by preparing layers and modules.

REMEMBER

Don't just stop with evaluations. Follow the lead of companies that ask customers to go online and write reviews. Ask people in your audience to write testimonials of how your presentation has helped them change from what was to what (now) is. With their permission, you can turn those testimonials into wonderful stories for future presentations.

4 It's Showtime

IN THIS PART . . .

Present like a pro, dress suitably and comfortably, practice the art of practicing, handle technology snafus, be inclusive, and overcome stage fright.

Find out why collaboration is about people and not technology, storyboard and rehearse as a team, and give and get peer feedback.

Articulate bad news, field questions, plus determine when to take questions and how to deal with difficult audience members.

Understand how and when to inject humor (or not), show your lighthearted side, and what to do if nobody laughs.

Strive for inclusion and diversity across ethnicities and generations, present in another country, and know conversion rates.

Journey from standup to virtual seamlessly, maintain on-screen savvy, and practice proper etiquette.

IN THIS CHAPTER

» Dressing comfortably and confidently

» Getting in enough practice

» Handling technology snafus

» Creating a culture of inclusivity

» Getting help for stage fright

Chapter 13

Poised to Present

Don't strive for perfection. We're not human topiaries to be pruned and preened.

—JO BOWLBY, A BOOK FOR LIFE

Striving for perfection can be exhausting. You'll never think you're good enough. Instead, strive for mastery — being as well prepared as you can be. When you strive for mastery, you embrace the process rather than limiting yourself by an ideal.

This chapter leads you through dressing the part, the art of practicing, using notecards, punctuating with your voice, dealing with technology snafus, creating a culture of diversity and inclusivity, and putting you on the path towards mastery.

Okay. Once you've completed the Start-Up Brief (Chapter 3) and prepared your stories and storyboard (Chapter 7), you're ready for your dress rehearsal to ensure that all details of your presentation are prepared and coordinated.

When your audience sees you as poised (even if your knees are knocking), they'll be receptive to both you and your message. Picture yourself as a swan gliding gracefully across a lake. Poetry in motion. What onlookers don't see is that under the water, the swan's webbed feet are paddling fiercely. When you're poised, your audience won't see your nervousness.

Making a Great First Impression

Like it or not, audiences are making conscious and unconscious judgments about you before you utter your first word. This section provides some general advice so that you can make a great first impression when your audience gets their first look at you.

Dressing for the occasion

The rule of thumb is to dress a notch above your audience. For instance, in the millennial tech world of computer geeks, you may anticipate people in the audience wearing hoodies and jeans. Wear slacks and a button-down shirt or sweater. In the financial people typically "dress up." Follow their lead and wear a suit, sport coat, or sharp-looking dress, as you see in Figure 13-1.

When you dress suitably, you're making the following statements:

- I'm a confident professional.
- I respect myself, and I respect you.
- I pay attention to detail.

FIGURE 13-1: This presenter is dressed comfortably and confidently.

JackF / Adobe Stock

REMEMBER

Avoid clothing that's too tight or revealing, flashy colors, and accessories that might distract the audience or make jingling sounds. If you're presenting virtually, stay away from busy patterns or overly bright colors. Wear something appropriate from the mid-chest up. (What you wear below is your concern.)

Wearing a name badge

Name badges (also known as nametags) are conversation starters. If you think everyone in the room will know you, remember that not everyone is good with names. A name badge can save someone the embarrassment of coming up to you and saying, "I recall meeting you at [xx], but I don't recall your name." If you're wearing a name badge that's easy to read, that person instead can greet you with a confident smile and handshake while saying "I recall meeting you at [xx], Johanna, and it's good to see you again." This creates instant warmth and familiarity.

Here are a few things to make you and your name badge stand out:

- **Avoid the squint factor.** Your name and affiliation should be easy to read from several feet away. It's wise to have your first name larger than your last. That's how people will address you, making it easier for them to recognize you and start a conversation. (Too many people use their business cards as badges. Most aren't easy to read unless you're standing right up close.)
- **Wear the badge on the right side of your upper body.** The reason is that when you shake hands with someone, your right hand naturally moves towards the other person's right side, so having your badge on the right side makes it easier for them to see your name and (hopefully) remember it.
- **Keep it professional.** Make sure your badge isn't crooked, sideways, or upside down (yes, we've all seen that). It implies a lack of respect for yourself, the occasion, and your attention to details.
- **Make your name visible if your badge is attached by lanyard.** There's no protocol for wearing name badges dangling around your neck. You may consider shortening the lanyard with a knot in the back, so your name is in view during a conversation, the same as it would be with a stick-on or pin-on badge.

TIP

Before you start speaking at your session, remove your badge. Your audience knows who you are. The clip-on kind never stays straight and can wreak havoc with stage lights. However, wear your badge before and after your session if you're mingling. Many people may be looking for you and will seek you out.

Wearing a mic

If you'll be using a lavalier (clip-on) microphone, attach it to the collar of a button-down shirt, to a tie, a scarf, or along the neckline — somewhere close to your mouth. Before you start your presentation, experiment with different placements to find the best one for the particular room. Also make sure the mic is secure and won't move around while you're speaking.

Be cautious of clipping it to a jacket lapel midway down your body because the sound quality may be poor, and it will change each time you turn your head.

Practicing the Art of Practicing

REMEMBER

Your audience is no more comfortable speaking in front of a group than you are; therefore, they'll be very supportive. They're attending your presentation because of you and/or your topic and are silently cheering you on.

Practice the presentation the way you'll deliver it. Talk aloud with the same passion as you would during the session, move around normally, and smile to increase endorphins (giving yourself a feeling of well-being).

Here are a few things to keep in mind:

- Practice in front of a mirror. This will enable you to see how you present yourself, your expressions, and gestures. It will also give you an idea of how the audience will see you.
- Highlight the key points with natural hand gestures, arm movements, facial expressions.
- Modulate your voice so you emphasize key points. Then pause briefly to let the points sink in. (Listen to how TV newscasters do that so effectively.)
- Stand tall and lean slightly towards the audience. Move around comfortably with authority. This will camouflage any nervousness.
- Record yourself on video and/or audio for instant feedback.
- Time yourself. You may talk a little faster during the session because your adrenaline will be pumping.
- Practice with your visuals.
- Practice without your visuals so you can carry on if technology goes awry.

When you're reasonably confident, see if you can practice in the venue where you'll make the presentation. So, if you'll be delivering your session in a conference room in your company's building, schedule some time there.

Practice well enough so you can give all your attention to the audience. That doesn't mean reading from a script. It doesn't mean memorizing every word. And it doesn't mean relying on notes or slides. They're just props. As you practice, keep a record of anything that doesn't seem to work. For example, are there any words you stumble over? Is the flow smooth? Did you group together words that look good on paper but don't sound quite right when spoken? In any practice situation, don't hesitate to analyze, re-analyze, and make adjustments.

The following sections go over various strategies to keep in mind as you practice toward mastery.

Practicing in front of people and getting feedback

SHERYL SAYS

I'm typically asked, "How many times should I practice?" My answer is, *Until you feel comfortable.* After you do, then it's time for a mock audience. Whether you're presenting as part of a team or going solo, it's always valuable to rehearse your talk before one or more trusted colleagues or mentors. Ask them to put themselves in the audience's place and use the following checklist to give you feedback in these areas:

Delivery

- ❑ Did my opening and closing have impact?
- ❑ Was my key issue clear?
- ❑ Was the call to action strong?
- ❑ Were any parts unclear or confusing?
- ❑ Were my points arranged in logical order?
- ❑ Did I share stories to highlight key points?
- ❑ Were there appropriate transitions between points?
- ❑ Did I use jargon or words you didn't understand?
- ❑ Did I clarify terms and concepts?
- ❑ Did I maintain eye contact?
- ❑ Did I speak too quickly? Too slowly?
- ❑ Did I display nervousness?
- ❑ Was I convincing?
- ❑ How was my pace?
- ❑ How did you feel during and after the presentation?
- ❑ Did you see yourself as the hero? If not, how could I have made it so?

Visuals

- ❑ Did my visuals make sense and enhance the presentation?
- ❑ Were they interesting? Boring? Helpful? Distracting?
- ❑ Did they contribute to the storyline?
- ❑ Did I provide appropriate transitions?
- ❑ Did they add meaning to my explanations?
- ❑ Was all the spelling and grammar correct?

Using notecards

Notecards (also known as cue cards) may add to your credibility as a speaker. If you read from a full sheet of paper, it may appear as if you don't know your content, and nervousness may cause the paper in your hands to make a rustling noise. Notecards won't make any noise, and they look more professional.

Following are some tips to keep in mind when using notecards:

- » Use either 3-x-5 or 4-x-6 cards.
- » Number each card so you can always reassemble the order, if needed.
- » Include two or three key words or phrases on each card as triggers.
- » Use large print for readability.
- » Use a highlighter for words or phrases you want to emphasize.
- » Practice with your cards as well as with any other props you'll be using.
- » Try not fidgeting with the cards and resist bending or flipping them.
- » Hold them in one hand at a time or rest them on a podium.

Making your audience the heroes

Notice how often the words *you* and *your* appear in advertisements. Advertisers know the importance of focusing on the audience, not on themselves or their products. (That's why so many of us have drawers full of never-used gadgets.)

REMEMBER

Your audience isn't interested in you. They're self-centered and want your presentation to be about them. Use *you* and *your*, much more often than you use *I* and *me*. Avoid self-absorbed terminology and statements that are speaker-focused rather than audience-focused. Here's an example:

Speaker focused: I'm delighted to tell you. . .

Audience focused: You'll be delighted to hear . . .

Knowing when to use positive or negative

Presenting yourself as an optimist is a winning strategy that will engage the goodwill of the audience. (The glass is half full, not half empty.)

Positive: With approximately 100 hours into [project], I'm pleased that we've completed 60 of the deviations. However, the remaining eight are very problematic in that . . .

Negative: With approximately 100 hours into [project], we still have eight deviations that need to be completed. All of these remaining deviations are very problematic in that . . .

Positive: I'm sure you'll be happy with the results.

Wishy-washy: I think you may be happy with the results.

Negative: I hope you won't be disappointed with the results.

STORYOPIA ARCHIVES: NOTING THAT PROS USE NOTECARDS

Professional speakers, dignitaries, and even heads of state use notecards — and even they have embarrassing situations from time to time. President Barack Obama, an eloquent speaker, was offering a toast to Queen Elizabeth in Buckingham Palace during a state visit. He was speaking from notecards. As he was nearing the end of his remarks, he set his notecards down and picked up his glass to begin his toast: *Ladies and gentlemen, please stand with me and raise your glasses as I propose a toast* (pause) *To Her Majesty, the Queen . . .*

At that point the band launched into "God Save the Queen," but Obama hadn't concluded his talk. He picked up his notecards and continued speaking over the music. This gaffe of not knowing when to quit made headlines across the globe; however, Queen Elizabeth took it in good spirits.

Lesson learned: Some of the best speakers use notecards. If they're good enough for the President, you shouldn't hesitate to use them. Also keep in mind that even great speakers have moments they wish they could take back, so don't worry if you make a mistake. You're in good company.

REMEMBER

There are times, however, when you need to present negative news and can't sugar coat it. Your goal always is to maintain the goodwill of your audience. Here's a sneak peek; check out Chapter 15 to find out more:

- Start with a buffer that may soften the blow. This isn't to fool them, but to put them in a more receptive frame of mind.
- Break the news.
- Give a justification.
- Redirect, perhaps to options.
- Remain positive and forward thinking.

Practicing strategic use of repetition

Human beings are quick to pick up on patterns. Repetition, used judiciously, gives words and phrases rhythm. It makes the tone more convincing, more emotional, and more dramatic. It tends to convince people of its truth.

When using repetition, choose words that are important and worth stressing. Words that are memorable. But don't overuse them or you'll lose the impact.

Here's an example of an energy company that wanted to stress ways in which customers can save. They used repetition judiciously, and their point went from boring to punchy.

Boring: Save on energy, maintenance, and taxes.

Punchy:

- Save on Energy
- Save on Maintenance
- Save on Taxes

Avoiding unnecessary redundancies

Keep your language tight. That means avoiding repetitive, repeated, and repetitious redundancies. Repetition and redundancies are different. Repetition refers to the same thing repeated over again (generally for emphasis, as in the second sentence). Redundancies describe something that's in excess, no longer useful.

STORYOPIA ARCHIVES: USING THE RULE OF THREE

The "Rule of Three" is a well-known writing and speaking principle. It suggests that when things come in threes, they're inherently funnier, more satisfying, or more effective than other numbers of things.

Here are a few of examples we're all familiar with:

- Friends, Romans, Countrymen, lend me your ears
- The ghosts of Christmas past, present, and future
- Stop, Look, Listen
- Location, location, location
- Lather, rinse, repeat
- Lights, camera, action!

Lesson learned: Use the Rule of Three to convey concepts more thoroughly, highlight your points, and increase the prominence of your message. (See what I did there?)

Here are a few to consider for your talk, your visuals, and your handouts:

- **Essential** — not absolutely essential
- **Opposite** — not complete opposite
- **Costs** — not costs a total of
- **Fundamentals** — not basic fundamentals
- **Thank you** — not "I wish to take this opportunity to thank you"
- **Status** — not current status
- **Concluded** — not arrived at the conclusion

Asking rhetorical questions

A rhetorical question is asked to make a point or emphasize a statement, not necessarily to elicit an answer, although some audience members may raise their hands or nod. You can use these types of questions for persuasive topics to challenge the audience's thinking and engage them. You may use them as a negative assertion, a metaphor for a question already asked, or to start a discourse. Here are a few examples of rhetorical questions:

- Do we really want our planet covered in plastic?
- What's more important than the health and safety of our children?
- Don't you hate it when your car is making a strange noise, you take it to your mechanic, and it stops making the noise?

Practicing pauses and punctuating with your voice

Can you read this: Spacesbetweenwordsareasimportantasthewords? Of course you can't; it looks like gobbledygook. It reads: "Spaces between words are as important as the words." Without spaces between written words, it's difficult, if not impossible, to read. . . Without spaces between spoken words, the same is true.

Spaces (pauses) are fertile ground that let words germinate and grow. Without them there would be no comprehensible language. A simple pause is one of the most versatile tools in your speaker's toolbox.

When you pause, even for a few seconds, you heighten the interest and impact for your audience. Here are a few ways to use pauses effectively:

- **Make your voice a punctuation mark.** Use short pauses after commas and longer pauses after periods, colons, or question marks.
- **Add emphasis to key points.** Pause before, during, and after statements you want to stress. This includes your opening and closing remarks.
- **Indicate a change in tone or topic.** If you get a round of applause or said something the audience found amusing, pause and enjoy the moment before you start again.
- **Reveal thoughtfulness.** Before responding to a question, pause briefly so you appear to be answering with care.
- **Add purposeful eye contact.** Use the pausing moments to make eye contact with the audience, specifically the person who asked the question.

Considering speech patterns and word choices

Your speech patterns and choice of words are critical. Omit verbal fillers such as *like*, *um*, *you know*, or other words that interrupt the flow of words. Pace your rate of speech. If you normally speak quickly, slow yourself down. Avoid words or expressions that read properly on paper but may be misunderstood when voiced. If you say, for example:

- The door wasn't locked. (If someone doesn't hear the *n't*, they'd hear "The door was locked.")
- The door was unlocked. (If someone doesn't hear the *un-*, they'd hear "The door was locked.")
- The door was not locked. (This would cause no confusion.)

TIP

Don't overuse "but" and "and." They're transitional words used to link ideas and signal changes in topic. They bring structure, flow, and cohesion, but if thrown in too often, they may be interpreted as fillers.

Getting in the Zone

About 10 minutes before your talk, go to the restroom. Put water on your table and take a sip. Breathe from your diaphragm. Visualize your success. Then walk on stage. Establish eye contact with your audience. Cast a smile. Say good morning, afternoon, or evening. Slowly turn your head from left, to center, to right, and back again. This connects you with your audience and grounds you before starting. Take a deep breath, and as you do, imagine yourself inhaling the energy of the room. Slowly exhale and begin speaking.

Looking Them in the Eyes and "Listening"

During the session, make eye contact with as many people as possible. If your audience is large, mentally segment them and choose one member from each section as your focus. Doing so communicates how much you care about that person's thoughts, and it invites dialogue. When shifting your focus from one area to another, don't follow a pattern or you'll appear unnatural.

While making eye contact, *listen* to your audience's facial expressions and other body language. That means listening with your eyes, as well as with your ears. Are they nodding in agreement? What makes them smile? Are they attentive and sitting upright? Are they checking their phones? Are they looking around the room, doodling, or chatting with neighbors?

TIP

If you seem to have lost their interest, pull something from your bag of tricks: Tell a story, ask a question, make them laugh, create a transition, ask them to write or think about something, or take a mini-break.

If you have a snoozer and others are starting to become listless (as in Figure 13-2), announce an impromptu break. Take a look at yourself, the surroundings, and your presentation. Is the room too hot or too dark? Are you speaking in a monotone or too softly? Are your words going over their heads? Are your visuals slidezillas? Is your presentation too long and too boring?

FIGURE 13-2: Will this tedium ever end?

gstockstudio / Adobe Stock

On the other hand, what do you do if you think you're on a roll and suddenly notice some*one* (and the key is *one*) is snoozing? If everyone else is attentive, don't take it personally. Perhaps that person was up all night with a colicky infant, flew in on a redeye, has insomnia, or suffers from a medical condition. First and foremost, don't point that person out. Keep going with your presentation.

However, if you notice someone's eyes starting to open and close or their head starts to bob back and forth, that's a sign the person may be starting to doze off.

You may rouse that person by trying to engage them with a question: *Devan,* (pause) *I know you're very knowledgeable in [topic]. Would you mind sharing some of your thoughts?*

Being Sensitive to Diversity and Inclusivity

Nobody should be made to feel embarrassed or hesitant to make a request during a meeting. For example, a presenter may say, *As you can see here . . . .* It should be comfortable for a person with visual impairment person to say, "I can't see that. May I please have a verbal explanation?" Many apps today are building products with inclusive aspects, such as screen readers, magnifiers, high contrast mode, keyboard shortcuts, relay service, and more. For example, captions are a lifeline to people with hearing impairment or for those whose English is a second language.

Running inclusive meetings isn't just about technology — although technology is part of it — it's about the authentic involvement of all participants regardless of abilities. Most of us make a common mistake when we set up large meetings and assume that all attendees will be able to participate fully. There may be attendees who have difficulty seeing, hearing, speaking, working a mouse, or have other issues that keep them from fully sharing.

Updating your terminology

Language is a living thing that changes with the times. As we welcome a new vocabulary, it shapes the way we think and view the world. Be mindful about using language that's appropriate today's culture. Here are a few examples:

- Chair (not chairman or chairwoman)
- Sales representative (not salesman)
- Legacy (not grandfather clause)

TIP

Check out the following website for an extensive list of appropriate inclusive terms: `https://www.nyc.gov/assets/mopd/downloads/pdf/Disability-Inclusive-Terminology-Guide-Dec-2021.pdf`

Avoiding online barriers

Zoom and Microsoft Teams are considered the most accessible apps. Accessibility features for real-time accessibility are in the early days, and there's still a lot to learn. However, apps are continually pushing out new updates and features.

STORYOPIA ARCHIVES: KNOWING WHAT YOUR CLOSED CAPTIONS WILL SAY

I was delivering a training session via videoconference but hadn't practiced with the real-time automated captioning captions. At one point I said, "I'll feel better when I send it." The closed caption read, "I'll feel better when I have sex." Yikes! I laughed along with everyone else and was glad the audience had a sense of humor.

Lesson learned: Always practice with the closed captions turned on, so what you say is what you get. And you must have a sense of humor.

Following is a checklist of things to consider so there are no (or limited) barriers for people to join a videoconference:

- Has the software been tested by people with different types of abilities?
- Is there real-time automated captioning?
- Does it allow for ALS interpreters?
- Are there keyboard shortcuts.
- Does it have the platform for chats, notes, Q&A — and are they accessible?
- Does it allow for computer-based and phone-based audio listening and speaking?
- Is there a relay service enabling real-time participation through a communication assistant?
- Are the interfaces customizable?

Dealing with Technology Snafus

SHERYL SAYS

My advice when it comes to technology: Predict the unpredictable. Don't rely on your equipment to always work. When it does work, treat it as a pleasant surprise. Although this is a bit tongue-in-cheek, practice as if losing your technology will happen. If (when) it does happen, it will seem like practice.

During face-to-face presentations

Following are a few of the many things that can go awry should Murphy (as in Murphy's Law) barge in with the crowd:

- Your file becomes corrupt.
- There are compatibility issues, especially from Mac to PC or vice versa.
- If you're using a web-based application, the Internet goes down.
- The sound card on the presentation computer fails.
- Fonts and formatting are askew.
- You finish your opening remarks, press the clicker to show your first slide, and a dialogue box appears asking for the password.

If you're a seasoned speaker, chances are you've dealt with technical glitches and have had Plan B ready. The unforgivable glitches are those that happen when you should have known better.

REMEMBER

Here are a few thought-out-beforehand remedies that will help you be the consummate professional rather than a fumbling amateur:

- BYOD (Bring Your Own Devices). Large venues often have systems ready to go, but bring your own device (laptop) as a backup.
- Bring a flash drive with your entire presentation loaded, even if it's been preloaded.
- Save your entire presentation to the cloud.
- Bring your own cables.
- Embed multimedia images into the presentation rather than link them.
- Make sure the screensaver is switched off so you don't have to keep re-entering the password.
- Always have Plan B (stories or props) in your bag of tricks.

During virtual presentations

Add virtual to the mix, and you have an entirely different set of possible snafus. Make sure you have the highest-speed Internet connection and the latest version of the software. Also, when possible, use the desktop client rather than your browser.

STORYOPIA ARCHIVES: HAVING PLAN B READY

I arrived early for a large presentation with my flash drive, laptop, and extra cables. Everything was set up in the room, and I tested all the equipment beforehand. A-OK. When the audience appeared a bit later, I gave my opening, then turned on the computer. Oops! The computer wouldn't turn on. I tried a few quick fixes, when Pete from the audience offered to come to the rescue.

While Pete was fiddling with the equipment, I pulled from my bag of tricks for Plan B: I had a relevant story that kept the audience engaged and amused while my "hero" restored my equipment. After Pete had performed his magic, I asked the audience to give him a round of applause. Fortunately, he had a great sense of humor and took a theatrical bow. The audience laughed and clapped. Pete turned out to be not only my hero but also my comic relief. Then, it was on with the show. (I had my laptop handy but was prepared to continue without any technology if I needed to.)

Lesson learned: Always be armed with a story or prop.

Over preparing and testing are key. Have redundancies in place in case of technical glitches: backup computer, tablet, phone, mic, and even a backup for Internet connectivity or cell service. Assign a co-host at the client's end who can help with technical difficulties.

- Open the slide presentation on the desktop.
- Join 20 to 30 minutes early to make sure everything is working properly.
- Close all other apps.
- Turn on the mic and adjust the volume. (If using an external mic, check that the connecting cable or the Bluetooth settings are on using the wireless mic.)
- Turn on the camera and check the lighting for glares and shadows.
- Open any materials you plan to share before the meeting.
- Be situated in a space free of noise (crying babies, barking dogs, and so on).

REMEMBER

Most important of all, if you have back-up plans in place, you'll be able to stay calm and composed in the face of technology snafus.

An Ounce of Prevention . . .

Think back to your childhood when you were learning to ride a two-wheel bike. You probably wiped out a few times and scraped your elbows or knees. Although a little embarrassed, you pushed through and learned to ride. With practice (your training wheels) and an ounce of prevention, your skills and confidence will improve. Mistakes, if we learn from them, help us grow. If you experience one or two hiccups, just smile, apologize, make a joke, or offer an explanation. But most of all, accept responsibility. Unexpected embarrassments happen to everyone in all walks of life.

Following are a few embarrassments people have shared with me that may have been avoided with an ounce of prevention. (I changed the names to protect the mortified.)

- Grace was practicing her talk just before she went on stage and got a massive paper cut right behind her thumbnail. Not only did it hurt like heck, blood ran down her hand and on to the front of her white blouse. There was so much blood, the FBI would have convicted her of something.
- **Pound of cure:** Always bring with you an assortment of first aid supplies. They come in handy for quick fixes, including shoes that rub against your heel or toe. And an extra shirt or blouse wouldn't hurt to have.
- Jacobi walked on stage waving at the audience as he was prepared to address a large convention. He didn't look where he was going and tripped on an uncovered floor wire. Not only did Jacobi sprain his ankle, but the embarrassment and discomfort in his ankle impacted his entire presentation negatively. He couldn't regain his composure.
- **Pound of cure:** In most venues, loose wires will be shielded with cable covers. Check the stage before your audience arrives to make sure none are accidents waiting to happen. Always carry with you a roll of gaffer tape to cover any loose floor wires that may have been missed. (Gaffer tape is preferable to duct tape because it doesn't leave residue.)
- Ivan was a relatively new employee and was delivering a slide presentation to an audience of higher level managers. He was selected because of his expertise in a specialized area. About 15 minutes into the presentation there was a thunder and lightning storm and the power went out (no back-up generator). Ivan had no stories prepared, no props, and no conversation starters . . . just slides he was intending to read.

STORYOPIA ARCHIVES: REMEMBERING THE SHOW MUST GO ON

During the 2017 Oscar ceremony, Warren Beatty, seasoned actor and presenter, announced that *La La Land* had won Best Movie. As the elated crew and cast were charging to the stage doing their victory dance, the accountant from PricewaterhouseCoopers ran onstage and shouted, *"Stop! He [Beatty] took the wrong envelope!"*

Jordan Horowitz, a *La La Land* producer, took the mic, waved one finger in the air and said, *"Sorry, guys, hold on. There's a mistake. Moonlight . . . you guys won best picture. This is not a joke."*

Lesson learned: Even professionals (actors, politicians, and presenters) make faux pas. But the show must go on. It's important to keep breathing. Hold your head high. Stand tall. Laugh at yourself. Learn from your mistakes. You will improve. And remember, it's not the end of the world.

- Ivan started blathering. It was almost like a *Seinfeld* episode — all about nothing. Managers started trickling out of the meeting. When the power came back on about 30 minutes later, Ivan was the only one left in the room. It was a setback to Ivan's career, *not* because he didn't deliver the presentation, but because he didn't have Plan B. He folded under pressure.
- **Pound of cure:** Practice delivering every presentation without the aid of slides, so you won't be caught off guard if something goes awry. Arm yourself with stories, conversation openers, and props. Also consider bringing printed copies of the important slides you want to show, so you can hand them out if necessary.

Embracing the Benefits of Public Speaking

Following are just some of the benefits of becoming a confident public speaker:

- Improve your professional and personal reputation.
- Increase your influence in decision-making processes.
- Gain the trust and respect of others.
- Advance your career.

- Become a valuable company asset and advance your career.
- Improve critical thinking and analytical skills.
- Be seen as an expert.
- Land your dream job or client.

If you shy away from public speaking for whatever reason, get a coach, take a public speaking course, or join a public speaking group. There are many ways to gain confidence. Book yourself into a college course or adult education class, enroll in a workshop or seminar, or get a personal coach. But here are some other ideas:

- **MeetUp:** Meet others in your local area who want to enhance their public speaking skills.

  `https://www.meetup.com/topics/publicspeaking/`

- **Toastmasters International:** This is a nonprofit organization, with local chapters, where groups meet to practice speaking. Speeches are critiqued by members in a positive and constructive way.

  `https://www.toastmasters.org/`

- **National Speakers Association (NSA):** This is another professional organization that has regional chapters to provide education, publications, and resources.

  `https://www.nsaspeaker.org/`

REMEMBER

If you're shrouded in a fogbank each time you present or even think about presenting, that goes beyond typical jitters. Perhaps you suffer from *glossophobia*, a severe fear of public speaking. If so, contact your doctor. Remedies may include cognitive-behavioral therapy (CBT), relaxation techniques, or medication. Don't let fear of public speaking limit your career.

IN THIS CHAPTER

- Prepping and rehearsing as a team
- Selecting the best setup
- Understanding the role of peer feedback

Chapter 14
Collaborative Team Presentations

A team is a small number of people with complimentary skills committed to a common purpose, performance goals, and approach for which they hold themselves responsible.

—KATZENBERG AND SMITH, BLUE STAR PLUMBING

If you've ever listened to a handbell choir, you'd agree they exemplify collaborative teamwork. A choir can range from a quartet to 50-plus ringers, each playing different handbells. Each person uses their skills and unique talents to blend as a single instrument to create a cohesive piece of music. Ultimately each ringer is responsible for playing their part correctly and on time. There will be practice sessions, and the oversight rests with the music director.

Putting together a team presentation takes the same type of collaborative teamwork. A team can range in size from two to many, with each person having a different responsibility. Each person uses their skills and unique talents to blend as a single unit to create a cohesive presentation. Ultimately, each person is responsible for participating fully and being on time. There will be practice sessions, and the oversight rests with the project manager.

In this chapter, you discover that teams are all about people. Technology is an effective tool to facilitate communication among team members, but it's never the focus. You also find out about formal and informal settings. Finally, at the end of the chapter, you find a hypothetical sales team meeting (with storyboard and all) that ties it all together.

Meeting the Team

The size and nature of the team depends on the type of presentation. Factors include the complexity of the presentation, the skills and expertise of team members, and the goal. It can be as simple as a two-person team with the following people:

- **Subject matter expert (SME):** Prepares the narrative, provides content for visuals, and delivers the session.
- **Graphic designer:** Creates the visuals that incorporates images and formatting.

Another type of team can be three to four people with a common goal:

- **SME:** Is similar to the function just mentioned, but may or may not deliver the session. (In the latter case, there would be an additional person, the presenter.)
- **Graphic designer:** Performs the same functions as just mentioned.
- **Project manager:** Bears ultimate responsibility for steps along the way and the outcome. For a small project, this person may be called a team leader.

At the other extreme, a team may be preparing a video presentation. Each of the following team members plays a different role in the success of the presentation:

- **Content creator:** Develops the narrative and provides input for visuals and handouts.
- **Researcher:** Gathers and analyzes data on the topic of the presentation.
- **Designer:** Creates the visual design and layout of the presentation, including graphics, images, and formatting.
- **Videographer:** Meets the expectations of the project manager by capturing the footage in a pleasing and technically sound manner.
- **Narrator (or moderator):** Provides the voice over and engages viewers with context and commentary on the visuals.

Knowing what makes a cohesive team

A group of people working together doesn't constitute a team. They may have different roles and independent responsibilities and accountabilities. For example, a person in the training department may engage consultants, and someone else in accounts payable is responsible for compensating them. Both are part of the company's team working for the betterment of the organization, but they work independent of each other.

A cohesive team is a group of people who work together *inter*dependently and hold each other responsible for achieving a common goal. The relationship is based on defined roles and responsibilities, trust and respect, flexibility and adaptability, varied perspectives, commitment to quality, accountability, and open communication.

Open communication is key. If team members aren't communicating effectively and sharing ideas, it can lead to confusion and inconsistencies. Factions can form, battle lines can be drawn, communication stops, suspicion rises, productivity and efficiency grind to a halt. It's the project manager who should ensure that the lines of communication remain open.

Understanding the role of the project manager

A project manager must assemble the right people. If one member of the team is unqualified, struggling, or performing poorly, it can negatively impact the entire team's performance. It's important for the project manager and team members to build a positive team dynamic and create an environment in which everyone feels valued and supported.

Once the team has been formed, it's the role of the project manager to build trust. Define rolls. Share a vision. Capitalize on the strengths of team members. Create team metrics. Make changes when necessary.

This can involve the following:

- Outlining the scope of the presentation and ensuring everyone understands their respective roles and the overall goal.
- Setting up a "Who's Doing What" checklist to identify tasks, responsibilities, processes, and due dates.
- Organizing activities according to priority, preparing contingency time, setting up rules for communicating, and everything else needed to keep the project on track.

- Coordinating the efforts of each team member and ensuring the tasks are completed on time.
- Being open to suggestions and ideas. If a team member expresses an idea, listen openly. If you don't believe the idea will work, explain why in a way that will encourage more ideas to flow.
- Communicating on a regular basis with team members and stakeholders in terms of progress or any changes in scope or timeline.
- Identifying strengths and weaknesses of team members to be sure each one is playing to their strengths.
- Holding team members accountable for their role through ongoing check-ins.
- Providing ongoing support and guidance.
- Attending "dress rehearsals" to offer guidance and constructive feedback.

Dealing with shirkers

Dealing with shirkers can be challenging, and it's the ultimate responsibility of the project manager to handle them. Sometimes, team members may shirk responsibilities because they feel overwhelmed or don't have the necessary skills or support to complete a task. In these cases, a project manager may offer support, such as training or additional resources. If the problem reaches the point where it's damaging the team's goals, disciplinary measures may be in order, although it's a last resort. That can result in the shirker being released from the team and perhaps the company, depending on the severity of the issues.

TIP

If you're a team member (not project manager) and realize that another team member may be having problems, consider approaching them to find out if there's a reason and find out how you can be supportive. Perhaps that person is overloaded with tasks, perceives unfairness, or is dealing with personal problems such as health issues or family matters.

Completing the Start-Up Brief Together

START-UP BRIEF

The entire team should be involved in filling out the Start-Up Brief found in Chapter 3. It will help to collectively think about the audience, purpose, key issue, and questions you'll need to address so you can tailor your presentation toward the audience's needs and call to action. You can do this in a number of ways:

- **Everyone fills it out in a room together.** This is the most efficient way because differences in opinion can be ironed out and all the details can be resolved in one sitting.
- **Each team member fills it out separately.** This will involve some back and forth, but technology apps will be a big help in identifying who said what.
- **One person is tasked with filling it out for everyone, then it's circulated for consensus.** This can lead to some disagreements, as team members may view things differently, and much time can be wasted. However, this is a possible last-resort option.

Once the Start-Up Brief has been completed, it's the project manager's responsibility to complete a project schedule outlining all the tasks, who's responsible for each one, and the deadlines.

Storyboarding as a Team

Check out Chapter 7 for elements of storyboarding. At this early stage, the storyboard should include the narrative, relevant stories, which elements each person will deliver, and the timeframes. The most efficient way to develop a team storyboard initially is to paste notes on a wall or board so each team member can move them around until you have a cohesive story. Here's how it's done, as you see in Figure 14-1.

- Write topics and brief notes about stories on individual sheets of paper or sticky notes. They can be one or two words, bullet points, or more fully developed phrases. This is a first pass and will have several iterations, so don't get bogged down in minutiae.
- Put the pages or notes in a coherent sequence on a board or wall.
- Create sub-notes (perhaps in different colors) that filter in a series of smaller sequences.
- Have each team member rearrange the Tell as they think it's appropriate.
- If there are large discrepancies, convene the group to iron them out.

TIP

This process can also be done virtually using Jamboard, a digital collaboration tool developed by Google that allows users to create and collaborate on a virtual whiteboard in real-time.

FIGURE 14-1: Collaborative team storyboarding with sticky notes.

Drazen / Adobe Stock

During the storyboarding process there will undoubtedly be differences of opinion. That's a good thing because each person has a valuable contribution to make. Be willing to hear each person's reasoning. Work out how to move forward in a way that's respectful and makes the most of each person's strengths. Ultimately, the project manager team member will have final say.

After the basics are in place, someone will transfer the storyboard to a computer. It's then the team's responsibility to identify data for slides and other visuals. They'll be placed in the Show column. (If more than one person is preparing slides, the template, fonts, and style must be uniform.)

Delivering Formal or Informal Presentations

Formal presentations are delivered with the speaker in front of the room facing the audience. Chapter 13 is chock full of tips about that. Also, check out Storyopia Archives at the end of this section for hints about standing behind a podium (or not).

If you're presenting to a small group of eight or fewer, you can make it more intimate by sitting around a table. The choice of the table's shape will depend on what's available. If you have table options in different conference rooms, decide on the table setup that will work best for your presentation. Here are some tidbits to consider:

- **Round table:** The advantage of a round table is that everyone is equal; no one sits at the head of the table. (You've all heard of King Arthur and the Knights of the Round Table. King Arthur wanted a round table so the knights in his court would be considered equals and wouldn't argue over status or rank. This represented chivalry in its highest form.) A round table provides a less form setting. It allows for good sight lines where all participants are visible to each other, so it's easy to communicate and engage.
- **Square table**: A square table provides a setting much like a round table, yet it adds a more modern look. With everyone seated around a square table, it's easy for participants to make eye contact and collaborate closely. However, if the table has sharp corners, people may have difficulty moving around it comfortably.
- **Rectangular table:** A rectangular table offers a different set of dynamics. It's more formal than a round or square table because there's a pecking order, but it's still less formal than being in front of the room. The person sitting at the head of the table is in the power seat — the symbolic person of authority, such as the president, C-level person, or other senior-level attendee. The seat on the opposite end of the table is the second power position. Both people are visible to others at the table. (Notice in the storyboard for the scenario at the end of this chapter that the visitors are seated in the power seats at opposite ends of the table.)

Sometimes for very large formal gatherings, rectangular tables are set up where the power seats are in middle facing each other. You often see this arrangement when heads of state meet foreign dignitaries.

STORYOPIA ARCHIVES: DITCHING THE PODIUM

The first few times I made presentations I stood behind a podium because I thought it would hide my nervousness. Although I tried to make the presentation interactive, the podium was a barrier between me and the audience. I wanted the presentation to be informal, but the podium gave the impression of formality and distance. After several presentations, I ditched the podium and started moving around the room. The same presentation engaged the audiences and made me more energized. By leaving the podium, I removed the barrier.

Lesson learned: Ditch the podium and move around the room. Here's why: If you hang on to the podium too tightly, you'll immobilize your hands, which will make you more likely to stumble over your words and make you tense up. The podium can create a "boxed in" look so you become a boring, inert image to the audience.

Using Technology to Aid Collaboration

There's no shortage of tools designed to help teams collaborate more effectively. Each of these tools has its own unique features and strengths, so consider the needs of your team and try out a few options before deciding which one is the best fit. Listed in random order, here are a few tools with their unique characteristics:

» **Prezi:** A presentation app that enables users to create visually appealing and interactive presentations. It offers a variety of templates and themes to choose from and lets users customize their presentations with images, videos, and animations.

» **Trello:** A project management tool that helps teams organize and track their tasks. It's primarily used for agile development processes so team members can collaborate on tasks and monitor progress in real time.

» **Slack:** A messaging and collaboration platform where team members can communicate in real time through chat, voice, and video. It also integrates with other tools to streamline communication and workflows.

» **Miro:** A digital whiteboarding and collaborative platform for teams to work together in real time on brainstorming, mind mapping, and other mutual tasks. It offers a variety of templates and tools to help teams organize and visualize their ideas and processes.

» **Asana:** A project management and team collaboration tool that enables teams to manage tasks, assign responsibilities, and track progress in real time. It has a variety of templates for different types of projects and workflows and integrates with other tools to help streamline workflows across different teams and departments.

Giving and Getting Peer Feedback

Before taking its show on the road, it's wise for a team to rehearse in front of trusted colleagues and, of course, the project manager. You can find lots of good practice tips in Chapter 13. This section focuses on peer feedback, rather than audience feedback (evaluations), which you can find more about in Chapter 12.

When giving peer feedback, describe rather than judge, give concrete examples, speak from observation rather than inference, and specify strengths and weaknesses without nitpicking. Be thorough, be professional, and be respectful.

Although this is less formal than an audience evaluation, it's important to include short- and long-answer questions. Peer feedback may contain any or all of the following (plus anything specific to your team or the presentation):

- **Short-answer questions**
  - Was the opening engaging?
  - Was the content focused?
  - Was there a smooth transition between presenters?
  - Did the slides and/or props add value?
  - Were there appropriate stories to enhance the presentation?
  - Did the presentation end on time and with an enticing call to action?
- **Long-answer questions**
  - What did each team member do well or need to improve?
  - What did the team as a whole do well or need to improve?
  - Were there any actions or behaviors that need tweaking? If so, please list them with suggestions.
  - Are there any other comments or suggestions?

Scenario: Setting the Stage for a Purchase

The following is a hypothetical scenario prepared by Naugle Company. They'll be making a presentation to ABC Corporation hoping to make a sale for an expensive piece of semiconductor equipment.

ABC Corporation representatives met Brooke, VP of Marketing at Naugle Company, at last month's trade show. They discussed some of the issues ABC needs to resolve before purchasing a multimillion-dollar semiconductor vacuum deposition system. The key issue ABC mentioned was lack of support from previous vendors.

Following an exchange, two of ABC's high-level decision makers will be visiting Naugle's facility. Naugle wants the visitors to return to ABC and give a glowing assessment to the person who'll sign the check — reporting that they found

Naugle to be the ideal company (with the right equipment) to accommodate their current and future needs. Here are the cast of characters:

Naugle Company: Hosting team (vendor)

As a result of brief meeting at the trade show, the Naugle team determined the following people need to be present:

Jon: VP Sales

Brooke: VP Marketing

Jesse: Manager of Technical Operations

ABC Corporation: Visiting team (sales prospect)

Rosa: Engineering Manager

Ramesh: Operations Manager

Filling out the Start-Up Brief and preparing handouts

In order to prepare for the presentation, Naugle must learn as much as they can about ABC, including its reputation, company leaders, "pain," level of technology, possible repeat purchases, plans for expansion, and anticipated questions. Naugle wants to show they're the best vendor to solve ABC's problems so that their reps return as heroes having made the right choice. Naugle's team will host an informal presentation and distribute a full-color handout that will include the following:

- Cover sheet with ABC's logo largely displayed. Naugle's logo will be beneath in a smaller size.
- Letter from Naugle's COO welcoming the visitors. It will include what Naugle's team learned about ABC and its fine reputation (flattery) and how Naugle anticipates a long-term partnership (making this a foregone conclusion).
- Testimonials from several of Naugle's high-profile customers, all of which have been pre-approved.
- Biographies of Naugle's top company leaders, highlighting their contributions to the industry, including patents and articles of note.
- Description of the process in words and photos.

TIP

Check out Chapter 10 to learn more about preparing, distributing, and binding handouts.

Storyboarding for this scenario

Jesse, manager of Technical Operations, prepared the storyboard. The following is a first pass, a loosely defined storyboard detailing how Naugle expects the presentation to progress.

Tell	Show
9:00 Informally welcoming our guests and chatting while enjoying coffee and pastries	• Coffee and pastries on table in back of room • Posters positioned strategically around the room, highlighting testimonials from delighted customers ... with key emphasis on the outstanding support we provide during installation and thereafter • Handouts on the conference table for Brooke to distribute before lunch
9:20 (Sit at conference table) **Brooke** (who set up the meeting) will formally introduce our team. **Jon** will say a few welcoming words and invite the visitors to share their concerns and needs. ** A key issue they've had in the past (as we learned at the trade show) is they haven't gotten proper support from previous vendors for this very expensive, complex equipment. <u>We must focus on our outstanding customer support.</u>	<u>Rectangular table arrangement</u> Rosa will sit at the head of the table; Ramesh at the opposite end, facing her. Jon and Brooke will sit on one side in the middle; Jesse will sit on the opposite side, facing them.
10:00 Q&A: Open discussion of how we can help them to solve their problems. **Jon, Brooke, and Jesse** will share stories of how we've helped customers solve these same issues, such as having a senior member of our technical team at their facility during installation in addition to the high levels of ongoing support throughout the period of ownership.	Pointing discreetly to posters highlighting our superior customer support
10:45 **Jesse** takes visitors on tour of application labs to showcase the equipment, the processes, the staff, and answer questions.	Lab tour

(continued)

(continued)

11:45 **Jesse** returns to the conference room with visitors. **Brooke** announces that we've made lunch reservations at The Vista. Before leaving, she distributes the handouts to reinforce their visit.	Distribute handouts
12:15 • During lunch, informal discussions will continue. • Toward the end of the meal, Jon will wrap up with the company's strengths, as they relate to the visitor's problems. • He'll invite them to schedule a return visit and bring samples to run through our process . . . • They'll say they'll get back to us (we expect).	Lunch at The Vista
Debriefing: **Next step:** Brooke will immediately send each visitor a letter with the following. • Thanking for visiting facility. • Asking for their initial impressions. • Learning if there are any further questions or issues we can address. • Telling them we'll call next week to follow up and (hopefully) set up the return visit.	

Making sure the Naugle team focuses on the visitors as the heroes

As discussed in several earlier chapters, make your audience the heroes who bring home the gold — who make a key decision that saves a company large amounts of money or solves a critical problem. In this scenario, the heroes will be ABC's visiting team who finds "gold" in the presentation and recommends Naugle as the leading candidate — or only candidate — to fulfill their needs.

Shaping the scenario with storyopia

Rosa and Ramesh will be heroes for choosing the "right" vendor after the company's had problems with former vendors that have cost them lots of frustration, time, and money.

REMEMBER

Gartner research shows that the number one factor in a prospect making a decision is the quality of the presentation. Pepper your presentation with stories of how you and your product solved the problems of specific customers (clients), making them the heroes when they returned home. These heroes deal with the same problems your audience is looking to solve; these problems are universal. Focus on the value proposition, and they'll imagine themselves returning with the gold. Here are a few tips:

- **Know their obstacles and goals.** Tell stories that focus on slaying their dragons. That's their edge against their competition. Their bottom line. Their gold.
- **Highlight how your company is the solution.** The more compelling you present the prospect's struggle (quest), the more compelling your hero story will be. As you weave the story, show how ABC can overcome obstacles along their road to success. Naugle's part is assisting them along that road.
- **Tie in a success matrix.** Whether success to the prospect means freeing up resources for a new initiative, increasing market share, extending community outreach, reducing energy, reaching a fiscal goal, or whatever, make your story about how a heroes' welcome awaits them at the end of *their* story.
- **Use language about them.** *ABC will be able to . . . What do you think will happen when you . . . Can you imagine . . .* Include the words *profit, safety, commitment, proven, gain, benefit,* and so on.

Rehearsing the choreography

Rehearse as a team so everyone knows where to jump in, what to say, and what to show. Also make sure the sequence works, everyone is sticking to the timing, and transitions are seamless. Your goal is to show that the entire team works cohesively and efficiently on whatever task is before them.

WARNING

Be prepared for a no-show. In the worst-case scenario, a key member of Naugle's team may be unavoidably detained or unable to attend. Have a credible understudy ready to go. Just as in the theatre, the show must go on.

Team members should be able to predict the moves of co-presenters to avoid the awkward stares at each other when someone misses a cue. Have a subtle timekeeper to be sure speakers deliver their content in the time allowed. The presentation must end on time. Brainstorm beforehand what you can omit if you fall behind or get a late start.

Plan the Q&A. Invite ABC guests to ask questions throughout the meeting. This will make them feel as if they're an integral part of the discussion. Hopefully, by the end of the presentation ABC will no longer be a prospect but rather on the road to becoming a valued customer (client).

IN THIS CHAPTER

» Dealing with difficult people

» Handling questions like a pro

» Choosing the right approach when conveying bad news

Chapter 15

On the Spot: Fielding Difficult Questions and Delivering Bad News

A successful [person] is one who can lay a firm foundation with the bricks others have thrown at [them]."

—DAVID BRINKLEY, AMERICAN NEWSCASTER FOR NBC AND ABC

Most audiences will be cheering you on; however, occasionally there'll be a person who'll throw you a curve ball (fortunately, not as harmful as a brick). And on rare occasions, you may have a contrarian in the audience. You know the type. If you put them in a room alone they'd argue with themselves. While it's difficult to deal with cranky people — and thank goodness they're rare — it's important to stay calm, be professional, and never take it personally.

This chapter walks you through dealing with disagreeable people, fielding difficult questions while keeping your cool, and delivering and owning bad news.

Dealing with Grinches

All presenters discover that things don't always go as hoped. Sometimes you'll face tricky questions that catch you off guard. Other times, someone asks antagonistic questions meant to incite contention. And there are occasional grinches out there who are downright sourpusses.

Questioning starts, and "bang, bang" you get shot down by smarty-pants. The obnoxious participant. The know-it-all. The clown. The sniper. They come across with a one-two punch. They become visibly upset and agitated. Don't let that rare person get to you. Here are suggestions for taking the high ground:

- Don't take it personally.
- Don't engage in combat.
- Never respond with sarcasm.
- Maintain control of the questions.
- Stay on topic and don't let the grinch derail your message.
- Answer the question briefly then be quiet. (The tougher the question, the shorter your answer should be.)

Responding to a combative person

Remain the level-headed person in the room. As much as you'd like to say, *Put a sock in it*, these people can often be handled with one or two simple statements:

- *That's very interesting. Thank you for your comment.*
- *Let's discuss this after the session.*
- *We seem to disagree. Let's continue during the break if you'd like.*
- *Perhaps if you wait until the end, you may understand the reason I'm suggesting this.*
- *We do have other questions and more to cover, so we need to move on.*
- *I think we're getting a little off topic here. If there's time, we can revisit this later.*

TIP

When answering, don't look directly at the grinch or they may see your eye contact as an invitation to continue battling. Instead, look at someone on the other side of the room and go on with your presentation.

Defusing tension

Defusing tension is about creating a comfortable environment, finding common ground, and creating a positive atmosphere for everyone. By staying calm, positive, and focused, you can help to create a more relaxed and productive environment. Here are some tips:

- Reiterate your understanding of the questioner's view. *If I understand you right, you feel . . .*
- Find common ground. *We're aligned on much of this. We both think that . . . and . . .*
- Share where you disagree: *This is one place we differ is . . .*
- Explain what has shaped your view: *The reason for my perspective is that . . .*
- Answer with some leading questions such as: *Can you please tell me more about what's driving your question? That's very interesting. Is it this something you've experienced yourself? Is there a specific reason for your concern?*

Fielding Questions

Receiving questions from your audience is a sign that they're interested and engaged. Dead silence isn't what you want, unless you're delivering a sermon in a monastery. Remind yourself that questions expand the presentation and add value.

REMEMBER

Your audience can learn as much from each other as they can learn from you. And it's amazing how much you can learn from them. Some people are uneasy asking questions, so it's important to validate them for taking a social risk in front of the audience. Make eye contact with each questioner and turn your body in that person's direction. Consider prefacing your answers with the following statements:

- *Thank you for asking that.*
- *That's a question I've often asked myself.*
- *I'm asked that a lot.*
- *That question is a good one.*

When you answer a question, incorporate some of the key messages or calls to action. Then end with the following:

- *Did I answer your question?*
- *Is that the answer you were looking for?*
- *Do you need more detail?*
- *Would anyone else like to add to that?*

Deciding when to take questions

At the start of your presentation, make it clear when you'd prefer to have questions: throughout the presentation, at the end of each section, or near the end of the presentation. There are pros and cons to each, but it comes down to your degree of comfort.

Answering questions throughout

Let the audience know at the outset that they're encouraged ask questions or offer comments as you go along. By offering that, your audience won't feel as though they're interrupting you. You can say, *I'm sure you'll have questions or comments as we go along. I look forward to hearing each of them at any time.*

Pros

- You appear more accessible.
- Questions are "in the moment" and relevant to the topic.
- People can jump in as they need clarification or answers.

Cons

- You may get sidetracked and your presentation derails. One way to avoid question overload is to say, *I'll give you the short answer now, and we'll be getting into that later.* Or *That's a good questions, but if you don't mind waiting, we'll be getting to that later.*
- Your presentation can last longer than expected, so you need to be aware of when to put on the brakes and what to cut if needed.

Saving questions until the end of each section

Ask your audience to make a note of questions and comments, and you'll address them after each main point or section. This is a great way to engineer a midcourse correction if needed.

Pro: This is a good compromise between, throughout, and near the end.

Con: You must build in ample time.

Leaving questions until near the end of the presentation

Ask your audience to jot down their questions and save them for the end. When you near the end, announce, *We have about 15 [or however many] minutes left for questions.* As time gets closer to the end, *We have time for two more questions.* If you're presenting virtually, ask them to use the chat function.

Pros

- You won't be interrupted.
- You won't lose your train of thought.
- The session will more likely end on time.
- The audience has more time to gather their thoughts and formulate more detailed and insightful questions.

Cons

- The moment may have passed.
- People forgot what they were going to ask or it now seems irrelevant.
- Some people need to leave close to the end of the session. (Once someone gets up to leave, others follow.)

WARNING

Never wait until the very end to ask for questions — wait until near the end. If you wait until the end and someone makes a downbeat comment or asks a negative question, your session will end on a sour note. You always want to have the last word with a strong assertion of your main message and call to action.

Handling difficult questions

START-UP BRIEF

You can't anticipate every question you'll be asked, but if you fill out the Start-Up Brief in Chapter 3, you'll have prepared a list of probable questions. If you think many people will have the same question, deal with it right up front. *I know many of you may be asking (or wondering) why...* Let them know that by the end of the talk you hope you'll have given them the answer(s).

Here are some ways to answer the outlying questions:

- **Prepare a go-to message that focuses on the overriding theme of your presentation.** For example, if you're delivering a status report, your go-to message may be, *Remember that we're still on schedule and on budget.*
- **Pivot your answer back to your key message: What you want your audience to do, think, feel, or learn.** It may feel like repetition to you, but if you say it in a different way, your audience won't feel your answer is repetitive. If you think of a story, all the better. If a question is off-topic or not relevant to your presentation, you can answer if there's time or you can politely redirect the conversation back to your key message.
- **Actively listen to the whole question before you answer.** You don't have to answer each question immediately. As you see in Figure 15-1, stop briefly and think about the best way to answer it.

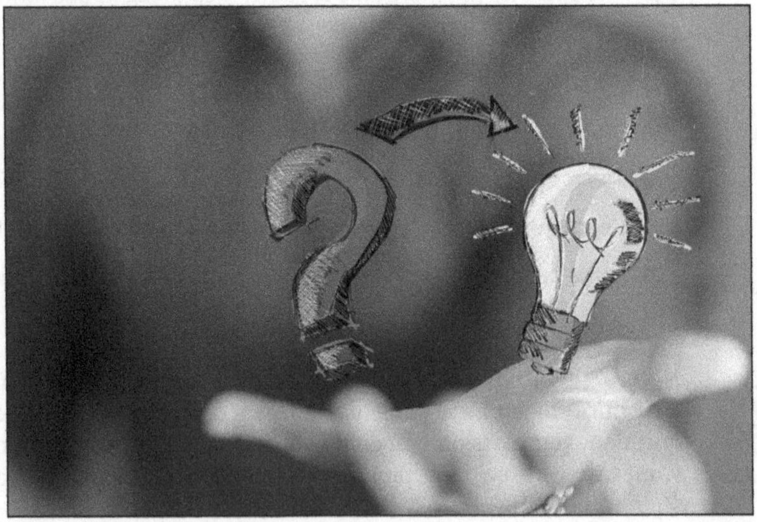

FIGURE 15-1: Stop briefly and think about the best way to answer.

vegefox.com / Adobe Stock

Not having the answer

Nobody has all the answers, and you're not expected to. Never try to fake it. Your audience can detect if you are, and you'll lose all creditability. If you can't answer a question, be forthright. This does *not* undermine you; it adds to your credibility and humanity.

Here are a few things to try:

- Be authentic with what you do know.
- Listen for the underlying question.
- State that you're not sure, and tell the audience when you'll have the information, where you're going to get it, and when you'll send it. *I don't have that information right now, but I'll email you an answer within the next day or two.*
- Defer the question by saying, *That's a very good question. Can anyone respond to that?*

REMEMBER

But most of all, stay in control of the narrative. Don't linger on areas you're unsure of. Give a short, clear answer and get back to your comfort zone.

Delivering and Owning Bad News

All leaders — whether they lead nations, corporations, departments, or projects — must sometimes deliver less-than-rosy news. Yes, it's uncomfortable. Yes, you may get pushback. What matters most is the way you handle the situation and yourself.

Owning the news

Take responsibility for the news, even if you didn't personally cause the situation. Provide your audience with insight, understanding, transparency, accountability, and empathy. Let them know you're in control of the situation.

- If the news is unexpected, make a bad news sandwich.
- If the rumor mill has been active, deal with the issue head-on ASAP.

Making a bad news sandwich

If you're not familiar with the sandwich approach, it works like this:

1. **Start with a soft slice of bread.**

   This means starting the presentation with genuine empathy, a compliment, or a positive statement.

2. **Pack the middle with the meat (the actual bad news).**

   Use a transitional word such as *regrettably* or *unfortunately* to address the "meat" of the matter.

3. **Close with a soft slice of bread.**

   Offer something positive or encouraging.

Using a direct approach

There's an element of gossip in every company. While light office gossip and a few comments here and there aren't harmful, a pervasive culture of rumor-mongering and trash-talking is detrimental to everyone. Bad news spreads quickly. Delivering bad news is never easy, but it's especially hard when you're a manager or team leader. This is every leader's least favorite task, but it's often a necessary one.

Is the company shutting down? Are you facing drastic budget cuts? Will you be announcing layoffs? Will headquarters be relocating to another part of the country? Are you revealing that one member of the group is getting a coveted promotion when you know others felt it should have gone to them?

Delivering bad news is a daunting job, but with careful planning you can soften the blow. Pay special attention to timing. It's best to deliver bad news as soon as possible. Colin Powell, U.S. Army General, politician, and statesman, said, "Bad news isn't wine. It doesn't improve with age. Sometimes you just need to do it."

- **Put yourself in their shoes.** Imagine how you'd feel if you were in their place and how you'd react. What are they losing as a result of the news? Use your understanding of their perspective to shape your talk.
- **Rehearse what you'll say.** Deliver this news (appearing to be) unscripted so you come across credible and sincere. Don't drown your audience in a sea of endless numbers and data dumps. Present the news in terms of critical takeaways. No slides. No notes. No jokes. Just you.

- **Stay calm.** This is often easier said than done, especially if the news is unexpected. Speak at a steady pace and make eye contact every few seconds or so. Don't lower your voice at the end of each sentence or you'll sound unsure of yourself.
- **Be honest and authentic.** Don't skirt the topic. Don't give false hope. Don't sugarcoat. Don't overly explain. Define what happened without blaming anyone or anything. And never say words like, *This all happened because* . . . or, *We knew this would happen eventually* . . . You'll earn points by taking charge and being forthright.
- **Don't talk corporate.** This isn't the time to use disguised, thick, insensitive jargon. Avoid talking about company policies or ideals. It makes you seem insensitive and far removed from the news. It also makes people feel like they are just a small piece in the corporate puzzle and are powerless to control their future, which in many cases they are.
- **Show you care.** Be sympathetic. Be understanding. Listeners might be angry, but it's your job to be calm. And be sure to turn your cell phone off so you won't be interrupted.
- **Allow ample time for venting.** Everyone has a different coping mechanism, and not everyone can take bad news calmly. Some people may get emotional. Some may show anger. Whatever the emotions, let people voice their feelings. Make yourself available to listen. Validate the emotions of your audience by repeating words or phrases they use. For example, if someone shouts, "I'm angry!" try to show that you understand by saying, "I understand you're angry, and you have every right to be."

STORYOPIA ARCHIVES: BEING HONEST — ALWAYS

Back in 1982, newscasts announced that seven people had died within minutes after swallowing Tylenol Extra-Strength pain relievers. This quickly became known as the Tylenol Murders, and panic spread quickly. Jerry Della Femina, then advertising mogul, was even quoted in the *New York Times* as saying he didn't think that Johnson & Johnson would ever be able to sell another product under that name." He was wrong!

The chairman of J&J at the time, James Burke, didn't wait for answers to the *why* or *how*. He didn't wait for an investigation. He responded swiftly and authoritatively, jumping out in front of the situation. His priorities were to protect consumers while saving the

(continued)

(continued)

product. Burke immediately stopped production and ordered that all remaining Tylenol Extra-Strength pain relievers be taken off the market immediately. J&J established communication channels with the Chicago Police Department, the FBI, and the FDA. Burke publicly offered the following:

- Counseling and financial assistance to families of the victims
- Exchanging other Tylenol products already in people's homes
- A reward leading to the arrest of the person or people who perpetrated this crime

Although the perp was never identified, this resulted in the FDA establishing tamper-proof guidelines for consumer products — an initiative undertaken by J&J. This immediate action by Burke redeemed the company, and it went on to be stronger than ever.

Lesson learned: Own the situation even if you didn't cause it. Honesty *is* the best policy.

Looking ahead when delivering bad news

I've heard it said that having a problem is like being stuck in a long, dark tunnel. The only way out is to go through it. And when you get out of the tunnel, look forward and plan for the road ahead. That's sagely advice in our personal lives and in business.

REMEMBER

Regardless of which approach you use to deliver bad news — sandwich or direct — end on a positive note giving your audience some hope and reassurance. Follow this basic plan when delivering bad news:

» Describe your plan.

» Explain what measures will be taken.

» State how this may be avoided in the future.

STORYOPIA ARCHIVES: PRESENTING A HOPEFUL FUTURE

Denise, a financial planner, needed to dispel the fears of her high-worth investors during a prolonged bear market. She wanted to speak to them personally, so she sponsored a series of breakfast meetings titled "Looking Ahead." (Feed them, and they will come.)

Denise's demeanor was very positive and upbeat. She told her audience how she's shifting some of their assets into "safer" investments. She prepared two powerful slides. Each one depicted the last two prolonged bear markets, showing how each time the markets rebounded. Her strong message was this: There's every reason to believe the markets will rebound this time as well. Her presentation was followed by a lengthy Q&A session, and everyone left the room slightly more optimistic (and with fuller stomachs).

Lesson learned: When delivering bad news, try to present a more hopeful future. Everyone likes an optimist.

IN THIS CHAPTER

» Giving the audience a giggle

» Practicing your punch lines

» Sneaking in some humor on a slide

» Handling the silence if your comedy falls flat

Chapter 16

Adding a Splash of Humor

A sense of humor cushions the potholes in the road of life.

—FRANK TYGER, AMERICAN CARTOONIST

Why do you think classic sitcoms are still streaming and in worldwide demand? It's because their short, humorous episodic plots are relatable. They showcase creative and amusing solutions to problems that mirror everyday life. They have people we identify with, and it's comforting to "see ourselves" on the screen. It makes us feel like our lives are more exciting. Through humor there are lessons to be learned because laughter is the best medicine.

Also think of comic strips. They've remained widespread ever since "The Yellow Kid" appeared in the *Hearst New York American* in 1896. The genre continued to grow because people of all ages have an insatiable appetite for humor. In both sitcoms and comics, there's enjoyment for everyone. Humor is a no-cost, easy way to soothe ourselves and fill the potholes in the roads of our lives.

This chapter helps you reflect on your audience, sidestep inappropriate humor, take cues from your audience, and avoid getting flustered if no one laughs. (I added splashes of lightness to the section headings in keeping with the spirit of this chapter.)

Invigorating a "Bored" Room

When you make audiences laugh — even chuckle — you've gotten into their minds. You've made a connection. You've jettisoned yawns. You don't have to be the king or queen of comedy to invigorate your presentation. When used *judiciously* (the key word), here are some of the things humor can do:

- Make the presentation more memorable
- Break the ice
- Illustrate and emphasize key points
- Reduce tension
- Foster a positive atmosphere
- Create a bond that brings people together
- Make the problem-solving process more enjoyable

Giving a Little Giggle

I've heard many people say, *I can't add humor. I'm just not funny.* Your audience isn't expecting to attend a comedy club, and they know you're not a stand-up comedian. Your role is to make them do, think, feel, or learn something new so they leave having new insights. There are loads of humorous situations — many from your own life — that can make the call to action more meaningful and memorable to provide those insights.

Adding a little giggle to your presentations isn't hard. Like most things, it takes a little understanding of how to do it, a willingness to try, and a little practice. You don't need side-splitting humor. If you can get your audience to laugh, chuckle, or smile, you're golden.

TIP

Check out Chapter 6 to help you recall such memorable moments. Think in terms of humor, ironies, metaphors, analogies, quotes, visuals, and memorable quips — not necessarily jokes.

Some things are universally funny (and this is subjective): TV sitcoms. Movies. Books. Comedians. Comic strips. Jokes and puns. Irony and satire. Observational everyday events. Parodies. Wordplay. Embarrassing situations. Unexpected outcomes.

SHERYL SAYS

When I first started presenting, I didn't add any humor to my sessions. I was too nervous to deviate from my "script." As time went on, I started adding a light-hearted story here and there. Then I became gutsy enough to open with a humorous slide that made the audience chuckle as they walked in. Over time, including humor became easier and more comfortable.

Mark Twain has been quoted as saying, "There are two types of speakers: Those who get nervous and those who are liars." I proudly admit to being the former! And if you check out Chapter 23, you'll see a list of well-known celebs such as Elvis Presley, Barbra Streisand, Katy Perry, and many others who also admit to nervousness before each performance.

Sliding in Lightheartedly

Let your audience know even before they even meet you that you have a sense of humor. Project a lighthearted slide they'll see as they're walking through the door — a slide that will make them titter and put them at ease. The slide signals that the session will undoubtedly be enjoyable.

Take a peek at Figure 5-1 in Chapter 5. That's a slide I project on the screen as the audience is walking into my Storytelling & Storyboarding workshop. If you don't want to look back, it's one of Jerry Seinfeld's famous quotes:

> *According to most studies, people's number one fear is public speaking. Death is number two. Does that sound right? This means to the average person, if you go to a funeral, you're better off in the casket than doing the eulogy.*

People chuckle. They relate to that thought, which brings an immediate connection between them and me . . . even before the session begins.

Show humorous slides (in moderation) during the presentation when they fit into the flow of your topic. For example, Figures 16-1 and 16-2 are clipart slides that can add whimsy at just the right times. Occasional clipart is fun, but don't overdo it.

REMEMBER

If you're using clipart or other graphics, learn if they're in the public domain. If they're not, either get written permission or pay for the right to use them.

FIGURE 16-1: Is this you? Harried? Always putting out fires?

shockfactor.de / Adobe Stock

FIGURE 16-2: Do you ever feel like a puppet and everyone is pulling your strings?

nuvolanevicata / Adobe Stock

Fashioning a Funny File

You don't have to go chuckle hunting to bag humor. You can find it in the most mundane and unexpected situations. It's important to appreciate these moments and find joy in the little things in life.

SHERYL SAYS

I find it helpful to capture these moments as they occur by speaking into my iPhone and noting them in my "funny file." When I need an amusing incident for a presentation, I have loads to choose from on a wide variety of topics. Your funny file could be a physical or digital file where you store things that happened to you or others. You've probably encountered situations that weren't funny at the time but were funny when you retold them. Think back to some of those situations. Perhaps you've experienced something similar to the following situations:

- You drove around a parking lot for what seemed like hours trying to find a parking space. Then you gave up, parked a mile away, and discovered (while walking back) that several spaces had opened up right near the store.
- Perry accidentally spilled coffee on himself during a job interview, leading to a comical exchange with the interviewer.
- Fran accidentally sent an intimate text message to the boss that was meant for their significant other.
- You rushed to get dressed, left the house, and someone at the meeting noticed you had on two different shoes.

These are the types of stories you can weave into a talk. They're humorous because things like this have happened to everyone (perhaps not the mismatched shoes). Also capture in your funny file cartoons, memes, entertaining images, or anything else that tickles your funny bone. As Jerry Seinfeld said, "The fact is, almost everything is funny. You just have to have a way of looking at it."

Popping Out a Prop

Consider introducing a whimsical prop as a memorable way to illustrate a point, add levity to a heavy subject, create a touch of entertainment, suggest a bigger picture, bring shock value, contribute subtext, or help the audience to better connect with the message.

Having trouble thinking of one? How about an oversized, outlandish, or unexpected item. It could be a jumbo watering can for an agricultural presentation, a colossal-sized pencil for a writing workshop, or a briefcase full of fake money for a financial planning seminar. Possibilities are limitless with a little imagination

STORYOPIA ARCHIVES: LETTING YOUR IMAGINATION RUN WILD

I attended a presentation given by a guy who sells promotional products for companies to distribute as brand recognition with their name and logo. Items ranged from funky (rubber chickens, custom bobbleheads, and whoopee cushions) to serious (tote bags, T-shirts, and mugs). After everyone was seated, the presenter walked into the room wearing a multi-colored beanie with a whirling propeller on top. He stood there briefly without saying a word and let his propeller spin. It was hilarious! He made lots of sales that morning.

That gave me the idea of a witty prop for a grant-writing workshop I was scheduled to present. I went online and ordered a "gag" check that was 30 inches wide. I filled in the amount of $250,000.00 but left the payee line blank. To open the presentation I showed the check and pointed to where the payee's name would be written. I said, *"This is where your name could go."* They imagined their names being written in as grant recipients — the heroes who brought home the gold. I had their full attention!

Lesson learned: If something humorous may add value to your presentation, check the Internet and let your creativity flow.

and the Internet. Think of what may be relevant for your audience, your topic, and your personality. Make sure your prop is easy to show and relate to. Don't be shy about being creative.

WARNING

Humorous props aren't appropriate for every type of presentation. They wouldn't work for somber topics because they may come across as flippant. Executives want executive briefings to be just that, "brief." And at formal presentations, visual aids may be better served with something more serious such as graphs and charts that send the message. The key is to use good judgment.

Ferreting Out Punchlines or Quotes

Instead of (or in addition to) elaborate stories, consider using short punchlines or intriguing, humorous quotes. You can find many by researching your topic such as, "salespeople quotes" or "legal quotes" as two examples.

- There are also websites specifically for finding quotes, such as BrainyQuote, Wikiquote, Quotery, QuotesLyfe, and Goodreads Quotes. Search by keywords or author's name.

- Use Twitter to search for hashtags related to your topic and scroll through tweets to find relevant punchlines or quotes.
- On Pinterest you can search for boards or pins related to the topic and browse through related images and quotes.

When in Hesitation, Skip the Citation

In other words, "When in doubt, leave it out." It's better to omit something if you're unsure how the audience will receive it.

START-UP BRIEF

This is where the Start-Up Brief in Chapter 3 is key to find out all you can about the demographics of your audience. For example, millennials may respond to humor about pop culture — baby boomers, perhaps not so much. Humor about tax ledgers won't work well if your audience has no clue about accounting.

Understanding the demographics can help to tailor your humor to make it relatable and engaging while ensuring that it's appropriate for the audience. Humor can be a powerful tool in communication, but you should always use it with mindfulness and an awareness of the audience's preferences and sensitivities.

WARNING

Avoid anything that has to do with sarcasm, sex, politics, race, nationalities, religions, genders, abilities, and wars. There's more:

- Don't talk about a local sports team unless everyone in the room is from the same geographic region.
- Be aware of humor with multinational groups that may be insulting to others.
- Don't go off on a tangent about a story that doesn't relate to your topic. It will be perceived as a waste of time. Humor is a vast garden with lots of flowerbeds to select from. Pick carefully.

It's critical to use humor very thoughtfully and in a way that's relevant to the topic and audience. Inappropriate or offensive humor can backfire and have a negative impact.

STORYOPIA ARCHIVES: PAYING A STEEP PRICE

After 20 years, Thomas left the rigors of the corporate world to become a motivational speaker, enjoying the flexibility his new consulting career afforded him. He was a jolly sort with a contagious laugh and sense of humor. During one presentation before a large audience, Thomas was asked a particularly challenging question. To relieve the tension, he responded with humor about a particular ethnic group. Thomas assumed his humor was okay because he was a member of that ethnicity, as were other members of the audience. His remarks were *not* okay. After the presentation, several members of the audience complained to the event's organizers, and they in turn complained to Thomas's booking agency. Those remarks ended Thomas's speaking career. The agency never again booked him.

Lesson learned: Inappropriate humor is risky and can have long-term consequences, which can harm your reputation and credibility. Thomas paid a steep price for his error in judgment!

What to Do if Your Audience Left Their Funny Bones at Home

You're giving an important presentation. At a key point in your talk, you add a splash of humor — and no one laughs. What can you do? What you shouldn't do is let the audience control your emotions. It doesn't matter whether they laugh; you're not there to be a comedian. You're there to change the way they do, think, feel or learn something. What you should do is be prepared for no one to laugh. If they do laugh, it's a bonus.

Throughout your presentation, pay attention to your audience's verbal and non-verbal cues. When you use humor, are they engaged, chuckling, or laughing? Are they staring at you blankly? If you hear laughter or giggles, it's a good sign that your humor is landing.

If you don't get the response you'd hoped for, perhaps the humor was funny to you but not to others. Perhaps you blew the delivery. Perhaps your audience left their funny bones home. If humor is an important part of your presentation, try testing it out beforehand with friends or colleagues to get a sense of what works and what doesn't. No matter — ignore the lack of laughter and move on, or take a rejoinder from stand-up comedians:

Hmm? My mother loved that story.

Okay, I'll scratch that one off my list.

Trying 30 Days of Chuckling

You know the expression, "April showers bring May flowers." Did you know that April also brings National Humor Month? That's no joke! And it's no coincidence that it starts on April Fool's Day.

This celebration was founded in 1976 by humorist and author Larry Wilde, director of the Carmel Institute of Humor in Carmel, CA. Its intent is to highlight the importance of humor in our everyday lives and to heighten public awareness of the therapeutic value of humor. In line with that, here are some fun ways to celebrate — and you don't have to limit yourself to April:

- Share a funny joke or story with someone you know.
- Attend a comedy club or watch a hilarious movie.
- Read an amusing book or cheerful article.
- Put jellybeans in your cereal.
- Hang out with friends who make you laugh.

REMEMBER

Laughter is a natural stress reliever that has many health benefits. It can improve relationships and help connect you with others. Laughter is a great way to bring a sense of joy and lightheartedness to all our lives, even in difficult times.

IN THIS CHAPTER

» Addressing a diverse group

» Taking your presentations abroad

» Converting accurately for non-U.S. audiences

» Blending your message for multiple generations

» Understanding how accessibility impacts your presentations

Chapter 17

Vive la Différence: Diversity and Inclusion

Diversity is all about us and about us having to figure out how to walk through this world together.

— JACQUELINE WOODSON, AMERICAN AUTHOR

Walking through a diverse world together means recognizing and respecting the differences among people and communities and working towards a more inclusive and equitable society for all. It means appreciating that diversity is a strength. When we seek out opportunities to learn from and celebrate various cultures and backgrounds, we find greater fulfillment both personally and professionally.

Many people think that diversity refers to different genders, ethnicities, and racial backgrounds. While this is true, there's much more. True diversity includes people of different religions, ages, cultures, sexual orientations, languages, educational backgrounds, skills, and abilities. A diverse workforce isn't a fad; it's here to stay. Diverse companies benefit from a greater range of talents and worldviews.

In 2019 McKinsey & Company, a global management consulting firm, found that the most diverse companies outperform their less diverse peers by a 36 percent profitability. There are several reasons for this:

- The wider range of perspectives and experiences can lead to better problem-solving and more innovative ideas.
- Diverse companies are more likely to understand and represent the needs and preferences of a diverse customer/client base.
- A diverse workforce can mitigate biases to promote inclusion, leading to greater employee satisfaction, retention, and productivity.

This chapter discusses how, with a little savvy, you can promote clear communication, build trust, open horizons, strengthen relationships, avoid embarrassment, and yield tangible results each time you present.

Presenting Skillfully to a Diverse Audience

When you stop to think about it, every audience is diverse. At the basic level, each person is different in their interests, how they learn, what motivates them, and so much more. The question becomes in what ways is your audience diverse?

START-UP BRIEF

Filling out the Start-Up Brief in Chapter 3 helps you understand who they are. Chances are your audience will be a mixture of interests, ages, ethnicities, and abilities, as you see in Figure 17-1, so find out as much as you can about them.

FIGURE 17-1: Faces of today's workforce.

Andrey Popov / Adobe Stock

Don't lose sight of the fact that there's diversity from region to region in the United States as well as from country to country. Some regions are known for being more liberal or conservative, while others may have distinct dialects or cuisine. Regions also differ in terms of climate, geography, and natural resources. These differences can have significant implications for issues such as economic development, social policy, healthcare, and more.

Even in countries where English is the primary language there are different spellings and expressions. For example, Americans take elevators; Britons take lifts. Americans have neighbors; Britons have neighbours. A friend of mine from London was on a cruise many years ago. She met a guy who offered to take her to breakfast the following morning. *That's wonderful,* she said, *Come to my cabin in the morning and knock me up.* The guy's face lit up. Her reference was a phrase that meant "knock on my door in the morning." However, to Americans "knocking someone up" has a very different connotation. (Oops!)

Speaking with clarity

Although you should follow these tips regardless of the composition of your audience, when speaking to a diverse audience you don't want to distract from the harmony, clarity, and impact of your presentation. Modulate your pace. Pronounce words clearly. Break sentences into short, definable sections giving your audience time to translate and digest what you say. If someone has an accent that's difficult to understand, ask them to please repeat their comment slowly, letting them know that what they have to say is important.

TIP

Here's how you can speak with more clarity:

- Avoid technical terms and acronyms unless they're needed. For example, when you fill out the Start-Up Brief you may find that your audience isn't from a single industry, so you may need to include a few explanations.
- Ask open-ended questions that don't require a *yes* or *no* answer. (In some cultures, it's impolite to answer *no.*)
- Avoid sentences with double negatives. (*I didn't say that I don't disagree with you.*)
- Be patient and try to follow ideas which may be different from yours.
- When someone does or says something that seems peculiar or wrong, give that person the benefit of the doubt. Ask yourself: *How else could I interpret these words or actions?*
- Avoid slangs and idioms. So if you think you'll *pass with flying colors*, you might *be in hot water*.
- Never use words or comments that may be offensive to anyone.

Paying attention to your body language

There remains a controversy over whether there's a universal body language. Some researchers have identified universal emotions such as happiness, sadness, surprise, fear, disgust, and anger to be universal. Others argue that those are cultural.

Suffice it to say that cultures use gestures in different ways. Some cultures are quite animated, stand closely, appreciate eye contact, exaggerate hand gestures, and openly express emotions. Others are just the opposite. Even a gesture as natural as pointing at something is considered rude and crude in some societies.

For example, some Asian audiences may close their eyes during a presentation. If you notice that happening, you're not putting them to sleep. They're concentrating on what you're saying. And they're not likely to interrupt with a question, even if prompted to do so. They may reply with a *maybe* or *yes* when they mean an outright *no* because they don't want to be too blunt. Know your audience and their customs beforehand.

Being content sensitive

Don't assume that people from different regions are familiar with your national, state, or local news, sports, or trends. If it's important to your content to include something local, provide context and an explanation. Also, avoid issues of politics, religion, sexual identities, and war. Be mindful not to offend, anger, or embarrass anyone — even yourself.

Pronouncing names correctly

Many people with difficult-to-pronounce names appreciate being asked the correct pronunciation. If you come across a name you can't pronounce, be straightforward and ask. *I want to make sure I say your name correctly. Would you please pronounce it for me so I can learn to say it properly?* People will appreciate your taking the time to get it right. Once you hear the name, repeat it, and write it down phonetically. Some people have simplified their names with nicknames and will say, *You can call me [nickname].*

WARNING

Never create a nickname for a person whose name you can't pronounce. It's rude and can be seen as disrespectful and dismissive of their culture and identity. It sends the message that their name isn't worth the effort to learn and pronounce correctly. In the extreme, it can be construed as form of *microaggression*, which is a subtle but harmful act of discrimination or offense toward a marginalized group.

Presenting in a Foreign Country

Learn all you can about the culture and customs of your host country. While you're there, you're essentially an ambassador for your country. One important thing you can do is study some key words to show respect for your audience and their language. Here are a few for starters: *Hello, please, you're welcome, thank you, goodbye, it's nice to be here.* (*Where's the restroom*? is also helpful.)

TIP

Use your smartphone to learn how to pronounce words in almost every foreign language. Even though your pronunciation may not be perfect, your audience will appreciate the effort.

STORYOPIA ARCHIVES: UNDERSTANDING YOUR AUDIENCE IN ANOTHER COUNTRY

Lorena was making a month-long tour to many European and Asian countries to train engineers on the use of a new piece of equipment her company developed and was marketing. She was the lead person on the development team; therefore, she was the most logical one to showcase the equipment worldwide.

Throughout Lorena's visits to the various countries, engineers asked many questions. They were eager to learn all they could while Lorena was at their facility. Then Lorena visited her last stop: Japan. During and after her training sessions, no one asked questions. "Excellent," she proudly thought, "I've become very thorough." After she returned to her office in the States, problems with the Japanese use of the equipment kept surfacing. "They didn't ask any questions," she recalled and wondered why there was any confusion. Lorena spoke with one of her colleagues whose family is from Japan. She learned why.

Part of the Japanese culture is not to question. As children, they're taught that asking questions of an elder challenges the elder's authority. That deference to authority continues throughout their working years (even when the person in charge isn't elderly). Japanese people are often ambiguous when answering questions. It's a way to maintain harmony and prevent loss of face. Therefore, presenters must be carefully attuned to their body language, which speaks for them. Lorena should have spoken with her Japanese colleague before her speaking engagement, so she would have understood the culture and knew how to recognize their body language.

Lesson learned: Learn all you can about your audience beforehand. This includes customs and cultures when presenting abroad.

Never underestimate the importance of preparation, including running something by a native speaker or checking the Internet for a translation. It doesn't take much to get a translation wrong and give a mistaken impression. Following are two well-broadcasted examples where a little a little extra preparation would have made a huge difference:

- *Ich bin ein Berliner* (*I am a Berliner*) was the opening of a speech given by President Kennedy in West Berlin in 1963 during the Cold War. It was one of the most famous speeches of the Cold War and won Kennedy much admiration among the German people. However, there was some controversy over his words. Apparently a "Berliner" is a type of pastry similar to a jelly donut. So some people heard Kennedy say *I am a jelly doughnut.* Regardless, his speech was memorable and appreciated by the German people.
- When Hillary Clinton was Secretary of State, during the Obama administration, she presented the Russians with a bright red button that, when pressed, called out *Peregruzka.* It was intended to call out "Reset," meaning a resetting of U.S.-Russian relations. The only thing redder than the button was Hillary's face when it was brought to her attention that *Peregruzka* means "overwork" or "burden." (Egad!)

Knowing Conversions

The United States differs from the rest of the world when using weights and measurements (metrics), temperatures (Celsius), dates (day before month), money (commas not periods), time (24-hour clock), etc.

Conversions are important when you're preparing slides or handouts or referring to weights, measurements, temperatures, and such. For example, you may be discussing water savings and would use the term *gallons*, which is your frame of reference. For a complete understanding by an international audience, write the liter equivalent in parentheses: 5,000 U.S. liquid gallons (18,927.06 liters). During your narrative, consider writing relevant conversions on a whiteboard or flipchart.

Storytelling Across Multiple Generations

Storytelling has the power to transcend generations. Many cultures have used oral folktales to pass on knowledge and values from one generation to the next. Additionally, stories can traverse thousands of miles and define the social constructs of a culture and its people. A well-told story can carry rich emotions and feelings that connect people and build relationships. It can educate, entertain, and connect people across time and place.

Today's business environment is enriched by its diversity. We have the most diverse workforce in history, and stereotypical differences between generations are exaggerated, overstated, blown out of proportion and whatever hyperbole you've heard touted. Multiple generations blend their backgrounds and talents. Vive la différence and la similarités.

The following sections help you look through a demographic lens to understand similarities and differences — always keeping in mind that audiences are people, not generations.

Being non-judgmental

Never judge people from other generations. Similarities abound. Older generations are staying in the workforce longer because of economic reasons or because they still have much to contribute. They have much in common with the younger generations. They jog. They bike. They practice yoga. They're vegetarians and vegans. And they embrace new technology with gusto.

Having said that, similarities may vary depending on specific cultural, social, and historical contexts in which each generation grew up. Each generation may manifest these similarities in unique ways that reflect their own values, beliefs, and attitudes.

Understanding generational dynamics

In presentations, it's wise to be aware of the subtleties between Baby boomers, Gen X, Millennials, and Gen Z so you can shape your stories accordingly. Each generation has own unique characteristic, ideas, and history that impact their expectations and understandings.

Here are some common descriptions of the various groups you may encounter:

- **Baby boomers** (1946–1964) grew up during the Vietnam War, the Civil Rights Movement, and the emergence of the counterculture. They're independent, competitive, resourceful, and value relationships. They work long hours and expect the younger generations to do the same.
- **Gen X** (1965–1980) grew up as latchkey kids with both parents working. They witnessed the *Challenger* space shuttle disaster and the fall of the Berlin Wall. They want to be included in decision-making processes so they can flex their acute problem-solving skills.

» **Millennials** (1981–1996) were raised by "helicopter parents" who hovered over them. They tend to be fickle and expect a work environment that gives them a sense of purpose and aligns with their values. They multitask on tablets and smartphones and embrace new gadgets.

» **Gen Z** (1997–2012) have been hard hit by Covid-19 with much higher rates of anxiety, decreased work hours, and the need for financial help. Work-life balance and personal well-being are very important. They want paid time off, the ability to take a mental health day, and a healthy work culture that encourages a sense of family and community.

These generalizations don't apply to everyone, but you should always be mindful of selecting age-neutral stories that all generations can relate to. This can include health and well-being, career development, history, technology, privacy and security, volunteering, finances, the environment, and more.

SHERYL SAYS

I didn't list the Traditionalists (also known as the Silent Generation [1925-1945]) because their numbers are diminishing rapidly in the workplace. However, they're responsible for developing today's space program, creating vaccines for many diseases, and laying the foundation for today's technological environment. They're considered the most loyal generation, and many remained with one company for their entire careers.

Blending the generations creates a rich exchange of ideas

What happens when you put multiple generations in one room? You're blending perspectives and a rich exchange of ideas. Each generation brings its unique experiences and viewpoints. By blending generationally diverse perspectives, it is possible to come up with new, innovative ideas that might not have surfaced otherwise.

Consider brainstorming, mentorship programs, team-building activities, training and development, open forums, and more. Try new things and novel approaches. When you seek out fresh topics with passion and incorporate some multigenerational strategies, your audience — regardless of their ages — will be tuned in and turned on.

Accessibility for All

Accessible for all is the practice of making information, activities, and/or environments sensible, meaningful, and usable for as many people as possible. When you consider accessibility, you need to ensure that everyone, regardless of their ability, can get the same (or nearly the same) experiences and interactions.

Making accommodations

With just a few preparations, you can help ensure your presentation caters to people at all levels. A little thoughtful planning on your part ensures that anyone who needs accommodations can fully participate and remain engaged. Here are some factors to consider:

- **Reserve seating:** During sign up, learn if there's anyone who needs special accommodations. If you can't learn that information and you're facilitating a large conference, put a few "Reserved Seat" signs up front for the people who have a visual or hearing impairment. That way, there's no need to make announcements that draw unwanted attention to anyone.
- **Lighting:** Many presenters darken the room, especially when showing loads of slides, but a darkened room isn't the best environment for anyone. You don't need to have someone trip over a backpack if they need to step out for an unscheduled break. Reduce the number of slides and increase the lighting.
- **Wheelchairs:** If your presentation is open to the public, be prepared for the possibility that someone may arrive in a wheelchair. Allocate a spot for a wheelchair ahead of time so you don't find yourself removing or rearranging chairs on the spot and embarrassing that person. Keep aisles unobstructed and wide enough for a wheelchair to pass through. And remember, a wheelchair is the person's personal space. Don't lean on it and don't push it unless asked.
- **Service dogs:** Don't talk to the dog or try to pet or feed it. The dog isn't a pet, and you don't want to distract it from doing its job.
- **Interpreters:** In the event you need an interpreter or transcriptionist, don't be distracted by their presence. Talk to the audience as you normally would. Keep pacing to a minimum and don't read from the screen.
- **Computer-assisted real-time translation (CART):** This is basically live captioning speech-to-text. It will be helpful for people with difficulties understanding regional dialects, accents, or unfamiliar vocabulary, as well as for people with hearing difficulties. Several software programs have built-in technology. If yours doesn't, consider vendors such as Rev, Verbit, Descript, TranscriptMe, and others you can find online.

WARNING

In a large room, don't assume everyone can see or hear you. Perhaps the acoustics are poor, there's background noise, people are too far away, or there are other reasons. At the beginning of your presentation ask, *Is there anyone who can't see or hear me?* If necessary, allow people to move before you get underway.

Delivering your presentation

When you deliver a presentation, you want all attendees to get the maximum benefit. Having good presentation skills and a sound presentation will take care of many issues, but there are a number of ways you can improve your environment to include everyone in the room.

- » Get the audience involved with memorable, engaging stories.
- » Use Accessibility Checker that comes with your presentation app to spot and fix issues. Most of the popular apps come with them. Examples may be low color contrast between text and background, issues with auditory components, and so on.
- » Provide multiple ways to learn such as lectures, discussion groups, Q&A, hands-on activities, and handouts.
- » Use captions when showing videos. If they're not available, speak key content such as the title, content, and credits. Share a summary of the video's content before you present it.
- » Use color combinations that are high contrast and can be distinguished by those who are colorblind, such as avoiding red and green.
- » Summarize key points.
- » Repeat questions so people who didn't hear them clearly can have clarity.

IN THIS CHAPTER

» Inviting attendees

» Getting camera ready

» Being inclusive and following best practices

» Offering interaction and substantive follow-up

Chapter 18
Journeying from In-Person to Virtual

Virtual presentations are about being engaging and telling a story, not just conveying information.

—NANCY DUARTE, SPEAKER AND AUTHOR

Journeying from in-person to virtual doesn't need to feel as if you're metamorphosing from working a room to speaking into a black hole. Although the experiences are different, if you're a good in-person presenter, you can easily transfer your skills to a virtual format. For example, being able to communicate clearly and confidently, engaging your audience, showing a sense of humor, and adapting to unexpected circumstances are all skills needed to present, regardless of the format.

In addition to leveraging your existing skills, there are many resources and tools to help you tailor your presentation style and content to suit the virtual format. This includes virtual whiteboards, slide sharing, break-out rooms, collaboration tools, and more.

This chapter covers several components to making virtual learning engrossing and long-lasting. It includes best practices: sending invitations and pre-work, getting screen ready, delivering synchronous sessions, being inclusive, following up, and more.

Storytelling to the Rescue

One key element of a good virtual presentation (or any presentation) is getting your audience's attention and keeping it. Great storytelling will forge that connection so you and your presentations are impactful, engaging, and unforgettable. Here's are some reasons storytelling can help you "work the screen" and create a connection with the audience:

- Captures and holds their attention
- Makes them feel they're part of the narrative
- Connects with their pain
- Links the key message and the theme of the presentation
- Increases the overall impact
- Remains memorable long after the event

Include visual stories so your audience can connect with and understand complex emotions and ideas in a way a narrative alone may not always accomplish. Just as with in-person presentations, visual storytelling creates a more immersive and memorable experience, leading to higher levels of engagement and retention. Visuals can include photos, videos, diagrams, props, virtual reality, augmented reality, and more.

WARNING

Don't go overboard with stories. Use them sparingly and make sure they're the right ones to stay with your audience after the presentation is over. People still shudder when they're required to facilitate or attend a virtual session. They think of the many webinars they endured where the facilitator babbled on and flashed one slide after another. It was much like the wizard in *The Wizard of Oz* — a talking head behind the screen. (When you think of it, many of these presenters were talking heads, boring audiences with slidezillas, when they presented in person.)

SHERYL SAYS

STORYOPIA ARCHIVES: FINDING REAL SOLUTIONS FOR VIRTUAL CHALLENGES

Having done in-person facilitation throughout my career, I needed to think of ways to make my sessions relevant via videoconferencing during the pandemic: I faced several challenges and found solutions that worked:

Challenge: Reducing each workshop from six hours to two hours. That's the maximum length of time you can expect to keep people's attention no matter how engaging you are.

Solution: Reorganizing, repackaging, discarding, and focusing on critical pieces of content to maintain a high level of engagement.

Challenge: Making each workshop interactive with lots of activities. Adding visual and narrative stories that added value within the limited timeframe.

Solution: Inviting everyone to actively participate by asking questions and encouraging them to share their own stories. I paid close attention to their body language, called on people, and created many activities for them to work on so they weren't just looking at the screen or checking their phones.

Lesson learned: Unleash your imagination and resourcefulness to successfully navigate obstacles and emerge triumphantly.

This chapter shares many additional ways I made videoconferencing work for me. I hope you can use some of these tips to make it work for you.

Getting to Know You

Offering a sneak peek of yourself and your presentation can generate excitement and interest before audiences walk into the virtual room. It offers a personal touch and helps you tailor your presentation to better meet their needs and expectations.

Sending electronic invites and follow-ups

The first touchpoint you may have with your audience is through an electronic invitation. This is your opportunity to make a positive impression and stimulate interest.

Following are some tips for electronic ivites and follow ups:

» Include a registration form. Mention that the session will be participatory, and encourage them to start thinking of their own stories as they relate to the topic. Send links to your social media sites, a promotional video teaser trailer, newsletter, blog, or bio. Include a questionnaire asking what they hope to do, think, feel, or learn from the session.

REMEMBER

It is also important to ask attendees to specify any accessibility needs so you can make accommodations beforehand. This may include closed-captioning, transcripts, options for font size and color contrast, and so on.

- Follow up immediately to confirm people's registration and include login instructions. If applicable, send pre-work (detailed in the next section).
- Send two reminders before the event — each with a different, distinct message (teaser perhaps). Send one a week in advance reminding them the event is just a week away. Send another the day before telling them you look forward to seeing them on [date]. Include the login instructions once again.

Sending pre-work

An advanced packet creates interest, gets the audience to a certain level of readiness, and helps you establish a connection with them. Pre-work can contain any or all of the following:

- **The agenda:** It's important for people to have a roadmap before they attend. They can prepare for the session or opt out if it doesn't suit their needs.
- **Something to read, listen to, or watch:** This can be a case study, article, podcast, video, blog, or anything else relevant to the topic. Give participants a series of questions you want them to answer and return to you. These can be questions about their experience as it relates to the topic, questions they may want answered during the presentation, or anything else important to them.
- **Workbook:** If you're conducting a training session, a workbook lets participants know the event will be interactive, and they won't be merely sitting there listening to you and watching slidezillas. Ask them to print the workbook out in advance, so they won't have to toggle between screens during the session. Instruct them to wait until the session to fill in any of the information.
- **Your bio:** The audience won't want to spend the first several minutes of their time listening to your personal pitch. Even if you sent a bio with your initial evite, this will refresh their memories. (Check out Chapter 11 on how to write a stellar bio.)

Being Ready for Your Close-Up

Nothing kills a virtual presentation faster than a presenter who fumbles with the technology, has poor lighting or sound quality, displays an inappropriate background, or wears eyeglasses that shine in audiences' eyes. Do a dry run. This is a performance, so make sure you know how to make it work.

What do people see when they view you on the screen? Do they see the puffy bags under your eyes? Do your glasses look like solar bursts? Are your facial wrinkles magnified? Is your neck sagging? No, you don't need Botox and turtlenecks in the blazing heat of summer.

Try these quick fixes to improve your screen appearance so you'll be ready for *your* close-up:

- **Camera:** Many laptops have built-in cameras that suck in low light. They're super-wide-angle cameras that capture more of your background than you. Consider using an external webcam that connects to your computer or smartphone via a USB cable. (Logitech is the most popular brand.) The quality can be a step up from a built-in camera.

  Place the camera at eye level and look directly into it when you're speaking. Have the camera frame your face, neck, and shoulders. People are drawn to faces, so you don't want to lose that connection by being too far away. You also don't want your face to take over the whole screen so you appear to be a dismembered head. Practice your positioning beforehand.
- **Eye contact:** Look at the camera, not at the screen; otherwise, you won't be looking at your audience. Also try to place the camera at eye level rather than above or below your face.
- **Lighting:** To prevent screen glare, don't place lighting behind you because it will shine directly on the screen. The best location is either resting on or mounted just above your desk on the same side as any paperwork you may be using. Also, overhead lights and desk lamps work best with LED bulbs.
- **Glasses:** To avoid glaring lenses, lower your chin slightly but still make eye-level contact with the camera. You can also lift the earpieces a notch to increase the angle of the lenses to the light source. (Computer screens emit a blue light which can cause eye strain and be damaging to your eyes. There's an anti-reflective coating you can apply to your glasses. Or check out eyeglass manufacturers who tout new non-glare technology to help protect your eyes.)
- **Sound:** Make sure your sound emits clearly and isn't garbled, or people will tune out. Practice with the same technical configurations and location that you will use for your presentation. If possible, plug your computer directly into your modem using an Ethernet cable. This will give you the strongest signal and the most stable Internet connection.
- **Dress:** Avoid stripes, herringbone patterns, animal prints, very bright colors, and accessories that jingle. Choose clothes that you're comfortable in and would wear to an in-person presentation.
- **Hair:** Choose a hairstyle that will keep the hair out of your face, so you avoid casting shadows. This will also help minimize fidgeting and playing with your hair, which is distracting.

SHERYL SAYS

I'm part of a poetry workshop and wrote this poem after seeing all my "flaws" during a Zoom workshop. The title is a line delivered by Gloria Swanson in the closing scene of the 1950 movie *Sunset Boulevard.* I hope this poem will give you a giggle.

[Not] Ready for My Close-Up Mr. DeMille

It's weird to watch myself on Zoom
peering back across the room.

Is this really what people see
when on Zoom, they look at me?

Staring at me in the eye
wrinkles seem to multiply.

My eyes sport swollen, puffy bags
and oh my neck, once taut, now sags.

Touch up my appearance is supposed to fix
but it didn't work. Oh fiddlesticks!

I tip my head, yet glasses glare
beholding people's nasal hair.

Maybe Botox is the only cure
How much more can I endure?

Can't wait 'til we meet face to face
and end this ghastly Zoom debase.

Creating seated energy

One big difference between in-person and virtual is that you're sitting down rather than standing up and walking around the room. When we sit and speak, we have to **consciously convey energy and enthusiasm**. Here are a few approaches to creating seated energy:

- Make use of your facial expressions. Smile. Make eye contact.
- Use natural (not exaggerated) hand gestures to emphasize key points.
- Sit straight to convey confidence and alertness.
- Let your tone of voice convey excitement and passion.

Energy is contagious. When you create a stimulating virtual session by infusing excitement into your content and delivery, you'll energize your audience.

Being ready with an understudy

Every professional performer has an understudy, and you should too. Your understudy would be a co-host (also called producer or moderator) to assist you with the technology so that you can focus on your presentation. The co-host can have the same privileges as you (the host) and can be a backup should your Internet connection be lost. Here are some additional things co-hosts can: admit guests, share multimedia, mute or unmute the audio, manage breakout sessions, start and end recordings, and more. Basically, the co-host can perform any task you assign them.

Choosing a background

Most videoconferencing apps let you select virtual backgrounds from an existing library (as you see in Figure 18-1) or upload your own. This can be a fun way to add variety to your meetings and disguise a distracting or unprofessional background.

If you're meeting with upper-level management, consider a strictly professional background of a bookcase, open cabinet or other office-like pieces of furniture. If you're meeting with co-worker, let your background reflect who you are professionally and personally. For example, if you're a golfer and have your clubs in view, you'll build rapport with other golfers. Backgrounds are easy to change, so you can pick one that works for each occasion.

FIGURE 18-1: Using a virtual background means no one sees the dishes piled up in the sink behind you.

Krakenimages.com / Adobe Stock

Creating a Culture of Inclusivity

Running inclusive meetings isn't just about technology, it's about the authentic involvement of all participants. Most of us make a common mistake when we set up a large meeting and assume that all attendees will be able to participate fully. However, there may be attendees who have difficulty seeing, hearing, working a mouse, or having other issues that prevent them from fully taking part.

Many apps today are building products that include screen readers, magnifiers, high contrast mode, keyboard shortcuts, relay service, and more. For example, captions are a lifeline for people who having hearing impairment, people whose English is a second language, or anyone who has to turn off the audio because of a noisy background.

WARNING

If you're using captioning, be very aware of the text that appears on the screen. I'm part of a Patient Advisory Council for my health care consortium. We had a videoconference and the captioning was on. One of the doctors said, "It's important to keep our patients on track." The caption on the screen read, "It's important to keep our patients on crack." (OMG!) If a faux pas like that happens to you, you can ignore it hoping nobody noticed. Or you can say, *Let's backtrack for a moment because I need to make a correction. The text didn't reflect what I actually said.*

Zoom and Microsoft Teams are considered the most accessible apps. Accessibility features for real-time accessibility are in the early days, and there's still a lot to learn. However, apps are continually pushing out new updates and features.

REMEMBER

Following is a checklist of things to consider so you have no (or the least limiting) barriers for people to join a videoconference:

- Has the software been tested by people with different types of abilities?
- Is there real-time automated captioning?
- Does it allow for ALS interpreters?
- Are there keyboard shortcuts?
- Does it have the platform for chats, notes, Q&A — are they accessible?
- Does it allow for computer- and phone-based audio listening and speaking?
- Is there a relay service enabling real-time participation through a communication assistant?
- Are the interfaces customizable?

Conducting an Interactive (Synchronous) Presentation

A *synchronous* presentation is where the presenter and audience are engaged in real time, typically via videoconferencing or livestreaming. (Think of the term *in sync.*) This allows for interaction and dialogue between the presenter and audience. Gather the audience for a virtual session that will last between one and two hours. Attention spans wane rapidly after two hours. Ask your audience to unmute their speakers so the session can be truly interactive, as if they were in the same room. (Suggest, however, that they mute their speakers during the time they may have a distracting noise in their background.)

Knowing the maximum number of participants

The maximum number of people for a synchronous presentation may vary depending on the platform, Internet bandwidth, or hardware limitations. Some platforms may have a maximum number of participants for a synchronous presentation, which could be anywhere from a few dozen to hundreds or even thousands of people. It's best to check with the specific platform or service being used for more information on their limitations for synchronous presentations.

Finding ways to be interactive

Here are ways to make your session interactive to promote engagement and retention:

- **Share stories to make your audience heroes.** Check Chapter 4 for more on how you can create stories with audience heroes.
- **Present relevant visuals.** This can be slides, videos, props, or anything else that adds to the narrative.
- **Incorporate questions.** Let everyone know your preference for answering questions: before, during, or near the end.

- **Incorporate participatory activities.** People aren't wired to sit in front of their computers staring at a screen. They're wired to use their fingers. Rather than having them use their fingers to multitask (such as checking their phones), have them use their fingers to stay on task with activities.
- **Call on people by name.** Calling on someone can be as simple as saying, *[Name] would you please share [xxx].* This keeps participants alert and engaged because they don't know when they'll be called on.
- **Use humor.** Include humorous stories and anecdotes that relate to the topic. Serious points can be driven home with humor. (Use humor with sensitivity as outlined in Chapter 16.)
- **Use *you, your,* and *we.*** Words such as these will help each participant establish a personalized experience.
- **Allow for plenty of pauses.** Use pauses for emphasis to give the audience a moment to digest certain pieces of information.
- **Use transitions.** Transitions will add continuity to your message and carry the participant from one point to the next. For example, *Now let's take a look at . . . .*
- **Include a call to action at the end.** Stress exactly want you want the audience to do, think, feel, or learn.

REMEMBER

Make your presentation relevant across localities. You may have an audience joining from different parts of the country or world. Remember there are 24 times zones, and your mornings may be the evenings of others. Also, refrain from geographic references such as the *East Coast or on the West Coast.* Instead, be specific: *New York* or *California.*

Being Savvy On Screen

Sorry, go ahead, I didn't mean to interrupt you, two people say after interrupting each other, only to start speaking again at the same time. Then there's a 30-second cold war silence. The following tips are meant to help you have on-screen etiquette to avoid awkward interactions.

Dos:

- Find a quiet space without barking dogs or crying babies. (If either occurs, press mute so others won't hear the noise.)
- Test your technology well in advance.

- Arrive 5-10 minutes early.
- Dress as you would for an in-person meeting (at least from the waist up).
- Have all your materials organized and at hand.
- Use proper lighting.
- Use a professional-looking background.
- Maintain eye contact.
- Follow the ground rules for participant interaction.

Taboos:

- Don't smoke, eat, or slurp your drink.
- Don't multitask, in other words, don't check email, play Wordle, or engage in other activities.
- Don't talk over someone else. Wait for your turn or use the chat function.

STORYOPIA ARCHIVES: SHOWING YOUR FACE DURING AN ONLINE SLIDE PRESENTATION

I attended a two-hour Zoom session one evening and thought I'd been transported into the Land of Oz. There were two sequential presenters. Each kept their slide presentations on the full screen. I never saw either of their faces. During the interactive discussions of each segment, I felt as if I were talking to the Wizard of Oz — the man behind the screen. This led to lack of engagement, diminished connection with participants, and difficulty building trust.

Lesson learned: Keep your slides to a minimum and stop sharing the screen when you're not referencing a slide. Let participants see your face. When you are showing a slide, use the presenter view (or mode) so participants can see you.

Following Up with Your Audience

You may have just finished a fantastic presentation and are breathing a sigh of relief that it's all over. Your presentation needn't end the moment you step off the virtual stage. Follow-up is critical to reinforce your key issue(s).

- At the end of the presentation, ask the audience for suggestions about what they think should/may happen next to keep the momentum going.
- If you promised the audience any materials, send them out right away.
- Send an evaluation form as close to the presentation as possible. (Check out Chapter 12 for more information.)
- Follow up with a thank-you note, survey, or questionnaire.
- Set up peer-to-peer coaching where you pair up participants and give them an assignment to complete and/or a follow up.
- Ask managers to monitor progress or changes they notice.

REMEMBER

Great feedback will result from the following: Participants weren't bored because you had a strong opening and closing, an energetic style, comfort with technology, an interactive approach, and a desire to connect with them personally. They left with the feeling that the virtual session was just as rewarding and engaging as an in-person session would have been.

5

Specialized Presentations

IN THIS PART . . .

Structure a training session or workshop, include pertinent activities, do a needs assessment, understand the difference between soft and hard skills, accommodate varied learning styles, choose your words carefully, understand how AI plays into training, and evaluate success.

Fine tune an executive briefing so you nail it each time, abide by the 10/30 rule, and deliver executive sales briefings to seal the deal.

Craft your message for a conference, captivate the audience, check out the room beforehand, and network, network, network.

Nip and tuck someone else's presentation, make it your own with stories, amend the slides, and remove the elephant in the room (which may be you, the stand-in).

IN THIS CHAPTER

» Knowing the difference between *train* and *work*

» Using a Training Needs Assessment (TNA)

» Designing your session

» Gauging your success

Chapter 19
Structuring a Training Session or Workshop

I put myself in the student's place and remember the frustrations, doubts, determination, and desires I felt going through the initial learning process.

—TED MARTINEZ, BASEBALL ATHLETE

Think of the last time you challenged yourself to learn something new. A tough course. A foreign language. A sports activity. Remember the frustrations you may have felt. The oopses you may have made. It's all too easy to forget what it's like when you're trying to learn something. Put yourself in your learners' places to better understand the challenges they may be facing so you can provide them with the support and confidence they need to be successful.

SHERYL SAYS

The words *training, workshop, lecture, seminar, tutorial, simulation*, and others are often used interchangeably. To keep it simple, I'll use the word *sessions* in most instances.

This chapter delves into the value of a training needs assessment (TNA), understanding the differences between hard and soft skills, organizing and personalizing a session, plugging in an ROI, and understanding how artificial intelligence (AI) is impacting and will continue to impact training.

Understanding Your Audience and Making Them Heroes

Have you ever heard someone say they dread going to a mandatory training session? When asked why, they generally tell you they're expected to sit and listen to a boring speaker and watch a seemingly endless slide presentation. They forget everything they heard or learned shortly thereafter because their minds had gone numb. If you don't understand your audience, and if the session isn't structured to meet their needs, boredom and low retention will result.

START-UP BRIEF

It takes understanding your audience, purpose, key issue, and questions your audience will need answered. To do this, fill out the Start-Up Brief found in Chapter 3. It also takes preparing stories and a storyboard. Stories add elements that will be the basis for preparing a session so that it's relevant, productive, and memorable. Your learners will leave your session as heroes, bringing back to their companies what they've learned that may make them more productive or save time and money.

Edgar Dale, internationally known for his theory relating learning and memory retention, said:

> We remember:
>
> 10% of what we read
>
> 20% of what we hear
>
> 30% of what we see
>
> 50% of what we see and hear
>
> 70% of what we discuss with others
>
> 80% of what we personally experience

STORYOPIA ARCHIVES: KNOWING THE BEST METHOD OF DELIVERY AND CREATING HEROES

Betsy is a nurse unit manager in a large metropolitan hospital. The hospital received a new, complicated piece of equipment, and Betsy was tasked with training the staff on its use. Each person receiving the training would have to pass a proficiency test to be certified. Betsy prepared a slew of slides showing different parts of the equipment and was going to talk about each part as she presented the slide. She took much of her information from the instruction manual that came with the equipment.

Betsy signed up for the Storytelling and Storyboarding session to validate her approach. I asked Betsy why she was doing a slide presentation instead of taking people into the room where the equipment is housed. Her answer was: *Everyone uses slides for presentations. It's expected.*

Long story short: During the workshop Betsy prepared a storyboard outlining what she needed to teach. She realized that training would be more memorable and realistic if she took small groups into the room for hands-on learning. That's what Betsy did. She explained how to use the equipment and each person got a chance to participate. She generated a few stories about how other facilities benefited from the equipment's efficiency. She didn't show a single slide because she didn't need any. Each person passed the certifying test — first try! Betsy was a hero and she made each of her participants into heroes!

Lesson learned: Don't just resort to a slide presentation. Understand the best method to reach your audience for what they need to do, think, feel, or learn.

Performing a Training Needs Assessment (TNA)

TNA is the process companies use to identify performance requirements, skill gaps, and knowledge needed to make them and the company successful. It involves evaluating competencies, skills, and knowledge levels, then comparing those levels to the requirements and goals of the company. Its aim is to determine if there's a need for training. If so, considerations include: What type of training is needed? Who needs it? When is it needed? Who's best to facilitate it?

The responsibility for performing a TNA can vary depending on the company's internal structure. It can be the HR department, managers, or an external training needs analyst (which you can find online).

Here are some steps in a TNA:

1. Determining the purpose and objectives of the assessment
2. Identifying the target audience
3. Deciding on the types of data that should be collected (surveys, focus groups, interviews, questionnaires, observation, examining work, and/or competitive analysis)
4. Collecting and analyzing the data to identify knowledge, skills, and performance gaps
5. Prioritizing training needs based on the identified gaps
6. Developing and implementing a plan
7. Finding the expert to deliver the training
8. Evaluating the effectiveness of the session

REMEMBER

Training isn't always the panacea for poor performance issues. Training is often treated like a kitchen junk drawer that accumulates miscellaneous items that nobody wants to take the time to sort through. So they keep piling things up in the drawer. There's a false notion at many companies that when in doubt, you should train. They pile one useless training session on top of another. TNA can prevent that waste of time and resources.

Determining areas where hard and soft skill training may be needed

Before scheduling a session, identify the specific areas where employees may need improvement in both hard and soft skills. This will ensure that the session is relevant, effective, and aligned with the specific needs of the employee and the company.

Assessing hard skills

Hard skills are those needed for a person to perform a job successfully. They're specific, quantifiable, and clearly defined. Hard skills are typically listed on job postings and descriptions and show whether a person is fit for a specific position. These skills are acquired through formal education, training programs, apprenticeships, or on-the-job training. They may include (but aren't limited to):

- Computer skills
- Management skills
- User-interface design
- Project management
- Foreign language
- Accounting and bookkeeping
- Graphic design
- Business analysis
- Sales and marketing
- Specific equipment

Assessing soft skills

Soft skills are social skills that shape how we think, operate, work, and interact with each other. They're subjective in that they can't easily be measured. Soft skills are vital for career growth and promotions, maintaining a healthy work environment, and a future that will never be automated. Approaches used are self-assessment, peer feedback, and behavioral observations (often by managers).

Some people come by these skills naturally — others need to learn them. Soft skills may include (but aren't limited to):

- Written and verbal communication
- Teamwork
- Leadership
- Problem-solving
- Time management
- Adaptability
- Interpersonal skills
- Work ethic
- Listening
- Critical thinking
- Attention to detail

Getting a ROI

Simply put, ROI is an economic indicator used to track the effectiveness of training and measure its value. It's not about how happy learners were with the session; it's a financial metric that outlines the benefits relative to the cost of training. Measuring ROI can also help organizations optimize their training budgets and make informed decisions about which programs and employees to invest in.

Companies have different ways of calculating the ROI, but here are several factors that come into play:

Observational assessment:

- Assess the content and knowledge of the facilitator
- Use of learners' knowledge or skills following the session
- Completion of tasks following the session
- Use of procedures and regulations
- How teamwork, customer services, conflict resolution, etc. have improved
- Employee satisfaction, engagement, retention, or turnover

Business impact assessment:

- Training costs
- Sales data (market share, new accounts, etc.)
- Churn rates
- Customer service satisfaction
- Productivity and output

SHERYL SAYS

As a corporate training consultant, I know that my skills and content are part of the financial metric. From my perspective, however, I focus on the ROI of my clients, not just from a business impact assessment, but from an observational assessment. By learning how my programs are faring, I understand what is and isn't working in order to continuously improve my techniques and skills. And, to be honest, to get more gigs!

STORYOPIA ARCHIVES: SPENDING TRAINING DOLLARS WISELY

I was working with a large organization that was reaching the end of its fiscal year. Fred, the CEO, realized that several departments had a lot of training and development dollars that hadn't been used. The money couldn't be rolled over to the following year, so Fred decided to cram lots of training into one very busy month.

This organization had a group of employees who weren't performing up to expectations. The knee-jerk reaction was to throw the training dollars into soft skills for these employees. These people were skilled technically, so poor performance could have been for a number of reasons: lack of delegation, poor planning or communication, inadequate skills of managers, or a host of other reasons.

The TNA, however, determined that Leslie, the manager of this group was a good technician but lacked strong managerial skills. The company sent Leslie for extensive management training (a hard skill). Thereafter, the morale and productivity of the group improved dramatically. Employees were happier. Productivity spiraled upward. That turned out to be dollars well spent, and the company yielded a high ROI. Leslie became a hero, and the department's needs were satisfied!

Lesson learned: Use a TNA to better understand how to spend your training dollars wisely.

Arranging and Organizing Your Session

If your session is a half day or a few hours, try to schedule it first thing in the morning when people are most alert and haven't been distracted by other tasks and other people. The least productive time is immediately after lunch (from 1pm to 3pm). In the afternoon, you risk people not showing up because they may be involved in meetings (and such) and/or they're anxious to get home and don't attend.

REMEMBER

If an organization is hosting the session, they'll generally take care of the basics. If not, as facilitator, all or part of the following may be your responsibility:

- Selecting the venue
- Checking for computer access and/or hookups
- Making sure there's accommodations for people with special needs
- Providing food and refreshments
- Preparing name tags, name tents, and printed handouts

» Providing white boards and/or flip charts

» Arranging the room with tables and chairs

» Sending invitations, reminders, and post-evaluations

Personalizing the session

Personalizing a session can have numerous benefits, such as improving engagement and retention of information, increasing motivation, and catering to individual needs and preferences — creating a more targeted and relevant learning experience for each learner. Here are a few suggestions for customizing the experience:

» Craft relatable stories to help them empathize with the characters and the character's experiences. Relatability helps learners see themselves or their own experiences reflected in the story. This can create a sense of validation and understanding.

» Clearly communicate the benefits and how the session will help them improve their skills and achieve their goals.

» Offer feedback and coaching throughout the session to help them see their progress.

» Follow up after the session to assess outcomes. This will help you to continuously polish your session.

STORYOPIA ARCHIVES: PERSONALIZING EVERY PRESENTATION

Prior to presenting my business/technical writing session, I send each person an email asking them to respond with two or three of their writing challenges and what they hope to learn from the session. I arrive early and notate their comments on a flip chart, putting names next to their inputs. Most of the needs are the same from one group to the next, including:

- I have trouble getting started.
- I'm too long winded.
- Most of my emails don't get results.
- I need to grab my readers' attention.

- Occasionally, there's an outlier with a very specific need. If I can, I incorporate a solution into the session. If not, I'll let that person know that we can chat during the break and/or I'll provide references.

I tape the pages of the flip chart to walls around the room so I can see them. During the session, when I finish each of the Six Steps, I refer to the pages and say: *[Name] do you think [what we just covered] will help you to satisfy [the challenge]?* This personalizes the program and makes each participant feel the session was designed just for them. Many people add to the evaluation forms that they felt the session was highly individualized.

I also ask them to bring to the session a document they need to write or one they've written and may need to use again. In essence, they're following a step-by-step process, each preparing different documents relevant to their jobs. One of the activities, after they're written their drafts, is dividing them into small groups to critique each other's writing. Even though they're all there to learn, there are lots of things they already know that add value to others, and they incorporate some of what they learned earlier in the day. For instance, I have a unit on creating very descriptive headlines. That's one of the things they focus on to help each other. During that time, I'm walking around to each group sharing my thoughts on their writing.

Lesson learned: Personalize every presentation as much as possible so every person in the audience thinks you're talking directly to them.

Incorporating engaging activities

If your group is small (10 to 30 people), provide hands-on experiences in pairs or small groups as you see in Figure 19-1. When you start an activity, punctuate it with the benefit they'll learn. Here are some ideas, none of which take more than ten minutes:

- **Buzz groups:** Divide people into small teams and ask them a relevant question. Have each team come up with solutions, discussing the pros and cons.
- **Brainstorming:** This is done quickly. Someone serves as the scribe recording top-of-mind ideas. All ideas are welcome. No one is judged. This is useful to understanding alternative viewpoints.
- **Presentations:** Ask a group to design a brief presentation with one person designated to share it with the group.
- **Case studies:** This offers the value of real-life, relatable examples. It infuses problem solving, analytical thinking, decision making in complex situations, as well as managing ambiguities. Have them come up with suitable outcomes.

- **Roleplay:** This is typically done in groups of three. Two participants play specific roles (such as host Q&A, host and guest style) and the third person observes and critiques. Then they rotate roles until each person observes and critiques. If you have an even number of people, create groups of two, and the rest of the group can observe and critique.

Engaging activities can have several benefits: increasing retention, improving motivation and participation, enhancing the overall learning experience, adding enjoyment. When people are engaged it requires them to think critically, solve problems, and apply their knowledge in practical ways.

FIGURE 19-1: Working at tables in small groups.

Andrey Popov / Adobe Stock

STORYOPIA ARCHIVES: GETTING A CONTACT NUMBER

Early in my training career, I was asked to facilitate a workshop at a very prestigious university. Pat, the organizer, told me she wouldn't be there but assured me everything would be set up by the custodian the night before. I arrived an hour early — which I learned is important for a number of reasons. There was a large table in the middle of the room, but not a chair or custodian in sight. I started going through adjacent rooms; fortunately, they weren't locked. I dragged into my room two chairs from one room, three chairs from another, and so on. Also, there was no computer, as was promised. So it's good I brought my laptop. By the time the workshop started, I was achy and stressed (to say the least). I didn't have to call Pat, but I did have her number in case I'd needed it.

Lesson learned: Always get a number to call in case anything slips through the cracks. I have had to use those numbers on a couple of occasions.

Mining Session-Related Stories

Training and workshop sessions provide fertile ground for storytelling, and a good story is one of many tools in a facilitator's arsenal for an immersive learning experience. For example, the session may be about the common goal of corporate social responsibility and ways others have given back to the community. Stories help the audience create that common goal, a sense of community, and thoughts of how they can participate.

The following sections help you develop the journey by understanding why people attend certain sessions and tapping into past successes and botches.

Understanding why people attend

Remember that people attend sessions for a variety of reasons. Some are there voluntarily because they believe they have something of value to learn or because of your great reputation as a facilitator. Others attend because the session is mandatory and their arms were twisted. Still others need a certain number of credit hours and your program just happens to fit into their schedule.

Whatever their reason, when you make stories relatable to the learner's real-life workplace experiences, you can foster attitudinal change, simplify a complex topic, and convert an abstract concept into something concrete. You can also help the audience relate to the consequences of their choices to influence future actions and drive a desired action or outcome. One story example may be how someone in a prior session (on the same topic) applied the learning and received kudos from their manager. Or didn't apply it and regretted it.

Tapping into past victories and flubs

The best stories are the ones you've personally experienced or heard from others — both negative and positive. They can describe a journey to success, people who helped along the way, and when the wrong decision spelled disaster. These descriptions show your vulnerability and humanity. (Check out Chapter 4 to find out how to morph experiences into stories.)

Think of prior sessions (or individual learners) that may trigger stories with positive and negative outcomes. Stories can relate to any of the following:

- Time saved or lost
- Stronger collaboration/relationships

- Increased productivity
- Decreased turnover
- Improved work environment
- Developed leadership
- Reduced waste
- Stronger brand recognition
- Greater customer satisfaction
- Mastered technology or equipment
- Awarded the funding

Crafting a Storyopia Journey

Crafting a storyopia journey for a session is like baking a cake. If you don't get the core ingredients right, it doesn't matter how delish the frosting is. The journey on which you take your audience is a delicate balance of sharing just enough of what makes your story relevant and relatable, but not sharing so much so that the audience feels you're delivering an impromptu therapy session.

Including characters, settings, conflicts and resolutions

Many facilitators have the tendency to share every detail, turning a short story into a tome. The key is to be succinct. Here are some thoughts to structuring your story:

- **Character:** When the character, rather than the setting is of key importance, start with the character, rather than the setting (as mentioned in previous chapters). Ultimately, the main character moves toward the goals through work, discipline, and the ability to overcome obstacles (or not). The characters can be learners who attended other sessions, their managers and how they reacted to the learner's new-found knowledge, or anything else that's motivating. You may start your story with, *Let me share a story of how [fictitious name] completed this session and . . .*
- **Setting:** The setting can be the training facility, conference room, board room, factory floor, manufacturing plant, or any place the story unfolds.

- **Conflict:** Unfold the problems, roadblocks, struggles, setbacks, or challenges and how the character progressed against these odds. Incorporate the people, tools, skills, and processes that helped the character along the journey to success or failure. Either outcome provides a learning experience.
- **Resolution:** This is an opportunity to learn. What was the turning point that determined success or the realization there was a problem or miscalculation? Did the story ends in success or failure?

Sharing a cautionary story

If you're sharing a cautionary story, consider reversing the order and starting with the resolution — what wasn't achieved. Here's an example: Chavi's team was launching a new product. With a tight deadline looming, Chavi issued the directive to move forward without properly testing the product. Although the people working on the project were reluctant, they obeyed Chavi's directive. The launch was a complete disaster. There were constant complaints from customers, and they lost many. The company's reputation was tarnished, and Chavi was demoted.

Once you've gotten their attention, backtrack. A cautionary story can be a valuable lesson learned.

Accommodating Different Learning Styles

Learning styles and preferences vary among people, and not all people fit neatly into one category but are a composite of two or more. Generally speaking, these, are the most common types of learners:

- **Visual (or spatial) learners** garner information from pictures, diagrams, charts, and more. They don't necessarily respond well to photos or videos.
- **Auditory learners** learn better when the subject matter is reinforced by sound such as lectures or discussion groups.
- **Kinesthetic (tactile) learners** process information through experiencing or doing. They learn best through personal experience, practice, examples, and simulations.
- **Reading and writing learners** consume information through the written word, whether they write it or read it. They do best with written quizzes and written assignments.

REMEMBER

Although everyone has a unique learning style, what's common to all adult learners is they want to learn new skills, acquire new information, and improve personal and professional competence. You have the best chance of awakening motivation for people with all learning styles when you combine a mixed-learning approach. Each session should include practice, variety, and reinforcement.

TIP

When you want to show how easy something is to learn or take the fear out of something that's difficult, your choice of words can make all the difference:

- *So advanced, it's actually simple*
- *No complex commands to memorize*
- *Practically runs itself*
- *A streamlined approach to . . .*
- *Takes the tedium out of . . .*

Evaluating the Success of Your Session

Each session must be evaluated so the company knows how and where to spend its dollars. Evaluators can be the learners themselves, managers, project team leaders, other stakeholders, or even the organization that sponsored the session. Here are some things that go into the evaluation, which is typically part of the TNA:

- Was it necessary?
- Were the participants well chosen?
- Was the facilitator well chosen?
- Were the materials relevant?
- Did the session result in continuous improvement?
- Was there a high ROI?

There are many ways to conduct evaluations. This may include pre-and post surveys to measure the learners' knowledge before and after the training. This can provide valuable insights into the effectiveness of the session in achieving the desired results.

Other assessments may formal and informal on-the-job feedback from peers, managers, or focus groups. This may include the reaction and satisfaction of trainees, implementation, usage and retention, business impact, and ROI. (Check out Chapter 12 for suggestions on preparing evaluation forms.)

TIP

If you're interested in a formal evaluation, there are many on the market you can find online. The following are popular methods listen in alphabetical order:

Anderson's Value of Learning Model

Brinkerhoff's Success Case Method

The CIPP Evaluation Method

Kirkpatrick's Four Levels

The Learning Transfer Evaluation Model (LTEM)

The Phillips ROI Model

TIP

If you don't already subscribe to *Training* magazine's online and hard copy versions, get your free subscription at `https://trainingmag.com`. This 50+-year-old publication continues to be the premier resource in all areas of learning and development. Here's why this publication is a wise investment in your time:

- Stay current on trends and technologies
- Access expert advice from industry experts
- Join the platform for social learning and networking to exchange ideas among global learning professionals

And the publication accepts articles of interest, so you can submit valuable content and (if your article is accepted) see your name in print and become a noted knowledge source. It's great fodder for your bio.

Training, AI, and the Big Bang

The world is undergoing an information Big Bang called Artificial Intelligence (AI). Just as the Big Bang explains how the universe began with a massive explosion and expansion, AI has emerged as a massive explosion and expansion of capabilities, applications transforming and reshaping the world in unprecedented ways.

AI is the ability of computer systems to simulate and perform tasks that are commonly associated with human intelligence. This includes speech recognition, understanding natural language, computer vision, learning, decision-making . . . and that's just the beginning. In simple terms, AI is somewhat like a chatbox on high-octane and steroids combined.

Understanding how AI is reshaping training

Some information about AI is fact, some is fiction, and some is inspired by fiction. Although in its infancy, AI has the potential to shake up corporate training and learning. For starters, here's some of the reshaping AI already offers:

- Personalizing learning experiences by tailoring training to a learner's needs and preferences.
- Offering adaptive learning by testing test a learner's existing knowledge and adapting the learner's journey to fit their needs for pace, depth, and breadth of learning.
- Creating engaging gamified learning experiences that can motivate learners to absorb and retain knowledge in an enjoyable way.
- Integrating with existing training systems to provide recommendations on the best content to deliver based on a learner's skills and performance.
- Analyzing performance, generating insights on a learner's progress, and providing automatic grading. This can help trainers and managers tailor the learning experience to individual needs.
- Facilitating group discussions, peer learning, answering questions about specific training materials, and a whole lot more.
- Simulating realistic scenarios so learners can train in a safe and controlled environment.
- Automating certain tasks that are repetitive, time-consuming, or dangerous.

Adding value or replacing people?

Unlike the industrial revolution that automated manual labor and replaced muscles with hydraulic pistons and diesel engines, the AI revolution is automating mental tasks with superhuman capabilities. But is it poised to replace people? No. At least not in the foreseeable future. And hopefully never. With all the attributes of AI, there are many things only people can do:

- Exercise good judgment
- Provide compassion and emotional support
- Make moral and ethical decisions
- Build trust

- Generate original ideas and creative solutions
- Provide common-sense reasoning

Using AI for its good

AI is changing the landscape of many professions and professionals. Medical schools are using AI to perform things that have never before been possible. They're pairing virtual reality training with AI to simulate evolving scenarios that mimic real-life hospital situations. It's involved in diagnosing, drug development, transcribing medical documents, and the list goes on and on.

In the financial world, AI is helping to detect fraud, predict market trends, and develop investment strategies. Manufacturers are using AI to optimize production processes, predict maintenance needs, and identify quality control issues. This AI renaissance is also remodeling education, giving teachers the tools to help students find their own passions and talents.

In the legal profession, AI can quickly sift through large volumes of documents and identify relevant information, search vast databases of legal cases and other documents, produce accurate and relevant results, analyze and extract key information from contracts, flag potential issues, search historical data to predict the outcome of legal cases with a high degree of accuracy, and so much more.

We're the generation inheriting the unprecedented wealth from AI. It's our responsibility to ensure that AI remains under human control. From the United Nations to nations around the world, these issues are being tackled.

Being aware of AI's drawbacks

WARNING

With the inherent prowess of AI, there are many pitfalls to acknowledge:

- There's a risk of ambiguous or incorrect statements, overly wordy writing, and incorrect assumptions when questions posed are unclear.
- It opens up new avenues for hackers to potentially breach advanced cybersecurity software.
- There are ethical implications of using copyrighted or proprietary data to train AI generated models.

- There's a lack of transparency as to how AI systems work, how it makes decisions, and what data it uses to come up with those decisions.
- It introduces privacy concerns. (Governments are challenged with passing privacy legislation to protect individuals against any adverse effects from the use of personal information in AI. They need to do that without unduly restricting AI's development. A very big challenge!)

SHERYL SAYS

I couldn't find a suitable quote to open Chapter 10 in any of my books on quotations, and an Internet search didn't come up with an appropriate one either, so I turned to an AI generator. A great quote popped up in a matter of seconds. Amazing!

IN THIS CHAPTER

» Avoiding what executives dislike about presentations

» Including the pertinent information

» Nailing executive sales briefings

Chapter 20

Nailing an Executive Briefing

Be sincere; be brief; be seated.

—FRANKLIN D. ROOSEVELT (FDR), 32ND U.S. PRESIDENT

As chief executive of the United States, FDR knew the value of sincere, brief communication. In just 6½ minutes, he delivered one of the most memorable speeches ever given by a U.S. President — his legendary "Day of Infamy" speech declaring war on Japan in 1941 after Japanese forces bombed Pearl Harbor. FDR included powerful words such as *surprise offensive* and *this form of treachery.*

The circumstances surrounding FDR's speech were dire, yet the lesson learned about brevity in public speaking is applicable: clear, concise, and brief communication is essential. This short speech galvanized the nation during a time of crisis and is remembered to this day.

If you deliver an executive briefing that's clear and concise — if you include well-chosen, powerful words such as *transformational* or *sustainable* — you too can have a galvanizing impact on your audience. This chapter shows you how to do just that.

KISS-ing the Message (Keeping it Short and Sweet)

Executives — the highest-level people in a company — are typically pressed for time. They're tasked with satisfying an array of stakeholders that could include a board of directors, investors, customers, employees, suppliers, creditors, government agencies, and others. In essence, they're responsible for a robust bottom line and meeting corporate objectives. They value brief, to-the-point communication.

When briefing them, have a succinct introduction followed by main points that are supported by relevant examples or data. Avoid unnecessary details that could distract from the main message. In the words of George Burns: "The secret of a good sermon [briefing] is to have a good beginning and a good ending, and to have the two as close together as possible."

REMEMBER

You add value by preparing a compact narrative in an easily digestible way. This is essential to having an impact on how the executives perceive and act on your information.

Are these folks heroes? Unsung heroes? Some are, and some aren't. Executive heroes are leaders who mobilize organizations to achieve bigger things. They overcome obstacles and help others to be leaders and heroes. They celebrate milestones, recognize achievers, value input, and encourage passions outside of work.

Executive Beef-ings

Executive briefings are meant to be just that — *brief.* No minutiae. Forget the attention-getting opening, humor, extraneous details, and engaging stories, unless they're pertinent to getting your point across. (One example may be a process that's gone awry and how the problem could have been avoided with the information you'll be sharing.)

WARNING

The following are a few beefs executives often have regarding presenters and briefings:

- **Not reading their body language:** They don't know when to stop talking, don't deviate from the script, and fidget when execs engage each other.
- **Death by PowerPoint:** They show endless, often unnecessary slides rather than sticking to relevant details.

- **Lack of presence and confidence:** They often seem ill at ease and cower when asked questions. They show no passion for the topic.
- **Taking too long to get to the point:** Their narratives are long-winded, filled with repetitive phrases, irrelevant information, and unnecessary details that distract from the main idea.

Now that you're aware of what not to do, the next section covers how to put together a briefing that will grab your audience's attention and make you shine.

Welcoming the Chance to Shine

Addressing this high-level audience can be nerve-wracking, but it can also be a big career boost. View this briefing as an opportunity to grow and increase your value to the organization. After all, you were the one chosen to make the presentation because you can supply key pieces of needed information. The executives see you as a valuable asset and are asking for your expertise.

TIP

Not sure how making a presentation like this can help you? Here's some potential added value for you:

- Be viewed as a subject matter expert (SME)
- Bolster your visibility
- Open new possibilities
- Improve your credibility and reputation
- Extend networking opportunities

Your chance to shine begins with a stellar briefing that shows you know your audience, understand what data to include, and can start and end skillfully.

Learning your audience's persona

START-UP BRIEF

Fill out the Start-Up Brief found in Chapter 3 to help you understand your audience's persona. Executives can be a unique group, and you need to know them. What are the interpersonal dynamics in play? What are their nonverbal cues? What are their takeaways? What's the most effective way to brief them? How do they prefer to interact during briefings? Whom do they turn to for advice?

STORYOPIA ARCHIVES: BEING BRIEF AND ON POINT

Arjun is the engineering manager at a large semiconductor company that manufactures chips. He came in one Monday morning and noticed that more than $100,000 worth of scrap in the deposition lab had been produced over the weekend due to defective film. This had been an escalating problem, and the company had spent many thousands of dollars for consultants to come in to recommend solutions. All but one of their recommendations was put in place, and none of them solved the problem, so it continued to escalate. The last recommendation, the purchase of new evaporators, was deemed far too expensive.

Arjun called a meeting of the executives. He prepared and showed a single slide. It was the cost-benefit analysis to show them the excessive amount of money the company is losing each month by not purchasing the new evaporators. His message was, *I'm here to ask for your approval to purchase the evaporators we need because it's costing the company $[XX] each week we delay.* Arjun had garnered their attention.

Result: The executives had a discussion among themselves during the meeting, made some calculations, and Arjun was authorized to look into purchasing the evaporators.

Lesson learned: Keep your talk brief and let the executives take over whatever portions they deem necessary.

REMEMBER

Here are some ways to look into their professional backgrounds beyond the Start-Up Brief: check LinkedIn, connect with colleagues in the same industry, or ask trusted resources within the organization. You can also make some assumptions. For example, if most executives in your audience have a finance background, you'll want to cover any financials such as cost, expected ROI, or operating margins. Pay special attention to the following:

- **Understand what they *need to know* about the topic.** You don't want to tell too much or too little.
- **Determine the call to action in quantifiable terms.** Talk in terms of percentages, dollars, or timeframes.
- **Mull over the questions you must address and be prepared to answer:**
  - How will my proposal impact strategic objectives over the next six months? A Year? Three years?
  - Will it reduce expenses? If so, by how much?
  - What's the potential revenue benefit?

Finding an ally beforehand

Having a high-level person who shares your opinions and supports your ideas at the briefing can be extremely beneficial. They can help ensure that your message is heard and understood by the other audience members. Additionally, having an ally can provide a sense of security and confidence, which can be especially important if your topic is new, controversial, or will impact the budget.

TIP

Here's a suggestion: Before the meeting, share your ideas with a potential supporter (preferably one who'll be at the briefing) and ask for their input and feedback. This can help you refine your ideas and build support during the briefing.

BLUF-fing your opening

Put the **Bottom Line Up Front**. That means to lead with the value proposition, information this group cares about — the bottom line. Be very specific, such as what follows:

- *Good morning. I'm here to ask you to approve a $500,000 investment in new [xxx] equipment for next quarter. This will ensure that we [justification].*
- *The XYZ project is hemorrhaging money. Unless we [specific call to action] now, this project will triple in cost by the end of the year, costing us an additional [$. . .].*

In your storyboard, include areas of the organization that will be impacted and the potential effect on revenue, consumers, employees, and other issues stakeholders care about.

REMEMBER

At the outset, agree on timing. You may have been given 30 minutes for your presentation, but in the lives of these busy folks, things change quickly. Open the presentation by asking, *I understand we've scheduled 30 minutes. Does that timing still work?* If it doesn't, be ready to make some quick adjustments that you've planned beforehand.

Adding supporting data

After a powerful opening, move onto the supporting details and background information using the inverted pyramid method. As you see in Figure 20-1, the widest part at the top should represent the most substantial, interesting, and important information. That may include the ROI your request will bring in terms of revenue increase, cost reduction, protection from risk, competitive advantage, or other business drivers.

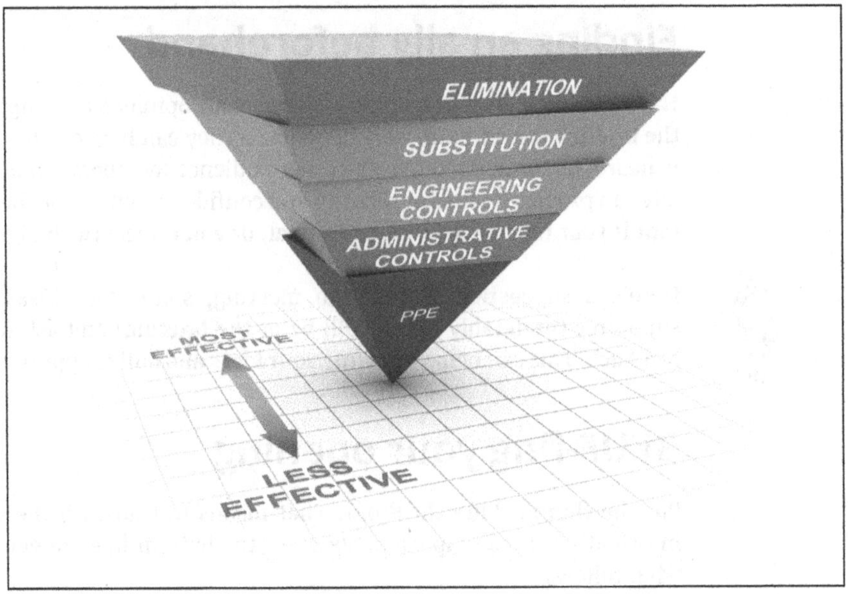

FIGURE 20-1: The widest part at the top is the most important information.

Olivier Le Moal / Adobe Stock

Phrasing skillfully

At this level, senior leaders depend on numbers for decision making, not minor details. Use graphs and charts, as needed, to highlight percentages, dollars, timelines to present outcomes, and what the data supports. Along with the visuals, include a narrative that may be something like this:

- *I'm here to*___________
- *It's important because* ___________
- *Just to give a brief background* (only if necessary)_____________
- *What we're trying to achieve is*______________
- *Because of* ___________ *I propose that* _____________
- *The way going forward is to* _______________
- *If we don't, then the consequences may be* _____________

Showing if-then scenarios

Show strong evidence that your position is important by offering a slide or handout with an if-then scenario. This means *if* the situation or event occurs, *then* the action or response will ensue. Both positive and negative if-then scenarios are intended to change outcomes. Which kind you prepare should depend on the goal you're trying to achieve. If your topic is a "hard sell" and may be met with objections, a negative outcome scenario may work better.

Leading to a negative outcome:

> ***If*** you don't stop smoking now,
>
> ***Then*** you increase your risk of cancer, heart disease, stroke, lung diseases, diabetes, and chronic obstructive pulmonary disease (COPD), which includes emphysema and chronic bronchitis.

Leading to a positive outcome:

> ***If*** you stop smoking now,
>
> ***Then*** you can increase your life expectancy as much as a decade and lower your risk of cancer, heart attack, stroke, and lung disease.

TIP

Although references of time may be the same, think is terms of gravitas. A decade has more gravitas than 10 years; a month, more than 4 weeks; a half century, more than 50 years; and so forth.

Applying the 10/30 rule and being ready to pivot

The 10/30 rules means if you have 30 minutes, plan for 10 minutes of content and the rest for interaction. Executives are notorious for interjecting, expressing their concerns and pushing back. Read the room and make changes to accommodate what's going on in the moment. Be flexible and ready to pivot. Expect questions and energetic discussions even before you've presented all your material.

During your presentation, the audience may multitask, make quick calculations, challenge your data, or switch topics. Your job is to let the conversation flow if it strays from what you rehearsed. Also, be prepared to defend potential roadblocks, challenges, or objections.

WARNING

There may be times the audience steers away from the topic and you haven't covered your key points. If this happens, stay calm and composed, and try to bring the briefing back to the topic. Here are a few considerations:

- Ask a question related to the topic. This may help them refocus.
- Be direct, but polite. *We have only ten minutes left, would it be okay for me to continue? I have just two more points to cover.*

» Put up a relevant slide or distribute a handout. (This means being armed with Plan B.)

Fortifying a robust conclusion

End your presentation with the call to action and next steps. Tie your key point into the call to action in terms of tangibles such as dollars or percentages and timeframes.

Strong and tangible: *We need an additional $1.5 million dollars in Q2 in order to . . .*

Weak and non-committal: *We need additional funds for . . .*

Rehearse. Rehearse. Rehearse.

Practice your presentation multiple times until you feel confident with the materials and your delivery. Use a timer to track its length. Then rehearse in front of a trusted team. Have them pelt you with unexpected questions and scenarios. They can help to prepare you for derailments so you gain more confidence. And be prepared to make changes as you rehearse. Then practice again.

Executive Sales Briefings

Executive sales briefings and executive briefings have different types of audiences and goals. While executive briefings typically provide high-level information to senior members of a company, the focus of executive sales briefings is to make a sales pitch and build relationships.

Your goal is to overcome customer resistance, improve your creditability, influence a faster decision, shorten the sales cycle, and seal the deal. A recent study by the Association of Briefing Program Managers (ABPM) shows the incredible value of executive sales briefings in bringing the deal to a close:

» 71 percent of customers made the decision to purchase products or services discussed.

» 75 percent said the briefing influenced their decision.

» 46 percent said briefings shortened the purchase cycle by an average of 30 percent.

- 72 percent said the amount of their purchase increased by an average of 36 percent.
- 76 percent said they discovered additional solutions that appeared to be useful to their company.

Because the stakes are high, how can you ensure success? The following sections help zero in on that. Find out what keeps them up at night, provide social proof with customer testimonials, and know how leading questions can wrap up the deal.

Finding their pain, needs, and desired outcome

Many companies today are in either growth mode, trouble mode, or somewhere on that spectrum. It's likely that your potential customer is as well. Research the company and the people you'll be meeting. Find out the company's strategy, priorities, competition, pain points, hiccups, and where they and the industry are headed.

Here are some ways to learn all you can about your audience and their company:

- Visit the company's website to view their products/services, mission, values, and history.
- Look for recent news articles, press releases, and social media posts.
- Talk to your sales and marketing teams. They often have keen insights, perspectives, and best practices about the prospect's industry, competition, and customers.
- Check out profiles of Fortune 500 executives at `https://fortune.com/ranking/fortune500`. It includes company names, website links, and other pertinent details. (There's limited free information and more with a subscription.)

Including testimonials to shout your praises

Use actual customer stories to illustrate points, highlight successes, and reinforce key messages. These types of stories — testimonials — provide social proof that work wonders to market your products/services. You can do this verbally, with slides, audio/video testimonials, inclusions in handbooks, and more. Get creative while remaining professional.

Creating a storyboard

Create a storyboard that includes success stories you've had with customers or clients in their industry. The stories can be negative or positive, depending on the point you need to make. Be clear about how your offerings and the ROI for your service or product is different (better) than those of your competition. Then put together materials and a plan that meets the customer's needs. Here are some tips:

- Include dynamic gerunds (verbs ends in *ing)* on the slides and/or cover of the handout. They can be *increasing, streamlining, incorporating, improving, maximizing, accelerating, galvanizing, securing,* to name a few.
- Use the potential customer's name as often as possible without it appearing as if you're pandering.
- Show you understand the customer's pain, needs, and desired outcomes.
- Tell stories. Tell stories. Tell stories. Nothing shouts "winner" like success stories.

Check out Chapter 7 to see a sample storyboard for an executive sales briefing.

Questioning that can lead to sealing the deal

As kids we always asked questions. *Why not? Can I? How come?* Somewhere along the road of life, we were discouraged from questioning. Perhaps it's because so often we heard, "Because I said so." I learned long ago — and you probably did as well — that the only stupid questions are the ones never asked.

There are many types of questions you can ask during an executive sales briefing to show you've done your homework. Questions are not to determine *whether* you can help (otherwise you wouldn't be presenting to this high-level audience) but *how* you can help. Here are some questioning styles that will encourage your audience to elaborate and keep the conversation moving forward:

- **Discovery questions:** Create questions that may introduce something you didn't already know. Avoid questions with "yes" and "no" answers because you don't want anyone to feel trapped by an answer.

  Examples: *What's your timeline for achieving these goals? How will you determine your return on investment (ROI)?*
- **Tie-down questions:** These types of questions are intended to clarify (tie down) the position of the person answering.

  Examples: *How does that compare with what you're paying now? How might this work for you?*
- **Leading questions:** These questions are posed to gently guide the audience toward your product or service.

Examples: *How are you currently handling this? How would this fit into your short-term goals?*

» **Closing questions:** As part of your closing, pose questions that reiterate the key points the audience mentioned up to this point. This shows you've been paying attention.

Examples: *How are you feeling about what we've discussed so far? If we were to move forward today, where would the equipment fit?*

Hopefully your briefing entices the execs to seal the deal and sign on the dotted line just as you see in Figure 20-2. (And if it's done with a smile, all the better.)

FIGURE 20-2: Your end game is having them seal the deal.

insta_photos / Adobe Stock

STORYOPIA ARCHIVES: TALKING *WITH* YOUR AUDIENCE, NOT *AT* THEM

On a referral from a colleague, Dev, the CEO of Marric Associates contacted me. The company was making an executive presentation to three senior members of Adam's Stores in the hopes of single sourcing facility management and maintenance for all Adam's Stores throughout the East Coast.

Dev wanted professional help preparing a slide presentation because this prospective customer had the potential of becoming one of Marric's most lucrative accounts.

(continued)

(continued)

When I arrived at Marric's office, I was taken into the conference room where the meeting would take place. I noticed a comfortable, well-lit room with a round conference table that could seat eight people.

Fast forward: I convinced Dev that a slide presentation wasn't the right approach. *You want to talk* with *your guests, not* at *them,* I explained. After much cajoling, I prepared a spiral-bound handbook with the following:

- A cover titled, *Saving the Day for Adam's Stores,* with Adam's logo largely displayed and Marric's logo below it in one third the size
- Welcoming letter from Marric's CEO
- Testimonial stories — in the form of letters — from big-name clients telling how Marric saved the day during a major problem and mitigated what could have been a disaster (several were also blown up into posters and placed strategically in the room)
- Several pages of services Marric provides that were chock full of color photos and key words
- Six forms (such as Inspection Reports) with Adam's Stores prominently displayed on each form — as if they were already doing business together
- A back cover listing client referrals with names and contact information (all pre-approved)

Each executive from Adam's Stores received a copy of the handbook and there was productive interchange among all parties. I also suggested that Marric order lunch for the guests. (Food is always a plus, even if it's coffee and pastries.)

Result: The three senior executives of Adam's Stores took their handbooks back to headquarters. Within two days it was agreed that Marric was the company that best suited their needs. Marric was awarded a multi-million-dollar contract.

Stories sealed the deal: Once the two companies started doing business together, Marric learned that the deciding factor that made Marric stand out from its competitors was the presentation accompanied by the saved-the-day testimonial stories in the handbook. Those stories were not just shared at the meeting, but they were in the handbook to be read over and digested.

Lesson learned: Talk *with* your audience, not *at* them. Use handouts (not slides) to reinforce what you want them to recall and share. And never underestimate the value of testimonial stories to build trust and credibility. They provide social proof that others have had a positive experience with you.

IN THIS CHAPTER

- » Understanding how presentations, symposiums, and conferences differ
- » Getting ready for your conference
- » Avoiding mishaps in your message
- » Assessing results and nailing networking
- » Becoming a keynote speaker
- » Networking at a conference

Chapter 21

Presenting a Paper at a Conference

If you can't explain it simply, you don't understand it well enough.

—ALBERT EINSTEIN, PHYSICIST

How does a conference (also called a symposium) differ from other types of presentations? It's a large event where attendees meet to share ideas and experiences. This term applies to various types of gatherings, but is often used for business, academic, educational, ecological, scientific, social/cultural, peace, and trade gatherings, to name a few. Conference organizers typically plan a full agenda of events that include keynote speakers, panel discussions, breakout sessions, and social events. Attendees can be a few dozen or several thousand, and they can come from all over the world.

In this chapter, you'll learn where to find stories to liven up your session, prepare for a conference, become a keynote speaker, network, and evaluate results.

Presenting at a Conference

Do you recall your first introduction to making presentations? It was probably in grade school when you brought in something for show and tell. Then in middle school and high school you stood in front of the class and delivered oral presentations. When you went to college, perhaps you took public speaking or presented academic work in a classroom or at a special event.

The main difference between presenting in school situations and presenting at a conference is this: When you were in school, you were trying impress one person — an instructor who would be giving you a grade. At a conference, you're the expert and are addressing an audience who wants to know what's in it for them. The similarities between the two are that they involve good presentation skills, stories to enhance the presentation, and visuals that add value.

Presenting a paper at a conference is a great way to introduce your work to colleagues, try out a new idea, hone research questions, and get feedback from a community of like-minded people. If you're nervous about presenting, remember you were selected to speak. That gives you instant credibility.

The audience will want to know why your presentation is worthwhile and what's in it for them. Audiences at conferences are typically technical or specialized, but that doesn't mean they're stuffy. They have the same need for stories, clarity, brevity, and relevancy. They also have a sense of humor and can appreciate a presentation that isn't a snooze-fest.

STORYOPIA ARCHIVES: INCORPORATING APPROPRIATE HUMOR

Beatrice's company had developed a new drug, and she was asked to deliver her paper at a medical conference. She signed up for my Storytelling and Storyboarding workshop to learn how to interject stories. Her concern was: *The audience is all doctors, so I can't lighten up the paper or add humor.*

I was puzzled by her dilemma and responded: *My son is a doctor, and he has an awesome sense of humor. Just because doctors aren't funny in the examination room doesn't mean they don't appreciate the lighter side of something in other settings. Approach the audience at a conference the same way you'd approach them if you presented to a small group. They're people first and professionals second.*

During the workshop Beatrice prepared several stories of how well the trials were going and she even thought of a humorous incident which she planned to share. I never heard how her talk went, but she left the workshop full of confidence to deliver her session at the conference.

Lesson learned: Never be intimidated by the audience's profession or the number of people in attendance. You were asked to present because you're an expert. And no matter who's in your audience, there's always a story to be told and appropriate humor to be shared.

Stories, Science, and Conferences

A scientific conference is an event where researchers, students, and scholars gather to present papers. They discuss research, issues and trends, findings, influence policy making, and share novel ideas and technologies. When you bring these great minds together, it can play a critical role in shaping the direction of research.

Conferences can be themed or general and are held regionally, nationally, and internationally. They encompass the fields of aeronautics, anthropology, astronomy, biochemistry, biology, botany, chemistry, ecology, genetics, hydrology, medicine, metallurgy, microbiology, neurology, optics, pharmaceuticals, physics, climate science, and the possibilities are nearly endless.

Storytelling is the soul of science communication

The common thread that binds all these sciences and scientists is storytelling, and this is being stressed more than ever. In an October 14, 2019, article in the *Journal of Science Communication*, authors Marina Joubert, Lloyd Davis, and Jenni Metcalfe wrote "Storytelling: the soul of science communication." They state there's a renewed interest among scientists to explore storytelling as a way to make sense of science and science-related issues.

The scientific community has redefined what it means to present, and savvy schools are preparing scientists to deliver narrative talks that reach broader audiences. They stress that the basics of all narrative talks encompass understanding your audience, bringing emotion, using metaphors and analogies, keeping it simple, and bringing the elements of any story: character, setting, conflict, resolution. Sound familiar?

Knowing where to find stories

Depending on the specific focus of your conference, look for stories in scientific journals, news outlets that cover scientific research, and scientific organizations that host conferences and events. Collaborating with other scientists or researchers in a particular field can also offer valuable insight into potential stories.

WARNING

Check out social media platforms such as Twitter and LinkedIn for discovering ongoing conversations around specific scientific topics that lead to stories. Be sure, however, to check and recheck anything you find on social media. It's full of disinformation.

Developing an Abstract

Conference organizers typically want to see an abstract of your paper. An *abstract* is a brief summary (between 250 to 300 words) that highlights your argument, evidence, and contribution to the historical literature. Be clear. Be concise. Be clean. Although the abstract is about your paper, it says a lot about you (such as how clearly you can express yourself).

Choose keywords for your abstract. What are the main concepts that you're exploring or analyzing in your work? Which general and specific key words capture the broad themes of your research and the specific details of your work? The abstract should answer these basic questions:

- What problem or data gap is your research addressing?
- What method or methods are you using to overcome this problem or fill the data gap?
- What data have you generated or are in the process of generating?
- What findings are you planning discuss?

TIP

Although there are many good resources for writing an abstract, here are three:

`https://akcongress.com/blog/conference-abstract/?lang=e`

`https://www.enago.com/academy/important-tips-for-writing-an-effective-conference-abstract/`

`https://blogs.lse.ac.uk/impactofsocialsciences/2015/01/27/how-to-write-a-killer-conference-abstract/`

Getting Ready for the Conference

When preparing your conference, first find out as much as you can about the audience. The theme should give you a big clue. Most conferences use mobile apps, and that's a great way to find out who's attending so you have a good idea of how much background to give so that your key points make sense.

START-UP BRIEF

Also fill out the Start-Up Brief in Chapter 3 to help you fill in the rest.

And be sure you know your time constraints and prepare accordingly. There's typically a moderator (also called commentator, respondent, or discussant) to assure that people start and finish on time. If there isn't one in attendance, be prepared to adapt. For example, if the speaker before you overshoots their timeslot, that may cut into yours. Know in advance what you can eliminate if you need to.

REMEMBER

After you introduce yourself or are introduced:

- State your purpose, goal, and why your work is important.
- Open with a relevant, memorable story. It can be about your research or something else the audience will relate to.
- Present a brief literary review for context.
- Give the audience a roadmap of your talk with the main point(s).
- Conclude by reiterating the main points and the importance of your research.

The following sections cover different aspects of conference preparation in more detail: structuring your message, preparing and delivering your presentation, making your presentation interactive, checking out the room, anticipating questions, and avoiding a mouth that feels like a desert during a drought.

Structuring your message

Does your initial draft suggest anything new about your topic? New findings? New technology? New therapies? Are there any interesting new patterns or emerging themes? Do you have a broader awareness of your topic's complexities?

Structure your delivery in the following order:

1. **Describe your thesis.**
2. **Compare it.**

3. **Associate it.**
4. **Analyze it.**
5. **Apply it.**
6. **Argue for or against it.**

Preparing and delivering your presentation

Your presentation can take the form of reading your paper aloud, preparing a visual preparation, or a combination. When you have the option, a combination works more effectively because it can be quite boring for your audience to listen to you speak for 15 to 20 minutes (the most common span of time).

Following are suggestions for summarizing a longer paper into a shorter talk:

- If you'll be reading your paper, it takes about two and a half minutes to read one double-sized page in a 12-point font. If you have 15 to 20 minutes for delivery, you can read approximately eight to ten pages.
- If you're delivering a slide presentation, follow the same guidelines as for any presentation. However, avoid extracting text for bullet points and pasting tables and figures into slides. Show creativity and include graphics.
- Write with the audience in mind. Writing a paper for a conference is different from writing for a journal. A conference paper is meant to be *heard,* not *read.*
- You may have time to make only one major point. State it. Develop it. Repeat it.
- Extract your argument, evidence, and conclusion from your larger body of work.
- Don't spend too much time on information the audience already knows. After three to four minutes of introducing your topic, get to the nuts and bolts of your thesis.
- It's fine to use quotes but don't say *open quote, close quote.* Instead say, *As [Name] has stated. . .*
- Allow time for questions provided that's part of the conference format.

Making your presentation interactive

Whether you're presenting to a group of 20 or over one thousand, make it interactive. Here are a few things to try:

- Take a poll and ask for a show of hands.
- Ask the audience to self-divide (if the group is large) and present a case study or something else to discuss relevant to the topic.
- Get off the stage, mingle in the audience, ask a question, and bring the mic to someone for an answer.
- Have people introduce themselves to someone next to them. (Many are there to network, and this is a great opportunity to meet others.)

Checking out the room

As early as possible, check out the room where you'll be speaking. This will save you from the last-minute panic of running across an unfamiliar campus, trying to find the room you're supposed to be in, and so on. Most rooms will be outfitted with everything you need, but there's no harm in making sure all the equipment is there and in good working order. And don't be afraid to ask for what you need. Here are a few scenarios and what to ask for:

- Open windows are letting in loud noises from construction vehicles on the premises. Ask for the windows to be closed if you can't reach them.
- Loose wires are on the floor. Ask for them to be taped down.
- The room is too warm or too cool. Ask for the temperature to be adjusted.

STORYOPIA ARCHIVES: TESTING THE MIC

Ronald Reagan, actor turned president, was known for his astute way with words. During the height of the Cold War, in 1984, he took a break from his reelection campaign to do a radio interview. For a sound check, he muttered into the hot mic, "My fellow Americans: I'm pleased to tell you today that I've signed legislation that will outlaw Russia forever." (Laughter) We begin bombing in five minutes." (More laughter)

News of his flippant remark reached the news outlets, but there was no laughter. Reagan's supporters tried to save face and blew off the remarks as Reagan's sense of humor. However, this became an international embarrassment as foreign news services referred to him as "an irresponsible old man." Fortunately this didn't result in the Russians feeling they needed to strike first. Instead, they publicly denounced his

(continued)

(continued)

comments and had much fodder for their propaganda mill. Immediately following these thoughtless remarks, Reagan's approval rating dropped precipitously. (But he did win the election by a landslide.)

Lesson learned: Never say anything irresponsible into the mic in jest. That can lead to damaging your reputation, hurting others, and even legal consequences. Stick with the old standard: *Testing, testing 1, 2, 3* or *Can you hear me clearly?*

Anticipating questions

Expect questions. If you don't know the answer, ask if anyone in the audience does. You can't be expected to know everything. Also ask for a question to be repeated if you don't understand it. (Chapter 3 will help you anticipate questions the audience may ask and need answered, and Chapter 15 offers advice on dealing with difficult questions.)

Don't worry if there aren't any questions. Whether there or aren't, it's not an indication of how good or bad the paper or your delivery was. If there are uncomfortable silences, be prepared with a few questions you may ask of your audience.

Preventing parchedness

A byproduct of speaking for long periods of time can be the feeling that you're speaking with a large wad of cotton in your mouth. It can lead to stumbling over your words, slurring, or mispronouncing words. Here are some ways to avoid feeling like your mouth is as dry as the Sahara Desert:

- Stay away from coffee, alcohol, or tobacco for several hours before your presentation.
- Bring a bottle of non-bubbly water to the podium and pour small amounts at a time into a paper cup. Take small sips from the cup during a pause. (Taking swigs from a bottle is unprofessional.)
- Try a dry mouth solution, which comes in a gels, sprays, or pills. (My fav is a product called Biotène that I've used successfully in spray and gel form.)

Avoiding Boos and Taboos

I always like to present a glass that's half full — sharing things that are positive — but here are some boos and taboos to help you avoid the half-empty glass:

- **Starting with "Can you hear me?":** Know beforehand that you can be heard by checking out the room and testing the equipment. Station someone in the back of the room and test the mic for sound quality and unwanted noises. (There's always someone floating around the venue you can ask to step in for a few minutes.) If audience members in the back of the room can't hear you during the event, it's disruptive if people move to different seats.
- **Planting yourself behind the podium:** You're not a potted plant, so don't just stand there. A podium is a physical barrier that separates you from your audience. Bring your audience into your presentation by going to them. When I present at a conference, I move about the room, especially during a crescendo when I want to share something decisive.
- **Ending with, "That's all I have":** Thank your audience for coming. If you have a handout that's saved for the end, remind them to take one. Let them know you'll be around for questions and comments. Check out Chapter 6 for memorable endings.

Taking Center Stage as a Keynote Speaker

It's up to the conference organizers to get a keynote speaker and decide the lineup of speakers based on their relevance, influence, and the overall structure of the conference. Every conference will have one or two keynote speakers. If there's one, they'll be the first to present. If there are two, the other one will wrap it up at the end. Having a keynote at the beginning and end will hopefully encourage attendees to stay for the entire conference and not trickle out over the course of the day.

Becoming a keynote speaker

Keynote speakers can be celebrities, academics, educators, humorists, motivational speakers, or whatever expert is relevant to the event. Many are contracted through speakers bureaus that have extensive rosters with a broad spectrum of disciplines and a wide range of budgets.

Being a keynote can bring beaucoup bucks and opportunities to travel to interesting places, but it's not for everyone. It involves being a road warrior for extended periods of time, which can be grueling. And the pressure to surpass expectations for each audience can be overwhelming. If this sounds like your dream job, here are some tips:

- Find your niche and unique skill.
- Hone your presentation skills until they're killer presentation skills.
- Take advantage of networking events and opportunities to speak before groups.
- Market yourself and have a strong social media presence.
- Prepare a 3- to 5-minute demo video (somewhat like a movie trailer) of one or more speaking engagements. Send it to several speakers bureaus so they can see you in action. (Check the Internet and you'll find lots of local and national speakers bureaus.)
- Search the Internet for gigs and conferences. Also check out colleges, universities, and other educational institutions in addition to local charities.

Being the opening keynote speaker

Opening the conference is the most desired slot. This speaker should take the audience on a storyopia journey to a place they haven't been before and inspire them to take action towards their goals and aspiration, making them heroes. Here are some attributes a keynote speaker needs:

- Having lots of charisma
- Bringing a great message along with a sense of humor
- Being able to captivate the audience and build enthusiasm
- Showing passion for the topic
- Setting the tone for the rest of the conference

Making the lasting impression

Being the last speaker in a daylong conference can seem daunting. Many people have may have left, and the speaker is talking to a partially empty room. However, those who've stayed are there because they're interested. The last speaker is the closing speaker — the speaker who'll leave the most lasting impression.

Here are a few dos and don'ts if you find yourself in this position.

Do:

- Play to your strengths and stick to what you're good at without trying to mimic other speakers.
- Grab your audience's attention immediately with a story, quote, anecdote, or visual that will let them know the session will be worthwhile.
- Start with something interactive to get your audience involved immediately.
- Maintain a high level of energy and enthusiasm.

Don't:

- Emphasize how empty the room is, or you make the audience feel as if they're also-rans for staying.
- Run over the intended time. You never want to do this, but it's especially important when you're the final speaker.
- Use the session to pitch your service or product. Rather, discuss challenges your audience faces.

TIP

End your session with a *save story*. As you near the end of your session, let the audience know you have a great story to tell but you're out of time. (This is a tactic, not poor timing.) Recommend that they catch up with you after the session. That would be during drinks, dinner, or whatever follows. In this way, you reconnect with them and they remember you not only for your presentation but also for the conversation and interesting story afterwards.

Networking at a Conference

One of your most valuable takeaways from any conference may be the new relationships and contacts you make through networking. Here's how to network effectively:

- **Get a list of conference dinners, meet-ups, and parties.** Attend as many as possible.
- **Try to learn in advance who'll be attending.** If there are specific attendees, vendors, or speakers you hope to meet and talk to, do your research ahead of time and make it a point to meet them.

» **Circulate and be approachable.** Don't spend all your time outside using your phone, laptop, or tablet.

» **Be ready with conversation starters to show interest.** You're not there just to pitch yourself, but to listen to others. So ask questions, such as, *Where are you from? Which session or speakers have you found engaging? What interested you in . . .?*

» **Have an exit strategy for ending conversations you wish never started.** For example, you may be chatting with Beau Braggart who has such a large ego, he needs his own zip code. Simply say: *It was nice talking with you but, I hope you'll excuse me. There are other people I'd like to meet as well.*

» **Have plenty of business cards to distribute.** Don't give them out to everyone you meet, only to people with whom you may like to re-connect.

» **Use your 30-second elevator pitch.** (Find out more in Chapter 11.)

TIP

Before and after the sessions, wear your name badge. Write your name in letters large enough for people to read without squinting. Wear the badge either on a lanyard or on the right side of your upper body or chest area, as you see in Figure 21-1. This is so when you shake hands, attention is brought to the right side of your body, making it easy for people to see and remember your name.

FIGURE 21-1: Place your name badge on the right side where people can easily see your name.

Krakenimages.com / Adobe Stock

REMEMBER

Networking doesn't end at the conference. Save the business cards you've collected and focus on the people you may be interested in having in your network. Send them an email or a LinkedIn invite. Depending on where they're located, arrange a follow up for coffee, lunch, or a Zoom session.

Evaluating the Results

As a speaker, you'll be interested in the evaluations for your presentation. Not all conferences voluntarily share them, so ask for yours. The sponsoring organization will also want feedback from exhibitors and sponsors, which you'll be asked to share. Questions may involve venue, food and beverages, hotel accommodations, speakers, overall experience, and more. This feedback will be useful in scheduling future conferences and speakers. Check out Chapter 12 for evaluation forms and feedback.

REMEMBER

Don't take it personally if you speak to a small audience. Some of the most influential papers are presented to small audiences. No matter what size the audience, a great presentation is a great presentation. If you want to mention the conference on your academic CV, no one will ask how many people attended.

IN THIS CHAPTER

- Nipping and tucking
- Personalizing the presentation with stories
- Acknowledging the elephant in the room (you)
- Coming from the corporate office

Chapter 22
Presenting Someone Else's Content

Stories are memory aids, instruction manuals, and moral compasses.

–ALEKS KROTOSKM, BROADCASTER, JOURNALIST, AND SOCIAL PSYCHOLOGIST

You arrive at work on Monday morning and learn that Jesse — who was supposed to make an important presentation at 1:00 — called in sick. People have flown in from different parts of the country, so it's too late to cancel. Your manager has charged you with filling in. You weren't involved in the preparation and know less than Jesse about the subject matter. Delivering a presentation is stressful enough, but delivering someone else's in a pinch — yikes!

If you find yourself in this situation, take a deep breath and follow the advice laid out in this chapter. It lays out the path to making you shine, getting rid of the elephant in the room (you), reclaiming the presentation as your own, sharing your unique stories, and much more. Don't worry. You'll get this!

REMEMBER

This isn't grade school where the kids play practical jokes on the substitute. These are adults who understand your situation; they'll be cheering for you.

Making This Your Time to Shine

Remember that you were selected for a reason. Perhaps you were part of the team who prepared the presentation. Or perhaps you're the subject matter expert (SME). Whatever the reason, you were selected because you can do it. Your presentation won't be identical to the original because you're a different person and bring your own unique talents.

Take a look at some people who were Plan B, who brought their own unique talents, and rose to star power when they had their time to shine:

» Child-star Judy Garland wasn't the studio's first pick to play Dorothy in *The Wizard of Oz*. The studio wanted Shirley Temple.

» Roberta Peters, soprano with the New York Metropolitan Opera, rose to stardom when she was the understudy and assumed the role of Zerlina in *Don Giovanni*.

» Harry Truman became the 33rd President of the United States upon the death of Franklin Roosevelt. Truman will long be remembered as the President who ended World War II.

» Backup quarterbacks have taken starring roles. The best known is Tom Brady who filled in as quarterback for the New England Patriots after Drew Bledsoe blew out his knee. Brady became the starting QB and has been nicknamed the GOAT (Greatest Of All Time).

So, when you think of yourself as Plan B, imagine the letter "B" representing **Belong**, **Bright**, **Brave**, **Bonanza**, and **Bat** it out of the **Ballpark**. With that can-do attitude, you too will shine.

A Nip Here, a Tuck There

Treat the presentation as you would a stunning second-hand item of clothing you acquired. It won't fit perfectly and may need alterations. Then, once it's altered, you can wear the garment with pride while maintaining its integrity. You'll have made it your own. Modify the presentation to fit your style and personality and "wear it" with integrity.

REMEMBER

You wouldn't be asked to fit into a size small if you're an X-large, so you wouldn't be asked to fill in for the presenter if you aren't a good fit. You may not be Jesse, but you *are* a good fit. Perhaps Jesse was planning to show a slide presentation. If you open with a relatable story, you've already elevated the presentation to a higher level.

Making the Presentation Your Own with a Story

Take the podium and share a personal success story or horror story from your bag of tricks. Check out Chapter 4 for details on incorporating stories: conveying a hero's journey, putting the backstory up front, telling a future story, sharing convergent strategies, or crafting a case study.

Modify the slides or use whichever are appropriate for *your* presentation. Slides the original presenter prepared aren't scripts. When facts and figures are interwoven with relatable stories, the audience will remember the stories (and you) long after they've forgotten the data. Going back to the opening quote at the beginning of this chapter, stories are memory aids, instruction manuals, and moral compasses. They'll serve you and your audiences well.

Don't Catch 'Em by Surprise

Either you or someone higher up should let attendees know as soon as possible that there will be a different presenter. This can be done through email, social media, or event announcements. Be sure to include a bio of the person who will be speaking instead.

If it's the last minute, make sure someone properly introduces the substitute speaker to the audience and provides some background information about the speaker's qualifications and expertise. Here are some things to include:

- Thank the audience for attending and acknowledge that the original speaker is unavoidably away.
- Introduce the new speaker by name, company, job title, along with relevant experience and qualifications.
- Highlight patents, publications, or anything else that adds credibility.
- Conclude the speaker's introduction by expressing full confidence in them and how the audience can look forward to a stimulating experience.

SHERYL SAYS

I've heard this done in the theater a few times. When a star wouldn't be performing, an announcement was made before the performance: *[Name] will be filling in for the role of [character] for tonight's performance.* That person's bio was inserted into the playbill. I've never seen anyone get up and leave and the performance didn't suffer in any way. Not having seen the original performer, perhaps the performer I saw was even better — just as your own performance may be better.

Dealing with the Elephant in the Room

The "elephant in the room" is a euphemism for something that's blatantly obvious to all, but it's not mentioned. When you think of elephants, remember how magnificent these creatures are and how dangerous they can be if not treated properly. They can go rogue and trumpet all sorts of trouble. Treat yourself with respect by dealing with the elephant in the room — you — and then moving on quickly.

SHERYL SAYS

Here's how it was magnificently handled by a fill-in presenter at a session I attended. He used humor and opened with the slide of an elephant, such as you see in Figure 22-1. Then he said with humor, *Good morning. I'd like to introduce the elephant in the room. That's me, although I am thinner and less wrinkly.* [Brief pause and chuckle from the audience.] *I know you were expecting [name], but I'm delighted to be sharing [topic] with you this morning. So let's get started.* Then he turned off the screen, having broken the ice, and continued with a story and delivered an awesome presentation.

"I suppose I'll be the one
to mention the elephant in the room."

FIGURE 22-1: I'm the elephant in the room and deserve respect!

cartoonresource / Adobe Stock

Don't Try to Wing It!

WARNING

Don't even think about taking someone else's content and trusting it to luck. It's unlikely you'll be asked to fill in immediately before the presentation begins, so there will be some time to prepare.

Here are some tips for getting on board quickly:

- First and foremost, don't try to wing it.
- Look through the slides and notes the intended presenter made. This will help you understand the flow, key points, and the audience's likely expectations.
- Talk to others from the team who may have been involved in the preparation.
- Go to the Start-Up Brief in Chapter 3 and identify all you can about the audience, purpose, key issue, and questions you may be asked. In particular, know the answers to the following:
  - What does the audience need to know and why?
  - What is the call to action (what the audience should do, feel, think, or learn)?
- Prepare some notecards to use as aids.
- Be prepared to adapt as needed. This can mean adding a few stories or activities from your repertoire.
- Stay calm and don't let the last-minute nature of the situation stress you out. Take a few deep breaths and get started.
- *Don't* tell the audience you didn't ample have time to prepare. (Even if you didn't, that's a big no-no.)

START-UP BRIEF

Amending the slides

Although you won't have total control of the slides because you lack sufficient prep time, you do have control of how to explain each slide and which ones to use. One suggestion is to jettison data-heavy slides if you don't think you can field questions about them. (There are probably too many of them anyway.) Add slides that address some of your own knowledge, sticking to the same format and template.

TIP

If you think some of the slides you jettison may be important, prepare them as a handout to distribute before the end of the session.

Including the audience

Garner as much audience participation as you can. Ask them questions. Ask them to share their own stories. Engage them in one or more activities. Share your own anecdotal experiences. Include an ice breaker. Look up a relevant statistic to open with. There are a number of benefits to including the audience and not trying to carry the presentation yourself:

- You'll hold their attention longer.
- They'll understand the content better.
- You'll pick up some talking points you can run with.
- They have as much to learn from each other as they have to learn from you.

TIP

Chapter 25 is chock full of ideas to make your session interactive. Check it out.

Taking a tip from artisans

SHERYL SAYS

As I was writing this chapter, I couldn't help forming an analogy between Japanese kintsugi and delivering someone else's presentation. In Figure 22-2 you see beautiful kintsugi pottery. Artisans join broken pieces of pottery with liquid gold. Rather than trying to hide the breaks and make invisible joints, they create a beautiful art form — kintsugi — creating a finished piece that's unique and more interesting than before.

You can take an otherwise bland presentation, break it into chunks, add your own personality, your own stories, and make it into a dynamic presentation in which you weave your golden threads — making your finished piece unique and more interesting than before.

FIGURE 22-2: Kintsugi pottery is unique and more interesting than before.

MARCO MONTALTI / ADOBE STOCK

Adapting a Presentation from the Corporate Office

You may be asked to deliver the dreaded, data-laden slide presentation prepared by the corporate office. If the company has its act together, the slides will have speaker's notes for the points the speaker is expected to make. But don't count on it. Presentations such as these are often bland, lifeless, and uninspiring. Instead of robotically boring with one slide after another, take ownership and alter the presentation.

You're not handcuffed to what the corporate office prepared. Make it your own by doing the following:

- Simplify the content.
- Make necessary alterations. (Even small changes can make a big difference.)
- Inject your personality.
- Tell your own stories.
- Add personal anecdotes.
- As already mentioned, know the audience is cheering for you.

Preparing as You Would for a Substitute Teacher

If you're in a position where someone else will have to fill in for you, do your best to prepare that presenter. It's like a teacher leaving lesson plans for a substitute teacher:

START-UP BRIEF

- Make sure the presenter understands what the audience is there to do, feel, think, or learn.
- Share the information on your Start-Up Brief (Chapter 3) so the presenter will understand your audience, purpose, and key issue.
- Point out the most important slides and/or handouts.
- Write down the opening first few lines.
- Jot down at least one story or anecdote.
- Make a note of key questions the new presenter can ask the audience to stimulate conversation.
- Leave contact information for yourself (or someone else in the know) who can answer questions beforehand or at any critical point.

6

The Part of Tens

IN THIS PART . . .

Think of Elvis, greet audience members as they enter the room, visualize your success, and consider joining a public speaking group.

Rustle up relatable stories, create a resource file, take your audience on an adventure, and end with a call to action.

Make your presentation interactive, gamify, get a debate going, and more.

Understand why presentations can fail and avoid those pitfalls, deal with technology snags, avoid slidezillas, and tell stories to make your audience heroes.

IN THIS CHAPTER

» Knowing you're not alone

» Making sure you're well prepared and in a good headspace

Chapter 23

Ten Hints for Combatting Stage Fright

If you suffer from stage fright, you're in good company. Rod Stewart, Andrea Bocelli, Donny Osmond, Carly Simon, Renee Fleming, Adele, Katy Perry, Rihanna, Ozzy Osborne, Luciano Pavarotti, Eddie Van Halen, and so many others admit to suffering from stage fright in varying degrees. However, here are a couple of doozies:

- Barbra Streisand suffered from such extreme stage fright that she stopped giving live performances for 27 years. She recalls at one time forgetting words to a song. "I simply drew a blank," she stated. Overcoming stage fright took a lot of work, but she did it, although she still gets healthy jitters.
- The King of Rock 'Roll, Elvis Presley, suffered from stage fright throughout his entire career. According to Elvis's sideman, Scott Moore, it was during one of Elvis's early performances that his legs were excessively shaky from nerves. He couldn't stop the shaking, so he exaggerated the movement. The crowds went wild. Thus, his iconic hip swing gyrations were born, creating a cultural revolution that reshaped the face of rock 'n' roll.

This chapter offers some tricks of the trade to make jitters subside.

Think of Elvis

Think of Elvis and all the other celebrities in the opening paragraph who've suffer from stage fright. And it's not only celebrities. Mark Twain said he suffered from severe stage fright. He was to give a speech in front of a large crowd in San Francisco, and he peppered the audience with friends, instructing them to laugh at his jokes. Although you probably won't do that, people find all sorts of workarounds.

SHERYL SAYS

I told the story of Elvis during a Storytelling and Storyboarding workshop. It saved the day for one of the participants. As one of several finalists, he was ready to deliver a critical presentation, hoping to be awarded a very large grant. Moments before he was to approach the podium, his knees started shaking. He was quickly reminded of the story I told of Elvis. He chuckled and his knees calmed right down. You never know how your stories will remain in the memory of someone in your audience. By the way, he was awarded the grant.

Greet People As They Enter the Room

After facilitating workshops for decades, I still get slight jitters beforehand. I found that by greeting people as they enter, I can get on with the show with ease and confidence. I think of the people I met as acquaintances, so I'm not presenting to a room full of strangers. It's somewhat akin to Mark Twain's trick of bring to his presentations people he knew so he'd see familiar faces in the audience.

Remember You're the Star

The audience is there to see you, hear you, and learn from you. It's because of your expertise that you were asked to be the speaker, so let your mastery of the subject matter guide you with confidence. You can guide your audience through what they should do, think, feel, or learn. Give yourself a break and believe in yourself. You can, and you should!

Build a Memory Palace

If you've ever read or watched Sherlock Holmes, you may have noted his technique of creating memory palaces to recall crucial information. When he's trying to solve a case, he'd think of the location, walk through the location in his mind, identify the features of the location, and make associations.

Build your own memory palace by thinking of an imaginary location where you can store mnemonic images, noting different points or stops within that location. They are the visual hooks to help you remember specific points in your presentation.

This is called *method of loci.* It's a 200-year-old memorization technique used by Greeks and Romans. This idea has been popular with storytellers as far back as Homer. The idea is to think of your house (your palace). It's a place you know thoroughly and can use as a mental storage system to deposit images. Here's an example: You're talking about a guy who wasn't allowed to perform to capacity for whatever reason. Perhaps his boss was a micromanager, he didn't have the right tools, etc. In other words, "his hands were tied." Imagine a person whose hands are tied behind his back sitting at your kitchen table. And that may jog your memory for a story.

Practice — Practice — Practice

Practice in front of the mirror as if you were speaking directly to someone. Or have someone record you. (With smartphones this is easy.) Pay attention to your facial expressions, gestures, and body movements. Practice in front of others. Practice until you're comfortable. Practice without slides in case there's a technology glitch.

Make a List of Specific Worries

When you worry about something, you often overestimate the likelihood that it will happen and you blow it out of proportion. If you're worried about arriving on time, leave enough time to allow for lots of traffic or a flat tire. If you're worried that the projector may not work, bring your own and know your materials well enough so you can go on without it.

Visualize Your Success

Positive thoughts can help decrease some of your pre-talk jitters. Imagine your talk going smoothly. Be as detailed as possible in your thoughts. See smiles on the faces of audience members and hear the roar of their applause. This isn't a bunch of psycho-babble. There's scientific evidence to support this technique. Check out this report on Forbes: `https://www.forbes.com/sites/eilenezimmerman/2016/01/27/survey-shows-visualizing-success-works/?sh=32ef793b760b`

Say Bye-Bye to Butterflies

Remind yourself that this presentation isn't about you — it's about helping your audience do, think, feel, or learn something about [topic]. They're coming to listen, not to judge. So just

- Take a few deep breaths.
- Focus on gratitude.
- Remember your audience is rooting for you.
- Pray, say a mantra, or give yourself a pep talk.
- Remember there's no difference between audiences of 25 or 2,500 people. (With larger groups, you just need to speak louder.)

Use Notecards

Notes make great prompts. You don't need to conceal them from the audience; they're a normal part of giving a presentation. Write trigger words or phrases in large letters. If you lose your place or draw a blank, you'll only need a few seconds to find where you were and get going again. Check out Chapter 13 for more about using and preparing notecards.

Join a Group

If you have a fear of public speaking join a group. You're not the Wizard of Oz who needs to hide behind a curtain, podium, or any other barrier. Toastmasters is the best known speakers group, and it's worldwide. For local groups, check out "public speaking support groups." You'll find many online and in-person groups.

REMEMBER

Many people experience some form of *glossophobia* (fear of public speaking) to varying degrees. Symptoms may include a combination of sweating, increased heart rate, dry mouth, muscle tension, need to urinate, nausea, and difficult breathing. If you're impacted by this, check with your doctor because there are several things that can help.

IN THIS CHAPTER

» Engaging your audience

» Taking readers on a journey and ending with a call to action story

Chapter 24
Ten Tips for Telling a Relatable Story

If the Martians you read about in Chapter 1 wanted to know the origin of a sandwich, you'd want your answer to be memorable. Would you (A) prepare a slide or (B) tell a story? *Yes, this is a rhetorical question.* You could prepare a slide such as you see in Figure 24-1, which would be mind-numbingly boring.

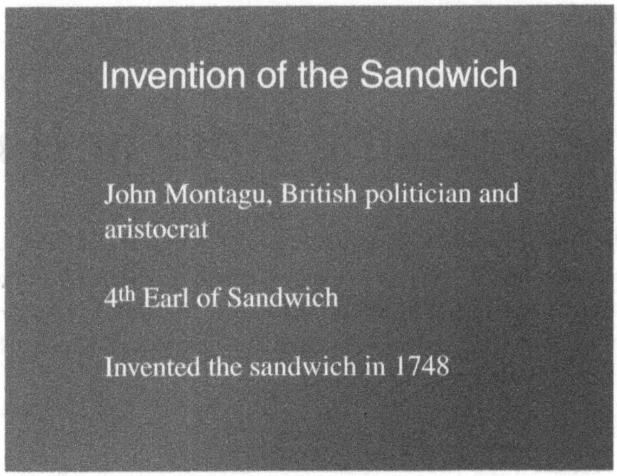

Invention of the Sandwich
John Montagu, British politician and aristocrat
4th Earl of Sandwich
Invented the sandwich in 1748

FIGURE 24-1: Why not tell a story instead of showing a boring slide?

Or you could tell this story of the Earl of Sandwich. In brief, history records that the sandwich was created in 1762 in England by John Montagu, the 4th Earl of sandwich. Montagu was known for being a problematic gambler, spending hours upon hours at the card table, and needing to eat. Learn the fun details, by checking out the following website: `http://www.open-sandwich.co.uk/town_history/sandwich_origin.htm`

This chapter provides ten tips to help you tell your own relatable stories.

Keep a "Resource" File

David Sedaris is a successful comedian and author known for his quick wit and crackling prose. He collects roadside garbage on a regular basis and tells stories of his "finds." Is there anything more mundane than that? Yet, he makes a good living at it. Your life is filled with stories from mundane experiences to outright adventures. Jot them down. You never know when you can incorporate one into a presentation.

Don't Open with a Slide Unless . . .

It's fine to open with a thought-provoking or memorable slide for the audience to view as they're entering and getting settled. If you open with a slide (especially when it's ho-hum and lists the name of the presentation, your name, and the date — YAWN), that's a telltale signal to your audience that the presentation will be a *snoozapalooza*.

Start with a Compelling Story or Hook

Tell a story that will feed into your audience's needs, desires, or fears. You never know where your words will end up or whose life will be changed because of them. Don't start with a long list of people to thank and don't bore your audience with a laundry list of your credentials. Too many presenters squander these all-important first minutes of their presentation.

Take Your Audience on an Adventure

"Once upon a time" conjures up childhood memories of tales that took us to places where anything was possible. These tales were filled with excitement, comfort, reassurance, and a sense of wonder. Whether the stories started with *once upon a time* or some other opening, they were magical and memorable. Openings can be:

- *Once upon a time . . .*
- *Isn't this crazy . . .* (arousing curiosity)
- *Picture this . . .* (as if they're at the scene)
- *Have you ever . . .* (putting themselves into a situation)
- *Did you know . . .* (leading question)

Embellish the Story

The difference between a boring story and an interesting one involves three things: authenticity, emotions, and embellishment. Sometimes you need to add a little flavor to highlight the moral of the story and make it more memorable, just as you add spices to a recipe to make it tastier and more flavorful.

Personalize the Story

Although you can tell stories from your experiences, you can also poach stories from the experiences of family, friends, business associates, or others (with their permission, of course. You won't need permission if you change the details so the actual people aren't recognizable.) Use the storyopia approach of sharing stories that take your audiences on a journey from what is to what could be. Have them imagine themselves journeying along the same path. For example, *Clients of mine found themselves in the same situation as you're in. They were . . .*

Start with One of the Five Questions

Don't try to tell a verbal novel. Get the audience involved with a single, interesting incident that starts with a hook — Who? What? When? Where? Why? How? For example:

- *Last year when I was . . .*
- *Back in 2022, my office buddy . . .*
- *I remember when I was in college . . .*
- *How do you think . . .?*

Make Sure Your Story Is On Point

Never tell a story for the sake of entertainment. You're not there to entertain but to persuade and drive your audience to do, think, feel, or learn something. If your story is about teamwork, start with the story about a team that succeeded or a team that failed. Either one will drive home a strong point. And if you can find humor in the story, all the better.

Circle Back to the Original Story

One of the most effective techniques of storytelling for presentations is to circle back to your earlier story and add a postscript. This can reveal a surprising twist or retell the story from another person's point of view. This can be an *aha* moment that brings your audience full circle to doing, thinking, feeling, or learning what you set out to accomplish.

End with a Call to Action

You may recall that Aesop's fables each ended with a moral to the story. Finish your story by saying, *My point is . . .* or *The reason that I'm telling you this is . . . .* Tie your story to your call to action: What you want them to think, do, feel, or learn.

Here's an example: A story about climate change could end with a call to action for the audience to reduce their carbon footprint by taking specific steps, such as using renewable energy, reducing consumption, and so on.

IN THIS CHAPTER

» Asking questions and encouraging debate

» Keeping your audience active — mentally and physically

Chapter 25
Ten-Plus Ways to Make Your Presentation Interactive

Is there anything more frustrating for a speaker (aside from a power failure or an embarrassing wardrobe malfunction) than looking at a sea of bored faces who are nodding off, scrolling through their phones, chatting with their neighbors, or fidgeting in their chairs? Keeping your audience's attention for long periods of time can be one of the biggest challenges even for seasoned speakers. This chapter provides ten-plus suggestions to help you avoid that frustration.

Ask Questions

One of the easiest ways to make your presentation interactive is ask questions. Follow up with people raising their hands. Doing so

- Brings them closer to the subject matter
- Increases interest

» Empowers them

» Makes them part of the presentation

Move Around the Room

Don't stand at the podium. Mingle with the audience. Move around the stage and room with purpose (such as handing someone the mic). Speaking from a podium gives you a place of hierarchy and removes you from your audience. By moving around, you're symbolically leaving your place in the hierarchy, making yourself more available and relatable.

Get the Audience Moving

An object in motion stays in motion, and a brain in motion stays in motion. This attests to our need to move thoughts and body. You know what I mean — awkwardly shifting in your seat needing to release some energy. To keep your audience moving, here are two suggestions:

» Ask each member of the audience to write a topic-related question and crumple the paper. One at a time they should toss it to another member of the audience to answer. This is somewhat like a snowball fight with one snowball (wad of paper) being thrown at a time.

» Ask everyone to get up from their seats and lead them in a few easy stretches. Even simple ones will get the blood flowing and will re-energize them.

Gamify the Presentation

Children love games, and, like kids, adults are more likely to remember something learned in a game-like manner. One suggestion is to pretend you're the host of Jeopardy. Display a topic-related statement on a slide and challenge the audience to answer it in the form of a question. Statements can be, "He was the first person to . . ." and the answer would be "Who was . . .?" Assign points for each correct answer. This can be done individually or as teams.

Do a Host-Guest Interview

Why do you think Oprah, Jay Leno, Ellen DeGeneres, Dr. Phil, Regis and Kelly, and other talk-show hosts like these have been so popular since the 1950s? They open minds. They allow people to spotlight their experiences. Here's how it works: You, the host, invite a subject-matter expert or someone from the audience to join you for a seated chat. You have a series of topic-related issues to discuss, and audience members (viewers) can pose questions.

Give Your Audience the Steering Wheel

Start your presentation by asking members of the audience to write down a question related to the topic. They you call on others in the audience to answer the question or find the answer. This is an awesome way to get your audience involved and make the presentation about them. It's about giving them the steering wheel and going in the direction that's right for them — even if you have to stray from what you planned. This strategy can cater to different learning styles and make the presentation more inclusive.

Get a Debate Going

Pick a controversial issue regarding the topic. Divide groups into "for" and "against" without knowing their feelings. Have them argue for or against the issue. It helps to understand an opposing point of view and may lead others to others to respect the point of view they're presenting. This is an incredible mind-opening activity that improves critical thinking, promotes resolution conflict, and offers new insights to complex or controversial topics.

Group for Scenario-Solving

Present two or three short scenarios and divide the groups into no more than five people. Let them discuss options and come up with conclusions. After five minutes have them share their solutions to the problem. This opens up new ideas and ways of doing things, much like a debate.

Create a Human Barometer

Ask the audience to stand. Then ask a controversial (but not sensitive) topic-related question. Ask those who agree to move to one side of the room, and those who disagree to move to the other. While they're standing, open a brief discussion. Then repeat the questions and ask if anyone changed their minds. If so, ask them to move to the appropriate side of the room.

Initiate Lightning Talks

Write down a series of topic-related questions. Fold them, and have each person select one. Give the audience one to two minutes to prepare a "data blitz" answer and have them share it with the audience. This works well in groups of 15 or fewer.

Speed Network

Get the audience out of their seats. Set a timer for one minute and have them introduce themselves to someone else. When the timer goes off, they move to another person. Doing this at the beginning of the session is a good icebreaker. Doing it during the presentation gets people up and moving. Many strong, lasting connections have come from getting-to-know activities such as this.

Incorporate Technology

With the emergence of audience interaction tools such as Mentimeter, Kahoot, and others, you can conduct real-time polls, quizzes, or surveys. This not only keeps the audience engaged but also gives you immediate feedback on your presentation.

IN THIS CHAPTER

» Weak opening and/or closing

» Not addressing the audience's needs

» Too reliant on slides

» Inadequate storytelling

Chapter 26

Ten Reasons Presentations Can Fail

You finished your presentation and discovered from the evaluations that the audience wasn't thrilled. What could have gone wrong? The following is a list of possibilities.

REMEMBER

Don't strive for absolute perfection. Instead, identify a few areas where you can improve. Start with those that are the easiest to correct and will have the biggest impact on your audiences.

Opening

Open your session with a bang. What can go wrong?

- Not starting on time
- Having a weak opening
- Making it about you (the speaker)
- Offering an apology for something

Audience

The audience is the reason you're there; they're the heroes. What can go wrong?

- Not assessing their needs beforehand
- Failing to engage them emotionally
- Lecturing — not including them in discussions
- Not providing new insights
- Not reading their body language

Verbal language

You must know your audience. What can go wrong?

- Using too much jargon
- Not showing enthusiasm for the topic
- Rambling and being too wordy
- Failing to pause for emphasis
- Using humor inappropriately
- Speaking in a monotone

Body language

Your body language speaks thousands of words. What can go wrong?

- Lacking eye contact
- Keeping your back to audience while reading slides
- Not smiling
- Not using gestures
- Standing in one place for too long (behind the podium for example)

Technology

Technology is just a tool; you must be able to stand on your own. What can go wrong?

- Not knowing how to use the technology
- Not having Plan B in case there are technical problems
- Dealing with file incompatibility
- Not being prepared to deliver the presentation without technology

Slides

Slides are great when used smartly. What can go wrong?

- Showing toooo many slides with toooo much information on each
- Relying too much on slides
- Reading from the slides
- Over-animating slides
- Displaying a glaring error
- Using them as a teleprompter

Storytelling

Lead your audience on a journey from what is to what can be: storyopia. What can go wrong?

- Not telling stories
- Telling too few or too many stories
- Making stories too long
- Telling irrelevant stories
- Not making the audience see themselves in the story

Questioning

Questions are a great way for your audience to interact. What can go wrong?

- Waffling when answering questions
- Allowing know-it-alls to monopolize the conversation
- Saving Q&A until the end and running out of time

Closing

Leave time for the call to action. What can go wrong?

- Rushing to get everything covered
- Overshooting the allotted time
- Ending with Q&A
- Summarizing the entire presentation
- Not stressing the call to action

Feedback

Feedback lets you know how you're doing. What can go wrong?

- Not including short- and long-answer questions
- Passing out evaluation forms too close to the end (several people may leave without filling them out)
- Not allowing for anonymous (honest) feedback on the evaluation
- Ignoring or dismissing feedback you don't want to hear

7 Appendixes

IN THIS PART . . .

Make sure you have all your ducks in a row with a handy presentation checklist.

Use the glossary to look up important terms and learn the lingo of storytelling and presentations.

Appendix A

Presentation Checklist

You wouldn't want to board an airplane if you knew the pilot hadn't reviewed the preflight checklist. You'd want any problems detected while you're still on the ground rather than in the air. Although your consequences at a presentation wouldn't be nearly as catastrophic as a flight, checklists work. When checklists are in place, you're not forced to remember every little detail of what needs to be done. Forgetting one of those details can be quite costly, or at least embarrassing. The following checklist outlines lots of important stuff for you to remember so you can deliver a polished, effective presentation that engages your audience and achieves your goals.

What to Bring

- ❑ Take one or two bottles of water.
- ❑ Throw in voice and breath accoutrements (lozenges and mints).
- ❑ Bring backup slides, cables, and extension cords.
- ❑ Include a laptop charger and HDMI adapter.
- ❑ Bring floor tape to cover exposed cords.
- ❑ Pack a remote laser presenter (clicker) to advance slides.

- ❑ Take plenty of business cards.
- ❑ Pack some pens for anyone in the audience who may need one. (If my name is on it, all the better.)
- ❑ Toss in a few plastic zipper bags to hold miscellaneous stuff.

Stories, Slides, and Props

- ❑ Have a number of stories prepared that I can plug in if there's a glitch of any kind.
- ❑ Verify that all names and numbers are correct on my slides.
- ❑ Make sure slides are limited to five to seven lines of text.
- ❑ Include graphics that are interesting and easy to read.
- ❑ Ensure that spelling, grammar, and punctuation are correct.
- ❑ Bring any props that add value to my words.
- ❑ Confirm that all the equipment I need will be in the room.

My Appearance

- ❑ Dress one notch above how I expect my audience to be dressed.
- ❑ Practice body language.
- ❑ Avoid anything to distract attention such as flashy colors and glitzy jewelry.

On the Morning of the Presentation

- ❑ Eat a hearty breakfast for energy.
- ❑ Get some light exercise.
- ❑ Make sure my laptop is fully charged.

- ❑ Double check that I have the right slides.
- ❑ Make sure I have ample business cards and handouts.
- ❑ If using notecards, make sure they're numbered.
- ❑ Arrive at the venue early to save myself additional stress.

Other Speakers

- ❑ Find out if anyone else will be speaking. If so, learn their names.
- ❑ Learn if their topic is related to mine.
- ❑ Know in what order I'll be speaking.
- ❑ Check if someone will introduce me or if I'll introduce myself.

At the Event

- ❑ Register and let the organizers know I've arrived.
- ❑ Test all my equipment.
- ❑ Make sure my slides are visible from every place in the room.
- ❑ Silence my phone.
- ❑ Hook my laptop and projector up immediately. (This is where problems may occur.)
- ❑ If time allows beforehand, meet and greet people who might be in the audience.
- ❑ Familiarize myself with the layout of the room and the equipment.
- ❑ Gauge the audience and adjust the presentation if necessary. (For example, if I'm presenting near the end of a conference, make sure my presentation is interactive.)

After the Event

- ❑ Make myself available so people can chat with me.
- ❑ Post slides, if appropriate.
- ❑ Distribute the evaluation forms (I or the host organization).
- ❑ Thank the organizers and ask for feedback.
- ❑ If my presentation was recorded, request a copy.

Additional Checklist for Virtual Presentations

- ❑ Make sure my audio and video are working.
- ❑ Check that I can put the video of myself and my slides up at the same time.
- ❑ Make sure I can look into the camera and not at myself.
- ❑ Raise my computer or webcam so it's at eye level.
- ❑ Notice if my main source of light is in front of me, not behind me.
- ❑ I'm not wearing stripes, patterns, or anything that may look distorted.

Miscellany

- ❑ Leave in plenty of time to allow for heavy traffic or anything else that can delay me.
- ❑ Double and triple check that I have everything I need to bring.

Appendix B
Glossary

Imagine Alice from *Alice in Wonderland* trying to decipher a weird language when she was thrust into her strange world. *Jabberwocky*, *galumphing*, and *outgrabe* were as weird to Alice as "scrum" and "metadata" may be to you. But Alice didn't have a glossary. You do!

SHERYL SAYS

There are three words in this list that are exclusive to this book. You won't find them anyplace else — at least not yet. I coined them. They are *storyopia, slidezillas,* and *wall-paper.*

artificial intelligence (AI): Leverages computers and machines to mimic presentations as well as problem-solving and decision-making capabilities of the human mind.

asynchronous learning: Learning that doesn't take place in real time but is available when learners need the training.

augmented reality (AR): Superimposes digital information into the user's real-world environment.

C-suite: Refers to most high-level executives; derived from the titles of top senior executives, which tend to start with the letter C: chief executive officer (CEO), chief financial officer (CFO), chief operating officer (COO), chief information officer (CIO), chief experience officer (CXO), and others who typically sit in corner-office suites.

clouds: Virtual spaces that exist on the Internet as storage where people can place their digital resources such as software, applications, and files.

collaborative software: Enables the sharing, processing, and management of files, documents, and other data types among several users and/or systems; can be used by two or more remote users to join work on a presentation.

CTA (call to action): At the end of a presentation, this is used to provoke an immediate response from the audience. (Many brochures, flyers, catalogs, email campaigns, and so on, also make use of a CTA.)

data storytelling: Conveying data that's not just in numbers, charts, and the like, but crafting a narrative that people can relate to — bring concepts to life. This is generally paired with data visualization.

data visualization: The graphical representation of visuals such as charts, graphs, maps, and so on, using specific apps such as Tableau, Microsoft BI, and Google Data Studio. They provide an accessible way to view trends and understand outliers and patterns. From this information, data stories can be woven.

digital storyboard: A sequence of drawings, frame by frame, done in specialized software that includes words and sketches of various scenes.

e-learning: A catchall phrase for a structured course or learning experience delivered electronically.

gamification: The application of games-design elements and principles in non-game contexts, such as learning and instructions.

hard skills: Quantifiable clearly defined skills needed for a person to perform a job successfully. They can include skills in computer, project management, graphic design, bookkeeping, and more.

HDMI adapter: An adapter that connects to the USB port on a computer and essentially adds an HDMI output to the computer. This allows you to connect your computer to your HDMI enabled display, like a TV or computer monitor.

microlearning: Small learning units and short-term training activities.

mood board: A collage of images, text, and samples of objects to indicate the overall feel or flow of an idea.

metaverse: Not a single entity, but multiple emerging technologies such as virtual, digital and 3D that merge virtual spaces and the physical world.

SFX: Special effects and/or sounds effects for video productions.

simulated learning environment (SLE) Simulations providing learners with procedures and routines in varying degrees of realism.

slidezillas: The presentation equivalent of Godzilla. Just as Godzilla is the towering, reptilian monster that plagued Japan, slidezillas are the data-laden technology monsters that have been plaguing audiences for decades.

soft skills: Skills that shape how we think, operate, work, and interact with each other. They can include adaptability, leadership, problem solving, and work ethic.

storyboard: A sequence of frames (words and visuals) that establish the narrative and associated visuals, outlining a presentation that will be delivered in person, by videoconference, or via video.

storyopia: Represents the ideal, like uptopia. It's the ideal story that takes the hero on a journey from what *is* to what *could be;* a journey to where the audience sees themselves as heroes along that same path.

subject-matter expert (SME): A resource person who had an in-depth knowledge of a certain subject of technology.

substack: An email newsletter platform. Its simple interface and ability to publish (and monetize) posts on the web have made it a game changer for writers of any skill level.

synchronous: Learning where the facilitators interact online simultaneously, such as via videoconferencing.

training needs assessment (TNA): Lets a company determine the knowledge, abilities, and skills employees need in order to make the employees and the company more successful in both hard and soft skills.

videoconferencing: A conference among people at remote locations via transmitted audio and video signals.

virtual reality (VR): Places users in a virtual environment that replicates real-world experiences.

wall-paper editing: Refers to pages of text and/or graphics that have been printed out — still in the draft stage — and pasted to a wall; ergo, the name wall-paper, a term I coined.

Web Content Accessibility Guidelines (WCAG): Provides recommendations for animated content and interactions.

word clouds (aka tag clouds or text clouds): A cluster of words in different sizes (looking somewhat like a cumulus cloud) used to pull out the most pertinent parts of textual data at a glance without showing charts and tables.

Index

D

E

F

G

H

I

N

O

P

Q

R

S

U

V

W

Z

Author's Journey

Sheryl grew up in New York City and still bears traces of her accent, which is very apparent when she says the word "coffee" (or as she pronounces it, *cough-ee.*) Sheryl stayed in New York with her husband while raising two sons, then she became a transplanted New Yorker and moved to the Boston area.

She was a child rhetorician, but not by choice! Sheryl was raised by a mother who was a stickler for speaking impeccably. When Sheryl was about five, her mother taught her to spell *schizophrenia* and *antidisestablishmentarian*, and she paraded Sheryl around like a prized show dog urging her to perform those words for anyone who'd listen. That experience must have had a subliminal impact because it instilled in Sheryl a love of words and the mastery of speaking in front of people — paving the path for her stunning career as a corporate trainer, business communications aficionado, and coach.

After receiving a combined Master's Degree in Business and English, Sheryl started her own communications company, Sheryl Lindsell-Roberts & Associates. In addition to corporate training, her career has spanned directing marketing and public relations campaigns, scripting video productions, writing technical docs, and authoring books. She's fiercely committed to helping people engage their audiences with storyopia, cut writing time by 30 to 50 percent, and deliver key information at a glance with strong visual impact. These are two of Sheryl's signature training sessions, which she often tailors for specific needs of clients:

- **Storytelling & Storyboarding: The Key to Stellar Presentations**
- **Write It So They'll Read It (business and technical writing)**

Writing is more than Sheryl's craft; it's her passion. One day she hopes to write the great American novel, but in the meantime, she's written 25-plus books for the business and humor markets. When she isn't in a typing frenzy riddling the market with new books, she dabbles in interior decorating. Other activities involve writing poetry, kayaking, cross-country skiing, snowshoeing, gardening, painting (pictures, not walls), practicing yoga, powerwalking, playing the violin, and globetrotting.

Her latest globetrotting adventure (during the writing is this book) took her to Egypt where she had the incredible experience of being infused with stories of Egyptian archeology and mythology. Guides wove together stories of kings and pharaohs. They merged bricks and mortar with ancient mysticism. These visual stories came alive like historical novels that have been frozen in time. Stories that continue to live on thousands of years later. Stories that will continue to live on thousands of years from now. This further supports the resilience of storytelling.

Sheryl's been a guest on radio and TV programs across the United States. She's been featured in many publications including *The New York Times* and is an ongoing contributor to *Training* magazine. To learn more, visit Sheryl at `https://www.linkedin.com/in/sherylwrites/`.

Dedication

I dedicate this to every person in every audience who's attended my training sessions, workshops, and presentations. I've learned as much from them as they've learned from me, perhaps more. I'm a student of endless learning and hope to continue learning from each person who'll walk through the door (or appear on my computer screen). I truly believe that if you haven't learned something new each day, you haven't been paying attention. Here are the first of a dozen things my audiences have taught me. (For the next dozen, you'll have to wait for my next book.) ☺

1. Presenting gets a lot easier after the first few times.
2. Take feedback to heart and learn from it.
3. Enjoy what you do, let it show.
4. Audiences love stories that relate to them; tell many.
5. Teaching is the biggest learning experience.
6. Never be afraid to show your vulnerability.
7. Laugh at yourself — we all blow it every now and then.

8. Challenge your audience but be sensitive.
9. Be flexible and adaptable.
10. Asking your audience questions is a great way to stay out of trouble.
11. Let your audiences know you appreciate them.
12. Audiences are there to learn from you and to cheer you on.

I also dedicate this to my best friend and harshest critic — my husband, Jon. When I want to refine stories or run an idea by him, I can always count on his perceptions. His analytical mind, coming from the engineering-scientific realm, will offer a view different from mine. I also appreciate his indulgence when we're in the middle of a conversation and he perceives my focus shifting from his words to new insights into whatever I'm in the midst of writing.

Acknowledgments: Building Storyopia

Foreword: John Wiley & Sons, Inc. (known as Wiley) was established in 1807 when Charles Wiley (John's father) opened a print shop in Manhattan. In its early days, the company served as a bastion for America's struggling yet superlative writers such as James Fenimore Cooper, Washington Irving, Herman Melville, and Edgar Allan Poe. Fast forward . . . that brings us to the story about the construction of this book.

SETTING	The overall structure for this book was set in many departments: publishing and editing, contracts and legal, sales and marketing, finance and accounting, design and development, production, and operations. It was also set online with meetings from several home-based offices.
CHARACTERS	**Tracy Boggier, Senior Acquisitions Editor:** This book became a reality through Tracy's keen vision. She believed in storyopia and storytelling in presentations, and she worked tirelessly behind the scenes, every step of the way, toward its construction and completion. **Sheryl Lindsell-Roberts, Six-time Dummies' Author:** This principal architect conceptualized the theme and produced detailed plans for solid construction with the highest-quality materials and craftsmanship. **Chrissy Guthrie, Development Editor:** Chrissy's vital role involved insightful ideas and design development as well as clarifying the intent and message to ensure that it met the *Dummies* (or in this case the *smarties*) high standards.

	Jennifer Connolly, Copyeditor: To ensure a clear flow of readability, Jenn polished the text to make sure no stone was left unturned in getting it right. **Kristie Pyles, Managing Editor:** Kristie functioned as the interior designer to provide guidance for layout and art. She also acquired the necessary permits. **Meir Zimmerman, Technical Editor:** To ensure the integrity of the project, Meir performed site inspections to safeguard against any weaknesses, omissions, or defects.
CONFLICT	Working with this A-team, conflicts were very few. But every story needs a conflict. So — along the way, when there were minor differences of opinions — we reached quick and amicable compromises.
RESOLUTION	United in the journey, we built an indispensable book that will transform novice or mediocre presenters into "it" presenters and turn audiences into heroes.

Publisher's Acknowledgments

Senior Acquisitions Editor: Tracy Boggier
Development Editor and Editorial Project Manager: Christina Guthrie
Copy Editor: Jennifer Connolly
Technical Editor: Meir Zimmerman
Senior Managing Editor: Kristie Pyles
Cover Image: © iStockphoto.com / Cary Westfall